The Philosophy
and Future of
Graduate Education

The Philosophy
and Future of
Graduate Education

Papers and commentaries delivered at the International
Conference on the Philosophy of Graduate Education at
The University of Michigan, April 13–15, 1978.

edited by

WILLIAM K. FRANKENA

Ann Arbor
The University of Michigan Press

Library of Congress Cataloging in Publication Data

International Conference on the Philosophy of Graduate
    Education, University of Michigan, 1978.
    The philosophy and future of graduate education.

    Includes bibliographical references.
    1. Universities and colleges—United States—
Graduate work—Congresses.   2. Education, Humanistic—
United States—Congresses.   I. Frankena, William K.
II. Title
LB2371.I53 1978   378'.1553'0973   80-14804
ISBN 0-472-09321-5
ISBN 0-472-06321-9 (pbk.)

Contributors

KENNETH E. BOULDING is distinguished professor of economics at the University of Colorado, Boulder, and director of the Program of Research on General Social and Economic Dynamics at the university's Institute of Behavioral Science. He is currently president of the American Association for the Advancement of Science and a past president of the American Economic Association. His recent publications include *Ecodynamics: A New Theory of Societal Evolution* and *Stable Peace.*

HOWARD R. BOWEN is an economist whose current specialty is the economic aspects of higher education. His career has combined service in business, government, and higher education. He has been president of Grinnell College, the University of Iowa, and Claremont Graduate School. He has also been president of the American Finance Association, the American Association for Higher Education, and the Western Economic Association. Among his publications are *Efficiency in Liberal Education* and *Investment in Learning.*

WALTER H. CLARK, JR., is interested in literature, the preparation of teachers, and the philosophy of curriculum. A former student of Israel Scheffler and I. A. Richards, he has published two books of poetry and a series of articles on aesthetic education. He is cofounder of Michigan's New England Literature Program which attempts to further the goals of undergraduate liberal education through intensive reading and writing in informal New England surroundings.

JOSEPH DUFFEY is chairman of the National Endowment for the Humanities. His career has included academic and government service, and he has served as assistant secretary of state. He is a graduate of Marshall University, Andover Newton Theological School, and the Hartford Seminary Foundation. Between 1960 and 1971, Mr. Duffey taught at the Hartford Seminary and Yale University.

WILLIAM K. FRANKENA is Roy Wood Sellars Professor of Philosophy in the College of Literature, Science, and the Arts at the University of Michigan. He is a member of the American Academy of Arts and Sciences and the National Academy of Education. His latest book, *Thinking about Morality,* is part of the Michigan Faculty Series published by the University of Michigan Press.

NATHAN GLAZER is professor of education and sociology at Harvard University and former professor of sociology at the University of California, Berkeley. He is author of *Beyond the Melting Pot* (with Daniel P. Moynihan),

Remembering the Answers, Affirmative Discrimination, and is the coeditor of *The Public Interest.*

STERLING M. MCMURRIN is E. E. Ericksen Distinguished Professor at the University of Utah. He also holds appointments at the University of Utah as professor of history, professor of the philosophy of education, adjunct professor of philosophy, and, until recently, was dean of the Graduate School. He was United States commissioner of education in the administration of President John F. Kennedy.

MAURICE MANDELBAUM is adjunct professor of philosophy at Dartmouth College. He has taught at Swarthmore College, Dartmouth College, and Johns Hopkins University, where he was chairman of the philosophy department and subsequently Andrew W. Mellon Professor of Philosophy. Among his published works are *Philosophy, Science, and Sense-Perception; History, Man, and Reason;* and *The Anatomy of Historical Knowledge.*

WILLIAM F. MILLER is president and chief executive officer of SRI International. He was vice-president and provost at Stanford University from 1971 to 1978. Before going to Stanford University, he had been the director of the applied mathematics division at the Argonne National Laboratory. At Stanford, he developed the budget equilibrium program and was the architect of the model which was an important instrument in the academic planning and financial management of that university.

JOHN PASSMORE is professor of philosophy at the Australian National University. He is a former president of the Australian Academy of Humanities, a fellow of the Australian Academy of Social Sciences, a foreign member of the British Academy, the American Academy of Arts and Sciences, and the Royal Danish Academy of Sciences and Letters. His latest book is *The Philosophy of Teaching.*

EUGEN PUSIC is professor of administrative science at the University of Zagreb (Yugoslavia) and head of the planning department for the Ministry of Welfare for the Republic of Croatia. He has been a fellow at the Institute of Social Studies, The Hague, Netherlands, and at the Center for Advanced Studies in Behavioral Sciences. He is president of the Yugoslav Association for Administrative Science and Practice and has been awarded the Rene-Sand Award for contributions to international social welfare.

ANTHONY QUINTON has been a university lecturer in philosophy at Oxford since 1950. He was a fellow of All Souls College from 1949 to 1955 and a fellow and tutor in philosophy from 1955 to 1978. Since 1978 he has been president of Trinity College, Oxford. His publications include *The Politics of Imperfection, Utilitarian Ethics,* and *Thoughts and Thinkers.*

LAURENCE VEYSEY is professor of history at Kresge College, University of California, Santa Cruz. He is author of *The Emergence of the American University* and *The Communal Experience,* among other publications. He is currently at work on a social history of America since 1920.

GREGORY VLASTOS has taught philosophy at Queen's University (Canada), Cornell, and Princeton. Since 1976 he has been Mills Visiting Professor of Philosophy at the University of California, Berkeley. His publications include *Platonic Studies* and *Plato's Universe.* He has been a member of the Institute for Advanced Study at Princeton and a fellow of the Center for Advanced Studies in Behavioral Sciences at Stanford. He was one of the founders of the recently established National Humanities Center at Research Triangle Park in North Carolina.

Contents

Graduate Education: A Case
for the Public Interest

Joseph Duffey

A major responsibility of the chairman of the National Endowment for the Humanities (NEH) is to articulate and defend the wisdom of investing public funds in the support of academic life. Of course that responsibility is not uniquely mine; nor is the Humanities Endowment really a lobbyist for the special interest of higher education. The legislated mandate of the agency is to encourage the curiosity and thoughtfulness of all Americans about the areas of inquiry we call humanities. The range of this encouragement is considerable, from sophisticated research projects for scholars to broadly disseminated programs for the general public.

While universities are vital to the inquiries of Americans about the great and timeless questions of humanities, the Endowment also supports the work of elementary and secondary schools, museums, libraries, the media, and voluntary citizens' organizations. From its inception the Humanities Endowment has been seen as having two fundamental purposes: to support scholarship, especially in academic settings, and to make the learning of the humanities available to a larger portion of our citizens.

The legislation creating the NEH lists several specific disciplines and authorizes funds for research, fellowships, and other higher education programs. These activities have always received a major share of the Endowment's funds. The Endowment has sometimes preferred to wear the costume of a patron of such popular programs as the *Treasures of Tutankhamun.* To their credit, the Endowment staff has labored long and hard to keep this division of purpose from becoming a source of conflict. My impression is, however, that we have had limited success in linking the public and scholarly aspects of the mindfulness of Americans about the humanities.

Audiences continue to grow for public television, radio, museum exhibits, library extension courses, and for discussion groups in such places as local lodge halls and senior citizen centers. I wish the same could be said for higher education. The number of students enrolling in courses and majoring in the humanities is declining and the number of faculty positions in these fields follows that trend. For younger scholars in the humanities who will not be able to teach, this is a grievous situation. I do not have to rehearse with this group the demographics and shifts in public policy that have led to this situation, but I do want to point out a paradox which has emerged.

On the one hand there is no question that the home of the humanities in American culture today is in our colleges and universities. Increasingly our literary and cultural criticism has come to be the product of college teachers and our learned publications issue from academe. Yet, paradoxically, the enthusiasm for the humanities is today stronger outside the academy than within it.

I am convinced that advanced scholarship in the humanities and programs of public dissemination suffer due to their isolation from each other. The scholarly community, when pressed, will say that public programs tend to be trivial, intellectually lightweight, and insubstantial. The layman, if he thinks of graduate education at all, thinks of it as a tool for career advancement through professional training. He too often regards the scholarship of graduate professors and students as trivial and irrelevant to the concerns of ordinary life.

There is little delight in this mutual daubing of one another with the tar-brush of triviality. It is discouraging to realize that our public exercise of mind is intellectually trivial, as it often is and it is equally discouraging to observe that our specialized pursuit of humanistic learning is also often socially trivial. I want to expand for a moment on the consequences of our trivializing.

Our elementary schools, for example, focus their energies almost entirely on the training of children in the technical skills of literacy and computation, without much concern for initiating them into our rich cultural traditions. While parents are calling for schools to return to the basics, there are few voices suggesting that what is needed is a return to complexity, toward helping our children to become capable of logical reasoning, of weighing alternatives, of tolerating ambiguity.

We are doing little better in our public life. Debate on the issues of our time is embarrassingly thin. Perhaps this is caused by our infatuation with the adversarial duel, exposé journalism, or the reduction of major problems to the so-called personalities behind the news. Americans are genuinely confused about public life. They seem to feel that public debate, heated as it is, is a sham entertainment, disconnected from any first principles we can all share.

Liberal learning plays a diminished role in contemporary life. Where once the humanities provided the terms for public debate, that hegemony has been usurped by technical jargon, commercially packaged blather, and "narcissistic psychobabble." This occurs despite the fact that a growing proportion of our citizens have a college education. Why have their educations left them so unprepared for the intellectual demands of adult life? A part of the answer must surely lie in the professionalization of the humanities on our campuses.

The proliferation of specialities and subspecialities within each academic discipline in recent years has fragmented the study of the humanities, which were once thought to involve a set of questions fundamental to all the disciplines. Research monographs and journal articles have pulled scholars, centrifugally, away from these common questions, and have subtly redefined humanistic scholarship on the model of the sciences and the so-called hard social sciences.

Each discipline of the humanities has thus become a world of its own, with its own social roles, economy, political culture, and language. This isolation, however, has lacked one essential ingredient—a stable level of economic support. The expanding arena of these disciplines has been purchased at the cost of their dependence upon government and private funding, and more urgently, upon the general economic conditions in the country.

The economic trials of higher education are only one sign of its social frailty today, of its isolation from public meaning. I would be the last to argue that every institution must serve a narrowly specified instrumental function in order to gain its legitimate sustenance from the society at large. Simply to preserve our cultural inheritance is an important responsibility for scholars. But the ends of advanced study cannot lie within themselves.

I look to this conference to help articulate new dimensions of public meaning for advanced scholarship in American life. I know that there will be much discussion here of the substance and structure of graduate programs, but I hope you will reach beyond these internal questions to address the larger public purposes which must underlie the social health of graduate study. The humanities can once again play an important role as the center of our common culture—not as an instrument for solving our social problems but as a language for exploring them.

How can this be accomplished? A start can be made within academic life itself. We need finally to rid ourselves of the pejorative connotations of vocationalism, so often thrown about by academic antagonists, and to rethink the relationship between the liberal arts curriculum and the student's need for professional preparation. The sophisticated technical preparation now required of professionals means that undergraduate learning is more and more preoccupied with stages of that preparation. It is reported that currently 70 percent of the students at some of our most distinguished colleges are enrolled in premed or prelaw programs. In our state and community colleges, there has been a continuing development of new and necessary technical specialities. Only one in sixteen undergraduate students today is majoring in the humanities.

Yet this appears to have had little effect on the preparation of college teachers. We continue to train our young scholars and teachers in the humanities to focus their intellectual energies on that scant 6 percent who pursue humanities concentrations, or on isolated courses which ornament the nonmajors' progress toward a degree.

What would it mean if the teaching we require of graduate students was based upon a better sense of the lives which all students might actually lead after college? If, for example, we want educated citizens to be able to articulate aesthetic judgments about a work of art, would that not entail a different pedagogy from training them to trace the historical influences impinging upon that work? If we want to help students defend or doubt the wisdom of government policies, wouldn't that mean a different way of teaching history from one which asked students to compare the interpretations of different historians?

When it comes to the professional and technical curricula themselves, our tasks are even greater. Is it not incumbent upon us, in teaching preprofessional students, to help them locate the key humanistic questions within the professional fields in which they will ultimately practice? All who are committed to the significance of the humanities should be aware of the need to assist students in thinking about the following:

ethical issues in professional practice;
political questions which surround the expression of that particular form of expertise in contemporary society;
the historical basis for the shapes which that professional world has taken;
the epistemological assumptions which are involved in its particular form of problem solving;
the relationship of the profession to our economic order; and
the set of social symbols and practices which characterize such work.

Finally, the lack of connectedness of the liberal arts and the professions today is being felt most poignantly by those Ph.D.'s who are leaving graduate school or college teaching for other means of gaining a livelihood. For such highly skilled, younger scholars in the humanities, the neglect within academic life of the intellectual core of other professions has contributed to their sense of confinement and a lack of preparation.

The dialogue of graduate education with contemporary professional thought might help reassert the centrality of the liberal arts for our common intellectual life. Another way of accomplishing that might be to encourage scholars to clarify the relationship between advanced study and the major issues of contemporary life. It is not primarily a matter of popularizing scholarly research; rather the task is one of contemplating how such research speaks to the timeless central questions of the humanities.

There are many examples:

the continuity or discontinuity of personal biographical development (which used to be called the problem of the freedom of the will!);
the cultural or biological determinants of behavior; and
the resilience of man's environment, and whether we will perceive our world as one of plentitude or of scarcity.

All these sorts of questions have important implications for public policy. But beyond these practical concerns, our best scholarship in the humanities—understood as philosophical reflection—presents a coherent vision of man based upon the fullness of experience. We need, therefore, to encourage professors to make time amidst their schedules of classes and examinations for such reflectiveness, and to set aside room on their bookshelves for that ancient and most honorable genre, the essay, which has been sadly displaced by highly specialized jargon in academic journals.

Still another challenge ahead for those who articulate the public meaning of advanced study has to do with the nature of the academic disciplines themselves. Each has its particular histories, each its debates about underlying philosophical assumptions, each an array of social forms which have nurtured its growth. My encouragement that these matters be considered is not an invitation to professional self-absorption. Quite the contrary. I would hope that such an exercise would lead us to understand the boundedness of what we study and how we work. We might then comprehend how knowledge in the humanities is always a process of moving among distinct languages and forms of knowing.

What we aim for was expressed best by Matthew Arnold a century ago. Those "happy moments of humanity," he wrote, come when "there is a national glow of life and thought, when the whole of society is in the fullest sense permeated by thought, sensible to beauty, intelligent and alive." Arnold's high ideal depended then, as ours does today, upon scholars coming to share their deliberations with the wider public.

I interpret our work at the Humanities Endowment to be related to the ideal of seeing that "the best which has been thought and said is current everywhere." We do not debase the humanities by seeing them in such proximity to the concerns of our ordinary lives, for at their best they offer us a deeper, perhaps tragic and ironic, but richer vision of the human condition.

Can what I have tried to suggest here be accomplished given our current institutional structures and needs? I will not argue that this is a simple task. It is hard, after all, to know just when we are as Socrates meddling in the public realm, and when we are being sophists to someone else's Socrates.

Beyond that, I am asking that one aspect of graduate education, which has been the breeding ground for all forms of American expertise, relinquish some of the special claims of the expert: that it work, in fact, against the overbearing claims of technical and professional expertise in American society; that it preserve the moral, political, and intellectual dialogue which may keep this from becoming a society overcome by technical imperatives. I do not know whether it is sociologically possible for a profession to act so much against its own narrowly perceived professional interests. That is in itself a humanistic question of a rather high order. But I am convinced that upon the answer to that question depends the immediate future of graduate education, as well as the future of learning in the humanities in America. And, most importantly, the future vitality of democratic politics in this society may also hinge upon our capability to respond to that challenge.

I. The Aims of Graduate Education

The College, the University, and Society

Maurice Mandelbaum

Although I was asked to engage in a discussion of graduate education, I have found it impossible to confine myself to that topic. Just as our colleges are deeply affected by the nature, successes, and failures of our lower schools, so graduate and professional education are affected by the way in which our college system functions—by who attends colleges, and by what they achieve while there. Furthermore, our universities are not solely composed of graduate and professional schools, but include within themselves one or more undergraduate colleges, and are likely to include research institutes, schools for paraprofessional and vocational training, and much more. Since these activities have an effect on one another, either directly or indirectly, graduate education cannot be considered wholly apart from most of the other activities carried on within a university. Of even greater importance is that all of these activities lead from our campuses into the occupations and ongoing concerns of contemporary society. Since no educational system is ever isolated from the other institutions in a society, it appears to me that any attempt to reflect on graduate education apart from the broader context in which it is embedded will lead to empty conclusions.

This is not to say that one must approve of the relations that have grown up between our colleges and universities and the forces that dominate contemporary society any more than one must approve of the education currently available in most of our schools in order to understand the problems that our colleges now face. In fact, perhaps a majority of those who have written most trenchantly on problems of education—whether in our schools, colleges, or universities—have been critical of existing social trends, believing them to be inimical to excellence in the educational system. One thinks, for example, of Veblen, Flexner, or Hutchins, each of whom was concerned with the reform of higher education in the United States. Unlike them, however, I do not propose to deal directly with questions that arise when we look to reform. I trust that this need not be taken as a sign of complacency. To guard against that misunderstanding, let me say that I know of no college or university which has the right to be complacent, which does not stand in need of one or another sort of reform. Some, I should say, stand in greater need than do others, but I do not subscribe to the view which is sometimes characteristic of educational reformers—that all colleges or universities, or all graduate schools, should conform to some one educational model, with each attempting to play exactly the same roles within society as other colleges, universities, or graduate schools do. My view on this matter springs from a belief that in a society which strives to be democratic there is need for democratization in education. Furthermore, I believe that if we examine any society we find that there is always diversification in the roles played by different individuals in that society; education, to be effective, should therefore also be diversified. This is especially true in societies with complex technologies such as our own, where there come to be fewer tasks that can be performed by individuals who lack certain basic skills that are not now to be acquired through either imitation or an apprenticeship system, but come only through schooling. Furthermore, the types of skills that are needed for many vocations have to some extent changed, and new types of curricula, and perhaps also of teaching, are needed to meet these changed needs. This is perhaps particularly true in the professions, and is I believe true in large segments of the teaching profession. As a consequence, we have witnessed, and can almost surely expect to continue to witness, an increase in specialization, in vocationalism, and in professionalization throughout our system of higher education. Let us first consider this matter with respect to the relations which have developed between our undergraduate colleges and our graduate and professional schools.

One change that seems to have been occurring is the gradual obliteration of the once-sharp line of demarcation that tended to separate the undergraduate college from graduate and professional schools. The clearest and most extreme example of this change lies in premedical training. Among many colleges that are attached to universities, and among a few which are not, there is now an increasing number of accelerated programs of medical education which permit undergraduates to enroll as full-fledged medical students prior to attaining the B.A. degree; the last year of college, and sometimes even the last two years, is a time in which students are also enrolled in medical school. Even where this overlapping of a college and a professional school is not formally acknowledged, from the moment a premedical student matriculates as a freshman he usually embarks on a program designed to be continuous with the professional training he is to receive in his postbaccalaureate studies. Nor is this situation

confined to medicine; it is also prevalent in engineering, and in varying degrees, often depending on the institution, it affects what
undergraduates do when they major in economics, business, psychology, or education, and to some extent what they do if they plan to
continue on to graduate education in other fields. At one time it might
perhaps have been said that a student's choice of his major was usually
not professionally oriented. In the ideal case the choice of a major was
supposed to be motivated primarily by an intellectual interest in a
particular field of study. However, in more cases than not, it in fact
turned out that students chose their majors for other reasons: they
had to choose some major in order to graduate, and the particular
major they chose, if it was not simply a choice of the lesser among
evils, was apt to be one they assumed would provide background that
could perhaps be useful in whatever career they might later decide to
pursue when their formal education was at last behind them and they
had received their B.A. degree. This picture is somewhat overdrawn;
there always were exceptions, and many majors, perhaps particularly
in the land-grant colleges, had a definite vocational bent. Now, however, the picture has so radically changed as to be almost unrecogniz-
able. Over the past decades, to an increasing extent, although there
may be signs of a slackening, fewer of our college students look upon
the B.A. as a terminal degree. For example, David Riesman remarked
that by 1972 the undergraduate college had in large measure become
a prep school for graduate schools, and he claimed that 80 to 90
percent of the students in Harvard College had, during recent years,
gone on to some form of graduate training.[1] Although the statement
and example may be extreme, there has undoubtedly been an increase in the proportion of advanced degrees as compared with baccalaureate degrees.[2] At the same time there has been both a widespread reduction in undergraduate distribution requirements and a
marked increase in the requirements for many undergraduate majors
in both the humanities and the social sciences. Thus, specialization has
set in, and though the requirements for majors in the natural sciences
have apparently not changed, they were already at a very high level.[3]
One may therefore say that in spite of the great emphasis on the need
for general education that followed the publication of the Harvard
Report on General Education in 1945, the earlier ideal of nonspe-
cialized general education for all undergraduates was gradually erod-
ing; the line between a college education and specialized graduate,
professional, or vocational training was being obliterated. I very
much doubt that statements now being made at Harvard and elsewhere, regarding the need for a return to a core curriculum, are

going to do anything important toward reversing this long-term trend.

We shall later have to consider some of the causes that have led to this change, and weigh some of its advantages against its often-stressed disadvantages. It is perhaps unusual, and by some it will doubtless seem perverse, to suggest that the present state of affairs does indeed have advantages. The lip service paid to what is designated as a liberal education is still very much with us, and has indeed dominated much of the discussion of higher education in this century. It is an ideal that had deep roots in English education in the nineteenth century. One need merely think of Cardinal Newman's *Idea of a University* and of John Stuart Mill's "Inaugural Address" when he became Rector of St. Andrews University, to recognize that two extremely able thinkers, who shared few other convictions, were at one in their insistence that liberal education at the postsecondary level should be protected against all influence of professionalization; that only after students had completed their university education should they turn their minds to those subjects which would directly serve the needs of their subsequent careers. Throughout Newman's discourses, for example, there runs the contrast between "liberal studies" and "the useful arts and sciences"; he regarded only the former as providing the proper subject matter for the curriculum of the university, or, as we should say, of the liberal arts college. The aim of a university, as Newman formulated it in the first sentence of his preface, was not the advancement but the diffusion of knowledge,[4] and, more specifically, of that knowledge which is universal, not particular, and is therefore not bound to practice.[5] One goal of this form of education was to develop a certain life-long habit of mind, the attributes of which were "freedom, equitableness, calmness, moderation, and wisdom."[6] Harking back to the original meaning of the term liberal as applied to education, Newman contrasted the liberal arts and studies with those arts which are "servile," the former being "philosophical" and the latter "mechanical."[7] As the Oxford *New English Dictionary* reminds us, the liberal arts, as contrasted with the servile and mechanical arts, were those "considered worthy of a free man," and all liberal pursuits were those pertaining to, or suitable for, "persons of superior social status." Thus, the liberal arts were "directed to general intellectual enlargement and refinement." Newman defended this conception of education in opposition to those who sought to measure the worth of education in terms of its "utility";[8] it is therefore at first surprising to find John Stuart Mill defending a conception of liberal education similar to Newman's.[9] Mill, too, stressed the effects of such an education on character formation, insisting that it is of primary importance for an individual to gain knowledge of the classical languages and literature, of mathematics, the experimental sciences, and logic, that he study morals and politics, and acquire an acquaintance with the arts, before being subjected to professional training. As he said,

> Universities are not intended to teach the knowledge required to fit men for some special mode of gaining their livelihood. Their object is not to make skillful lawyers, or physicians, or engineers, but capable and cultivated human beings.

And he continued,

> Men are men before they are lawyers, or physicians, or merchants, or manufacturers; and if you make them capable and sensible men, they will make themselves capable and sensible lawyers or physicians. What professional men should carry away with them from a University, is not professional knowledge, but what should direct the use of their professional knowledge.[10]

What underlies the views of both Newman and Mill with respect to their belief in the separation of liberal from professional studies was a profoundly conservative view of education. As we have noted with respect to Newman, the university was not a place which was to foster the advancement of knowledge; that was a function to be performed by individuals acting individually, or by learned societies or academies.[11] The university's function was teaching, but it was only such teaching as would serve to form healthy habits of mind—not teaching for the sake of purveying information or specialized learning; the habits to be formed were those which Newman identified with that intellectual culture and enlargement of mind which was characteristic of those whom he termed "gentlemen."[12]

Mill's conception of the function of education in civilization was even more explicit in its conservatism. His characterization of formal education identified it with "the culture which each generation purposely gives to those who are to be its successors, in order to qualify them for at least keeping up, and if possible for raising, the level of improvement which has been attained."[13] One might think that such a characterization would have allowed Mill to view professional and technical education as also being of importance, along with liberal studies. However, he held that even though such education does have importance, what is to be gained through it forms "no part of what every generation owes to the next, as that on which its civilization and worth will depend."[14] That there was implicit in Mill's view of civilization, no less than in Newman's view of the gentleman, a degree of socioeconomic elitism is clearly evident when he argued that geography and history do not belong within the scope of a liberal education since they are best come by through "private reading." They are, he adds, only appropriately taught in "elementary schools for the children of the laboring classes, whose subsequent access to books is limited."[15] The inference is inescapable: a liberal education is a type of education limited to a restricted segment of society. This view has indeed persisted into our own times, where liberal education, as opposed to goal-oriented vocational or professional training, is the type of education assumed to equip individuals for roles of leadership in society. With respect to that view, Laurence Veysey has given a thumbnail sketch of those humanists who favored liberal education in the late nineteenth century, opposing both the German model of research and specialization and the utilitarian-vocational ideal. Veysey characterized their position in the following way.

> In this generation, humanistic reformers were apt to retain an emphasis on the social and the moral as distinct from the intellectual aims of higher education. They continued to define education according to a single desirable formula for everyone. But the model was no longer taken from the classics or, in most cases, the tradition of Christian piety. It was that of the well-rounded gentleman or, sometimes, the citizen and potential leader of his society. A strong civic sense marked this camp of academic spokesmen, but unlike the utilitarians, its members firmly divorced the notion of public service from that of vocational expertise. Rather, they turned to the reviving English universities, particularly Oxford, as their contemporary source of inspiration. Their aim was to produce the kind of dutiful, disinterested national elite which they believed to be embodied in the British civil service.[16]

That there was this bias, and that it had permeated American education was one main theme in Thorstein Veblen's, *The Higher Learning in America*. To be sure, Veblen opposed the bias, advocating a new type of higher learning which would be free of its influence. What is of most interest in the present context is, however, that Veblen's views of the opposing forces in higher education paralleled the views earlier held by Newman, though they disagreed as to which of these forces was the more beneficent. Like Newman, Veblen insisted on drawing a sharp line between fostering liberal education and advancing learning. While recognizing that citizenship, as he termed it, was no less important than scholarship in the total system of education,[17] Veblen took it to be the function of the university to foster scholarship, not citizenship. He viewed it as disastrous for American education that both undergraduate colleges and professional, vocational schools had come to be administratively connected with the university. These were aspects of the educational system which had functions extraneous and inimical to the advancement of knowledge for its own sake. Newman and Mill had, of course, also advocated the separation of education from disinterested research, but their conception of the university was that of an educational institution, not a place dedicated to research. For them, teaching was at the heart of the educational enterprise, whereas Veblen believed that in a true university teaching would be confined to the master-apprentice relationship in which students were to be the co-workers of mature scholars and scientists, not pupils to be taught by lectures, drills, and examinations. From Veblen's point of view "the difference between the modern university and the lower and professional schools is broad and simple; not so much a difference of degree as of kind."[18] At least that is how, according to Veblen, it should be; and that, he thought, was the direction in which the whole movement of modern thought was tending.[19]

While Veblen did not discuss the German university, his views on the proper function of a university resembled, though in even purer form, the German model.[20] However, there were forces in the American educational system which worked against the development of universities as centers of completely disinterested learning. One important factor was the establishment of the land-grant colleges through the first Morrill Act of 1862. These colleges had practical missions, being intended to develop the arts of agriculture and manufacture, and to open up advanced educational opportunities to a broader spectrum of the population than had previously had access to them. This act gave a major impetus to our midwestern and western universities, and it was out of their development that what Clark Kerr has termed the multiversity arose. While the ideal of pure disinterested science took root within many of these institutions, as Veblen had foreseen that it would, this constituted only one of their many functions; they also developed large liberal arts colleges, professional schools, and a wide range of vocational programs and technical services. Further grants by the federal government, up to and including the programs of grants connected with World War II, established the multiversity pattern not only within the original land-grant institutions, but in every American university, both public and private. Nor was this development solely due to federal funding. The expansion of the services to be rendered by universities was to at least an equal extent fostered by acts of the various state legislatures. This cannot be attributed solely to the fact that the teaching and research carried on by the universities fostered the economic interests of the individual states; it also reflected a conviction that others besides those who wished to enter professions such as law and medicine should have a chance to benefit from the existence of the state university—they, too, should receive training that would help launch them on their future careers. Thus, the wish expressed by Ezra Cornell, the founder of Cornell University, can be taken, as Eric Ashby took it, to be a dominant theme in the growth of postsecondary American education: "I would found an institution where any person can find instruction in any study."[21]

The exponents of both the traditional liberal arts college and of the ideal of the German university have consistently aligned themselves against this conception of higher education, but their opposition does not seem to have checked the trend in that direction, nor have they been able to establish any new type of viable institution which holds great promise for the future. To be sure, there are graduate institutions, particularly among private universities, in which the broad coverage characteristic of the largest multiversities has been radically curtailed. As a consequence, the students at such institutions tend to be less heterogenous in their interests, in particular their vocational interests, than are the students in our state universities. Nonetheless, in those particular portions of graduate offerings which are common to all universities, such as doctoral training in the arts and sciences, or professional training in medicine or law, there is little if any difference in the kinds of training offered, whether or not they also offer types of vocational training generally scorned by those connected with our older private institutions. Similarly, when one considers the relationship that liberal arts programs bear to graduate study, the differences between other colleges and undergraduate programs in the arts and sciences which are offered by our multiversities are much less striking than the critics of the multiversity take them to be.[22] What has happened is that the range of choices in types of education has been enormously expanded ever since the land-grant college movement got under way. We must distinguish between this development and whatever changes have taken place within other areas of the curriculum and not assume that the addition of new areas of training and new types of college students is what has brought about change in what had formerly been the core of liberal education. Other changes in our society could well have brought about many of the changes within the traditional liberal arts curriculum, even if our universities had not developed schools and programs in domestic science, hotel management, business administration, library science, labor relations, hospital administration, or other vocationally-oriented specialties in addition to training in medicine and law.

It cannot be said that the critics of the multiversity have been oblivious of the fact that changing social conditions have contributed to that which they deplore. But the focus of their attention in dealing with these changes has been on those factors which they regard as having led to abuses within the educational system. In general, they have not seriously considered whether there have been some changes that should be commended even though these changes may have radically disturbed a previous equilibrium in the educational system. For example, in one series of lectures, *The University of Utopia,*[23] Robert M. Hutchins singled out for attention four features of society which he viewed as threatening to corrupt education: industrialization, specialization, philosophic diversity, and social and political conformity. In his discussion of these factors, he failed to consider whether there may also have been benefits accruing to education because of one or more of these changes in society. It might well be argued, for example, that specialization, at least in the sciences, is not without redeeming features; or that philosophic diversity has definite advantages if the alternative were to be a single, entrenched system of thought, even were it the Thomistic cast of thought so highly praised in these lectures. Nor did Hutchins' survey of the sociological factors which have radically changed education take up the question of whether, in spite of whatever losses there may have been, the extension of education to an ever-increasing segment of the population has not been a movement to be welcomed on moral grounds.

One basic difficulty that I find with many discussions of education is that although they recognize that differences and changes in social structure have an impact on educational systems in different countries and at different times, they tend to treat each educational system as if its value were to be assessed without reference to the entire social system within which it functions.[24] Consequently, while recognizing that education is influenced by institutional differences and changes, the standards of evaluation generally used do not take into account how well particular forms of education function within a particular system. Instead, these forms are judged in terms of whether they are seen as preferable to, or inferior to, another system of education that existed at another time or place, and which is then also considered apart from the context in which it grew and the society which it served.[25] I shall try not to commit this same error.

In attempting to understand and evaluate any segment of the process of education which exists at a particular time and place, it is necessary to obtain a clear comprehension of the background which those who are to be educated at that level will already bring with them. It is necessary also to bear in mind what particular ends that segment in the process is designed to serve. This is no less true of graduate education in general than of the first years of grade school, or of the undergraduate college, or of schools of medicine and law. In this sense any formal educational system, such as those with which we are acquainted in the West, forms a continuum, and does so even if the transitions from segment to segment are abrupt rather than gently modulated, for when a student goes from one stage to the next, however abrupt or gentle the transition may be, what he brings to that next stage will have been shaped by the experiences he had before reaching it. For this reason it is neither possible nor desirable to attempt to state what a graduate school, or an undergraduate college, or even a kindergarten should be unless one has some conception of that which the individual can be expected to bring with him when he enters it, and what it is that he can be expected to be going on to after he has left it.[26] Given the great differences in the nature and the standards of undergraduate training in the United States, one might think it impossible to say what postbaccalaureate education should be like, whether that education be in our graduate schools of arts and sciences or in professional schools such as those of law or medicine. However, our professional schools and our graduate schools of arts and sciences tend to solve this problem for themselves by means of their selective processes. In general they admit only those whose background and abilities appear to be such that the student, once admitted, can be expected to meet the standards set by the school. Similarly, graduate and professional schools aim to train their students for certain vocations, and not for others, although when there is an oversupply of those who have graduated from these schools many will not find openings in the careers for which they have been trained. Thus, the selective process and the career-oriented focus of the graduate and the professional schools in this country make it possible to understand and evaluate such schools in terms of their own standards.[27]

There is, however, another quite different difficulty that arises with respect to evaluating graduate schools, and it is with them rather than with professional schools that I shall be concerned. This difficulty centers on the fact that the aims and methods appropriate to graduate training are not identical in all disciplines. Putting the matter in an initially crude and approximate way, it may be said that the problems typically encountered in graduate training in the physical and biological sciences are extremely different from those that are apt to be characteristic of most humanistic studies.[28]

There are many ways of calling attention to these differences. One way is to compare the characteristics of a doctoral dissertation in the experimental sciences with a dissertation in English or American literature. Differences in length, in the types of research required, and of the usual role of the dissertation director in guiding the student's work are all so obvious that the point need not be labored. Furthermore, the focus of dissertations in the sciences is apt to be far sharper and more limited than is the case in most humanistic disciplines. One need merely attend doctoral orals in these areas and note the differences in the lines of questioning usually followed in order to have that contrast brought home. However, what I take to be the most significant difference between the training of scientists and of humanists is the fact that in the sciences there is a ladderlike progression which must be followed, at least in the earlier stages of scientific training: one cannot proceed in a science such as molecular biology without first having acquired certain tools which depend upon training in mathematics, physics, and chemistry, as well as biology. In the humanities, on the other hand, one can start at any one of a number of points and spread out in different directions; it is only the student's interests and needs—not the nature and the connections of the disciplines themselves—that determine in which direction he moves, and in what order he pursues these studies. The student of contemporary American literature, for example, may find himself first dealing with American political and intellectual history, then with some philosophical issues, with psychology or with anthropology, and with other literatures, but he is not bound to pursue all of these studies, nor to pursue them systematically, nor in any fixed order.

This difference throws considerable light on the undergraduate curriculum as well as on the relative lack of communication among some disciplines in our graduate schools. The undergraduate aiming for a career in medicine or the sciences must take a progressive series of courses in a fairly definite order if he is to prepare himself adequately for postbaccalaureate work.[29] He then fits in other nonscience courses as best he can in order to meet whatever distribution requirements there may be in the college he is attending, and to satisfy, in so far as time permits, interests of his own. He takes these nonscience courses in whatever order is most convenient for him, since they do not usually have—and in most cases need not have—any particular prerequisites.[30] On the other hand, the choices of science courses by undergraduates majoring in humanistic studies will usually be severely limited because of the fact that these students will not have acquired the tools which are presupposed by any but the most elementary science offerings, and usually these offerings are especially tailored to fit the limitations and the likely interests of nonscience majors. Thus, within our undergraduate colleges the "two cultures" phenomenon becomes entrenched. Furthermore, the same phenomenon permeates our graduate schools with respect to both students and faculty, for whereas scientists who have an interest in doing so may acquire a fair knowledge within one or another area in a humanistic discipline, humanists will not generally be in a position to acquire an equally advanced knowledge in any particular science.

There are those who, faced by this situation, advocate a reoriented curriculum for undergraduates in which the present degree of specialization will be curbed, and each student will receive broader training. Those who advocate reinstituting this type of program (for it was tried and has in large measure now been abandoned) sometimes fail to weigh the sacrifices that their proposals are likely to entail. I take it that no one would wish to extend the time it takes to train a doctor, which now stretches from his freshman year in college through his internship and residency, nor the time it takes to train a research scientist, which in most cases also extends from his freshman year through a postdoctoral fellowship. Yet this time would have to be extended if provision were to be made for gaining more than a perfunctory acquaintance with the humanities, the social sciences, and the arts during the student's undergraduate career.[31] Nor should I suppose that most persons who weighed the alternatives would, in the end, be willing to relinquish the fruits of the sciences which they now enjoy, even though they are often inclined to decry some of the consequences which have followed on our development of a high technology in medicine and in the physical and biological sciences.

In an essay entitled "Science and the Human Community,"

J. Robert Oppenheimer pointed out the rapidity with which both the quantity and the quality of scientific work has recently increased.[32] Those who inveigh against the supposedly heartless, mindless advances of science and technology would do well to stop and think of how much of what we now take for granted, and would not wish to do without, would be sacrificed if scientific specialization were to be universally discouraged in favor of that form of "limited liberal education which [formerly] had great charm and coherence," but was not, at least insofar as science was concerned, "really serious higher education at all."[33]

To be sure, Oppenheimer's praise for the quality of recent education did not extend to the humanities. His preference ran to the way in which philosophy, for example, had previously been taught.[34] Whether such a preference is justifiable is a difficult question to answer; we are here dealing with a scientist's preferences in a nonscientific field, and it would not be surprising if we were to find that present-day humanists much preferred the ways in which the sciences were formerly taught. I do not claim that in humanistic studies one is likely to find differences between former and present achievements which are as great as those to be found in the sciences; nevertheless, one should not underrate the advances that have been made in the breadth, the accuracy, and the sophistication of more recent historical scholarship, nor the value for the study of literature of the fact that contemporary humanists are apt to draw on a wider range of data relevant for literary interpretation and criticism than most of their predecessors had done.

Earlier I said that I saw some advantages in the fact that there was no longer a sharp line to be drawn between the undergraduate college and the graduate and professional school. I am now in a position to explain why this seems to me to be so. In the sciences at least, but also for those in the humanities who actually go on to graduate school, a well-constructed undergraduate program serves as the basis for the specialized study which one has a right to expect graduate education to provide. Where this background is lacking, graduate study will not truly be advanced study, since what can be accomplished at any stage in the educational process will, as I have pointed out, depend on what the student brings with him when entering that stage. What is wasteful in undergraduate education is that many programs which serve the legitimate interests of those who have already decided on their careers are also taken, perforce, by those who have no desire to continue their formal education. For the latter, an unspecialized liberal arts education may perhaps provide the richest background for whatever careers they subsequently follow. In this connection, however, there are two points that should not be overlooked.

The first is the fact, to which I have already alluded, that a decreasing proportion of students in our four-year colleges now end their formal education at the level of B.A., and past trends in our society suggest that this tendency is apt to continue into the future. Just as the college diploma supplanted the high school diploma in helping to gain access to better employment, so whether we like it or not the B.A. no longer carries the cachet it once did. It is therefore likely that further degrees will be sought by those whose interest in such degrees is not primarily educational but careerist, and I can see no reason why all universities should confine the advanced degrees that they give to those which up to now have been regarded as professional rather than vocational—as if our professions were not also vocations.

The second point to be borne in mind is that even though our liberal arts colleges claim to turn out well-educated individuals who, regardless of the careers they later followed, have profited from the culture they acquired, that type of education often failed, and failed very badly. Many liberally educated B.A.'s were in later life indistinguishable, so far as their intellectual attainments and cultural interests were concerned, from what they probably would have been had they never entered college. Of course, this was by no means true in all cases, but it should go without saying that one ought not to compare those who profited most from a liberal arts education with those who profited least from highly specialized training; when one compares the least-successful products of both, there may be very little to choose between them. Therefore, when I advocate a well-constructed undergraduate program that leads directly to graduate training for those who are to receive such training, I do not wish to be understood as advocating putting blinders on a person and training him to master a subject by repetition and rote learning. I am advocating a program designed to provide intellectual stimulation and the background and skills which it is necessary that he master in order to profit from graduate training and later be able, as a practitioner, to meet the demands placed upon him.

It is obvious that my advocacy of this position rests on the belief that there should not only be continuity between college and graduate study, but that the programs in our graduate schools, no less than in our law schools and schools of medicine, should look to the roles which their graduates are to play in the society to which they belong. If this is the case, our universities should guard against the danger of

diluting the seriousness and the quality of their doctoral programs
through admitting into them students whose objectives are different
from those of the majority of doctoral candidates, and who only wish
to pursue a terminal master's degree. It is of course a legitimate interest on the part of a university to wish to render service to its community by offering master's degrees for those whose occupations call for
additional technical training, as well as for those who have the time
and inclination to pursue programs designed for their personal, cultural enrichment. Nevertheless, unless the students in such programs
are excluded from the courses and seminars taken by doctoral candidates, the doctoral programs will be bound to suffer.[35] The purpose
of a doctoral program in the humanities, the social sciences, or the
natural sciences is to offer genuinely advanced training in an
academic discipline; those whose scholarly ambitions are more limited
ought to be regarded as being as much out of place in such a program
as a person with only amateur interests would be regarded as being
out of place in a graduate school of medicine or of law.

To hold that programs leading to advanced scholarly degrees
should be viewed in relation to the training they provide for subsequent careers is not to propose a radically altered Ph.D. program; it
merely suggests that some changes in present practices would be in
order. That no radical, wholesale alteration would be called for is due
to the fact that these programs have traditionally been directed toward training those who are preparing themselves for teaching or for
research, or for both. Nothing that I suggest should be taken as cast-
ing doubt on the need to continue preparing individuals for careers
of these types, and to do it through Ph.D. programs. Where change
seems most in order is not in the sciences but in the humanities, for in
this area little attention has been paid to the possibility of a linkage
between graduate studies and careers other than teaching. The development of such linkages would doubtless entail some cutback in
the amount of time spent in attempting to master every aspect of the
central discipline, with this time being allocated to work that would
help equip students to understand the nature and needs of certain
types of nonacademic institutions with which they might later become
affiliated. Among the types of nonacademic institutions which may
increasingly offer career opportunities for persons with advanced degrees in, say, the humanities, would be branches of federal, state, and
local government, museums, businesses, and public-service organizations. Also, adjustments in the conventional doctoral curriculum have
recently been widely advocated in order to make the training it af-
fords more useful for future teachers who have not the inclination to

commit themselves to careers in which scholarly research occupies a central position, but who nevertheless seek rigorous, advanced training in order to prepare themselves to teach. What sorts of curricular adjustments should be made to accommodate these and other persons, or whether degrees other than the doctorate should be made available for that purpose, is not my present concern. What I wish to indicate is that any adjustments that must be made if we are to accommodate those whose future careers do not demand that they complete all present requirements for the doctorate, but who nonetheless seek training beyond a master's degree, are adjustments which can presumably be made without abandoning our research-oriented programs which have been, and remain, as important for genuinely advanced teaching as they are for specialized research.

What does follow from what I have said is that throughout our educational system there be a continuing proliferation of options, and that the reform to be undertaken in our lower schools, in our two-year colleges, four-year colleges, and universities should be designed to improve the ways in which individual institutions fulfill their respective missions; that it should not be assumed that at each level there are fixed goals that every institution operating at that level should achieve. The justification for urging greater pluralism in our educational system rests on my already expressed belief that in the increasingly complex technical society in which we live, more education is needed for an ever-increasing proportion of our population in order that more individuals can put their capacities to work in a productive fashion. This already holds with respect to the need for more vocational training for those whose formal education does not now extend beyond the high school level; it will, I believe, also come to hold more and more with respect to the professional training of persons whose interests, abilities, and opportunities have led them to enter our colleges and universities. It is obvious, however, that the system of higher education which we originally inherited from the English and German universities is not competent to offer the necessary training: the types of career choices for which these forms of advanced education would help to equip students are far too limited to meet the demands of mass education in a complex industrial society. A readaptation to present conditions of the original goals of the land-grant colleges is what I believe is needed.

What Clark Kerr termed the multiversity is the form of institution best adapted to meeting such needs. In fact, it was the existence of these needs, and their rapid proliferation in the last decades, that has been responsible for the largely unplanned growth of the multiversity. This growth was greatly accelerated by demands placed on the educational system by World War II, and the role of the federal government in the growth of our multiversities has been so striking that Clark Kerr himself spoke of the multiversity as "the federal grant university." Without funding from governmental sources, both federal and state, the multiversity could not exist; and to this funding there have been added very substantial grants from industry and private foundations. The magnitude of this funding makes our system of higher education very heavily dependent upon it, and has caused a great deal of justifiable concern. While it is the case that such funding is not confined to multiversities, they have undoubtedly been its chief beneficiaries. As a consequence, one finds that in some quarters the attack on the multiversity rests primarily on its connection with government and industry because of the fear that the whole structure of education will be made subservient to what are claimed to be national needs, and that scientists and scholars will lose their independence and their ability to serve as critics of those segments of society on whose funding they depend.[36]

It cannot be denied that there are dangers in the fact that our present system of higher education is heavily dependent on government and industry, but no system of education is ever self-supporting: in its origins at least, it always derived its support from outside itself, whether that source was a church, a philanthropist, or a government. And unless we, today, are willing to do away with most forms of scientific training and research in our universities, we shall be forced to continue to rely heavily on some form or forms of governmental support.[37] Our problem, then, is one of placing enough bulwarks between sources of support and the objectives of research so that scientists can make relatively pressure-free decisions as to what is of scientific importance, and as to how work of that sort can best be carried on. To a very considerable extent a state of affairs of this kind has existed in our recent experience, though it must be admitted that it is constantly under pressure. In this connection, however, it is noteworthy that those scholars and scientists who have been outstanding beneficiaries of federal support have not proved to be too timid to be among the most outspoken of all recent critics of government and of industry.

Even so, relations between scholars and scientists and those on whose support they depend have not in all cases been amicable. It is not unnatural that even when government and industry allow a high degree of autonomy to those whom they help support, the decisions they reach as to which further programs should and shouldn't be funded may not be popular with all of the scientists who are affected. It is in these matters of priority, which often represent differences between basic and applied research, that conflicts between government and industry on the one hand, and the scientific community on the other, are most apt to arise. It is well to remember, however, that similar sorts of conflict arise at almost every point in the democratic political process. It behooves scientists to recognize that in such conflicts what is often at stake is a social and political issue, not always a question in which scientists as scientists have a special degree of competence. Furthermore, it is important to recognize that there is always some danger that scientists, because they are scientists, may tend to favor whichever of two alternatives is likely to yield the greater scientific payoff, failing to give equal weight to other forms of social benefit. It is for this reason, if for no other, that the education of scientists should not be exclusively technical. On the other hand, I do not believe that this argues in favor of the sort of broadly humanistic education most often identified with a liberal education. If one is to make responsible choices when faced by the complexities of modern life, it is surely of great importance that one be educated to think constructively, and with considerable technical sophistication, concerning social issues. Some humanistic studies may be of at least indirect help in leading a person to do so, but without a grasp of the nature and changing forms of our social institutions such indirect help as can be derived from earlier forms of liberal education may be of little service in our present perplexities. Consequently, I see merit in demands that our traditional conceptions of a liberal education be brought up to date and be more relevant. The difficulty in most appeals to relevance is, however, that they are apt to be based on the belief that once a problem has been identified, and its impact on human life has been deeply felt, the ways in which it should be solved will become fairly obvious. What is not appreciated is that the analytic training required to know how social problems can be solved, or how their disastrous effects can at least be mitigated, is no less exacting than the training needed in the most rigorous of the sciences. If I am not mistaken, what is now required in rethinking liberal education is how we can best make a start toward providing such training. In seeing this as a major present task I am not, I believe, perverting the goal of education; I am simply translating into contemporary terms something to which both Newman and Mill would have subscribed— that we bend every effort to finding adequate means whereby what is best in society can be preserved, and what is not can be changed.

NOTES

1. David Riesman, "Experiments in Higher Education," in Howard Mumford Jones, David Riesman, and Robert Ulich, *The University and the New World* (Toronto: University of Toronto Press, 1972), pp. 37-38.

2. United States Department of Commerce, Bureau of the Census, *Statistical Abstract of the United States, 1976* (Washington, D.C.: Government Printing Office, 1976), p. 146, table 244.

3. For a discussion of some distribution requirements and also for requirements for the major, cf. Laurence Veysey, "Stability and Experiment in the Undergraduate Curriculum," pp. 36-43. On the increase of specialization in the social sciences, cf. Neil J. Smelser, "The Social Sciences," pp. 126-30. For the level of specialization in the natural sciences, cf. Paul Doty and Dorothy Zinberg, "Science and the Undergraduate," pp. 179-80. Each of the above articles appeared in Carl Kaysen, ed., *Content and Context: Essays on College Education* (New York: McGraw-Hill, 1973).

4. *The Idea of a University*, ed. Charles Frederick Harrold (New York: Longmans, Green, 1947), p. xxvii.

5. Ibid., pp. 99-101.

6. Ibid., p. 90. Cf. his preface, pp. xxiii-xxiv.

7. Ibid., pp. 94-95 and 99.

8. Ibid., pp. 135-36.

9. I say "at first surprising" since when one takes account of the ways in which, and the extent to which, Mill altered the psychological theory of Bentham's utilitarianism, the view that he takes in the "Inaugural Address" regarding the role of liberal education in character formation is wholly consistent with his utilitarianism. (On the contrast between Mill's psychological theory and Bentham's, cf. my article "On Interpreting Mill's *Utilitarianism*," *Journal of the History of Philosophy* 6 [1968]: 35-46).

10. John Stuart Mill, "Inaugural Lecture," *Dissertations and Discussions* (Boston: William V. Spencer, 1867), vol. 4, pp. 387 and 388.

In an exceedingly able book, *The Promise of Wisdom: An Introduction to Philosophy of Education* (Philadelphia: Lippincott, 1968), J. Glenn Gray points out what Dewey had noted, that "liberal" as used with reference to education suggests that which is free and generous, and Gray expresses a preference for the phrase "a generous education" (p. 80 n.). Unfortunately, however, he traded on various associations which have grown up around the term "generous"; originally, as the *New English Dictionary* makes clear, its primary sense had nothing to do with sympathetic insight, freedom of inquiry, and the like, but was connected with noble lineage and high birth. Examined sociologically (although not linguistically), a similar connection may be said to have persisted in many of the private colleges which were dominated by the ideal of liberal education.

11. *The Idea of a University*, ed. Charles Frederick Harrold, pp. xxix-xxxi.

12. *The Idea of a University*, ed. Charles Frederick Harrold, Discourse VI,

"Knowledge Viewed in Relation to Learning." On Newman's concept of "the gentleman," cf. Harrold's preface, pp. xxi–xxiii.

13. *Dissertations and Discussion*, vol. 4, p. 386.

14. Ibid., vol. 4, p. 387.

15. Ibid., vol. 4, p. 399.

16. Laurence Veysey, op. cit., p. 7.

One can find many expressions of this view in more recent statements by college and university presidents. I choose one almost at random. It is to be found in the preface to *Liberal Education and the Democratic Ideal* (New Haven: Yale University Press, 1962), which is a collection of speeches by A. Whitney Griswold, a recent president of Yale. He said (p. vi):

> Not only does [liberal education] concern itself more directly and vitally than any other type of education with the good life that is the end of all political society; it also shows a like concern for the means whereby that society is to be governed and the good life achieved.

Newman, too, held that one important consequence of a liberal education was that it "produced better public men, men of the world, men whose names would descend to posterity" (*The Idea of a University*, p. 128).

17. Thorstein Veblen, *The Higher Learning in America* (New York: B. W. Huebsch, 1918), p. 21.

18. Ibid., p. 20. For his contrast between colleges and universities, cf. pp. 22–26; for that between universities and professional schools, cf. pp. 26–31.

19. Veblen recognized that there were strong pressures in our competitive system toward making universities more subservient to practical ends, but he believed that there was a "long-term idealistic drift" which would prevent the subversion of the higher goal of disinterested learning (cf. pp. 42–44).

20. Purer, because the German university included some professional schools. As we see in Abraham Flexner's acceptance of that model, "the learned professions," such as medicine and law, were deemed to belong by right within the university, but schools which emphasized "technical or vocational education," such as schools of business, journalism, or library science, did not. On what was supposed to constitute "a learned profession" cf. Abraham Flexner, *Universities, American, English, German* (New York: Oxford University Press, 1930), pp. 29–30.

21. Quotation from Eric Ashby, *Any Person, Any Study* (New York: McGraw-Hill, 1971), p. ix. For an independent general statement of some of Ashby's own views, the reader may well consult *Adapting Universities to a Technological Society* (San Francisco: Jossey-Bass, 1974). Particularly relevant to some points in the present paper are his characterization of the English model (pp. 3–4), his criticism of attempts to establish "general education" within our colleges and universities (pp. 11–12), and his insistence with respect to the introduction of mass higher education that "'More' does not mean 'worse', but undoubtedly 'more means different'" (p. 136).

22. The most vigorous opponent of a drift toward the multiversity has

almost surely been Robert M. Hutchins, who attacked what he termed "the service station conception of a university" in *The Higher Learning in America* (New Haven: Yale University Press, 1936), p. 6.

23. Robert M. Hutchins, *The University of Utopia* (Chicago: University of Chicago Press, 1953).

24. This seems to me especially true of Abraham Flexner's *Universities, American, English, German.* He recognizes (pp. 4–5, passim) that educational systems reflect differences in the national experience of the countries with which he was concerned, but he never examined these systems in terms of the other institutions to which they were related in that society. In short, a genuinely sociological point of view played no role in his analyses.

25. This stricture is obviously not applicable to the educational writings of either Dewey or Veblen, whatever may be one's opinion of the merits of their views regarding the role of education in modern society. Nor would I say that it is applicable to those works of Clark Kerr and Eric Ashby which I have cited, and from which I believe I have learned a great deal.

The best and most extensive available study of the role of higher education in contemporary American life is Howard R. Bowen's *Investment in Learning: The Individual and Social Value of American Higher Education* (San Francisco: Jossey-Bass, 1977). Critics of the present paper may be inclined to hold that I undervalue the beneficial social consequences that flow from the traditional ethos of higher education, but I do not disagree with Bowen's conclusions concerning this matter (Bowen, pp. 267–77). It should be noted that Bowen's conclusions apply to our system of higher education as a whole, not to any specific segment of it. In fact, as chapter 8 of his book makes clear, no major differences exist between the changes brought about in the social values of students who attend different types of nondenominational colleges or universities.

A somewhat similar objection to my thesis has been advanced by Richard Rorty, who kindly read the present paper in manuscript. After pointing out that I have not discussed the sociological role of academics, he argued that, by and large, theirs has tended to be a quasi-sacerdotal role which has been of importance to society. He suggested that because colleges and universities have been regarded as somehow apart from the mainstream of life, they have been viewed as better or purer than other institutions. As a consequence, academics have gained some degree of moral authority, the loss of which would be harmful. With respect to this criticism I feel that whatever moral authority is presently vested in university teachers, and in universities as institutions, it is not likely to be lost if they become more and more directly involved in the general life of society. In fact, it now appears that those academics who presently speak with greatest moral authority are not academics whose intellectual concerns are remote from the social issues of the day, but are precisely those who—like our atomic physicists and biological scientists—are engaged in research which has immediate social consequences. To be sure, the funding of scientific research raises special problems concerning the relations between the university and government and industry, but as

I shall later suggest, these problems are an inescapable aspect of modern scientific research: they are not tied to problems concerning the goals of undergraduate or graduate education.

26. If one assumes with respect to some particular stage that many individuals will leave the system of formal education after that stage, whereas many others will not, it follows from what I have said that an evaluation of what can be expected to be accomplished in that particular stage should be judged with respect to each of these groups, and not with respect to one of them only.

27. Whether these standards are themselves subject to further evaluation is not here at issue. However, from what has previously been said it should be clear that I believe that in evaluating the standards themselves one must look to the needs of the society which the schools must serve, rather than setting up standards which only conform to some ideal of what educated men should under all circumstances know.

28. This is crude and approximate only. It should be recognized that within each of these areas there is likely to be great diversity. For example, different problems arise in different humanistic disciplines, as one can note if one considers the sorts of training necessary in archaeology, in philosophy, and in comparative literature. There is also diversity encountered within the natural sciences, depending in part on whether the aim of the training lies primarily in teaching, in so-called pure research, or in the possible industrial applications of the discipline. When one also takes into account the diversity of both the methods and the objectives to be found among the various social sciences, it becomes obvious that the generalizing statements which I must make would have to be carefully qualified and greatly refined to be strictly accurate. I beg the reader's indulgence in this matter.

29. It is debatable whether all premedical school requirements are in fact essential for the pursuit of a medical career. It has sometimes been suggested that the emphasis on concentration in the sciences is little more than a screening device used by medical schools in relation to their selective processes. I am not in a position to assess what, if any, degree of truth is in this suggestion. To be sure, if every premedical student were enrolled in an undergraduate program attached to a specific medical school, and no undergraduate needed to prepare himself for admission to any medical school other than that toward which his undergraduate scientific training had been pointed, premedical requirements might be greatly reduced. However, with the exception of Brown University, this option does not obtain in any college or university with which I am acquainted. Furthermore, it is possible and perhaps even likely that intensive training in various sciences may better equip a premedical student to understand developments which later arise in medical research and practice than would any more limited scientific training which had been designed simply to satisfy minimal admission requirements.

30. It is also open to doubt whether the premedical student who takes nonscience courses late in his undergraduate career, when his professional interests have fully solidified, devotes as much energy to the materials in those

courses as he would were they directly related to his future career. If that is the case, a question arises as to whether such courses are likely to provide deep intellectual stimulation or greatly enrich his cultural background. In many cases they may contribute nothing more than a thin layer of veneer.

31. I find it ironic that we now hear distressed college and university administrators urging that we return to the period in which so-called general education was a widely adopted model, while they at the same time sponsor acceleration in premedical training and often take pride in how advanced their offerings in the sciences have become. Similarly, it should be noted that there has been a proliferation of courses in humanistic disciplines which are available to undergraduates, and this militates against the reintroduction of a program of core courses, such as formerly characterized liberal arts programs. I have not noticed that those who now wish to return to the basics in undergraduate education would be willing to remove some of the newer undergraduate options, such as those which relate to Far Eastern studies, to anthropology, or to problems related to ecology or the urban environment.

In this connection I must note that Glenn Gray's plea for a generous education which will promote wisdom and give us the capacity to apply knowledge to all aspects of our personal and social lives fails to show how such a goal can be achieved within the framework of a college career. In the chapter devoted to the curriculum in his *Promise of Wisdom* (Philadelphia: Lippincott, 1968), Gray acknowledges the need for specialization in order to cope with an increasingly complex technological society, but he insists that such specialization is wholly compatible with promoting general courses which can yield insight into the underlying principles and the interconnections of all the arts and sciences. What models for such general courses he may have in mind is left unclear, nor does he attempt to show how both objectives can actually be realized within a single curriculum by a single body of teachers, and with the time allotted to a student's undergraduate career.

32. In Charles Frankel, ed., *Issues in University Education* (New York: Harper and Brothers, 1959), pp. 48–62.

33. Oppenheimer, "Science and the Human Community," in Frankel, op. cit., p. 48.

34. Ibid., p. 49.

35. Unfortunately, there are at present many doctoral programs (at least in the humanities) in which no such line of demarcation presently exists. It is even more unfortunate that present financial exigencies at many institutions have led to the admission of an ever-greater proportion of terminal master's degree candidates into courses and seminars in which doctoral candidates take much of their work.

36. Cf. Robert Paul Wolff, *The Ideal of the University* (Boston: Beacon Press, 1969), pt. I, chap. 3, especially pp. 39–42.

37. In "The Community of Scholars," (in *Compulsory Mis-education and the Community of Scholars* [New York: Random House, Vintage Books, 1962]), Paul Goodman insists that "education is an instrument of social needs, and by and large . . . the powers of society get the education they want and deserve"

(p. 210; cf. pp. 211 and 225). His criticism of contemporary education is thus founded on his criticism of contemporary society, and stands or falls with his avowedly anarchistic ideals. That he is an opponent of the sciences and of modern technology is entirely clear in what he puts forward as his "simple proposal" for educational reform (*The Community of Scholars,* chap. 8). He advocates secession as the instrument of needed reform: a core of some five senior scholars should secede from each of twenty colleges and universities, taking their students with them, and setting up dissenting academies of their own. That such a proposal views the humanities, some social sciences, and the creative arts as being alone worthy of cultivation in a community of scholars is obvious. Almost all of those seceding scholars whose work lay in the sciences—and many humanists and social scientists as well—would have to leave behind them all the tools essential to their work.

Comments by William K. Frankena

Mandelbaum has put a great deal before us. I shall confine myself to graduate education and to philosophical questions about it, ignoring other aspects of Mandelbaum's paper, much as I admire them. I shall define graduate education as education or teaching that presupposes a bachelor's degree and falls under a graduate school proper rather than under a professional school such as law, medicine, engineering, education, or theology. I have to confess that, if I had written a main paper for this conference, I would have committed most of the errors Mandelbaum warns us against; my temperament and philosophical bent are so different from his. This will come out in my discussion of the contentions, in the way of philosophy of graduate education proper, which are explicit or implicit in what he says.

One of these contentions, which takes up much of the first half of Mandelbaum's paper, is that there should not be a sharp line of demarcation between undergraduate education and graduate education, such as there once was, with undergraduate education being liberal or general and graduate education being vocational or specialized. I shall not discuss Mandelbaum's arguments for this view. Our question is: What are its implications for graduate education? Mandelbaum uses it to point to the conclusion that the recent drift toward specialization and vocationalism in undergraduate education is all right and even desirable. One could, however, use it to support the conclusion that graduate education should not be wholly vocational and specialized. But Mandelbaum does not seem to wish us to draw out this implication; indeed, he seems to proceed on the assumption that graduate education should be wholly vocational in aim and specialized in nature. He does say, just at the end, that the education of scientists should not be "exclusively technical" (p. 26), should even be liberal in a more up-to-date or relevant sense, but this does not mean that their graduate education should include any nontechnical or humanistic studies.

I believe one of the main questions of the philosophy of graduate education to be precisely whether or not it should be wholly vocational, i.e., whether its aims should be wholly vocational and whether its means (methods, programs, etc.) are to be determined solely on the basis of their conduciveness to its vocational ends. If we say yes, as Mandelbaum seems to, we can still recognize and insist, and I gather Mandelbaum would, that there are several rather different kinds of vocations graduate education should prepare people for:

1. Teaching in undergraduate colleges or even more elementary schools.
2. Teaching at a graduate level.
3. The vocation of doing research, in any field whatsoever, within a university or outside it.
4. Other sorts of nonteaching and nonresearch careers in business, government, educational administration, etc.

But should we say yes without any debate even then?

Mandelbaum also defends, in the second half of his paper, the view that a university should be pluralistic in its aims and take the form of a multiversity. I agree with this as to the university as a whole, although I see no reason why every university should take such a form. The question for us is whether the graduate education part of a university should be pluralistic in its aims and take the form of a kind of mini-multiversity. I agree with Mandelbaum that graduate education should be pluralistic in its aims, at least in the sense of preparing people for the above four kinds of vocations. But, if we take seriously the possibility that graduate education should be even more pluralistic and include a nonvocationally oriented segment, then we can still hold that this segment of graduate education should not be pluralistically conceived but should be essentially the same for everyone, even if it should take the form of the more up-to-date or relevant liberal education Mandelbaum talks about at the end. It might, for instance, all take the form, to use Mandelbaum's words, of educating people "to make responsible choices when faced by the complexities of modern life . . . to think constructively, and with considerable . . . sophistication, concerning social issues" (p. 26).

I should also like to comment on the metaphilosophical view underlying Mandelbaum's paper and reappearing in papers by Pusic and McMurrin, that one should not engage in "any attempt to reflect on graduate education apart from the broader context in which it is embedded." One must not "treat [graduate education] as if its value were to be assessed without reference to the entire social system within which it functions."

In attempting to understand and evaluate any segment of the process of education . . . at a particular time and place, it is necessary to obtain a clear comprehension of the background which those who are to be educated at that level will . . . bring with them,

[and] ... also to bear in mind what particular ends that segment in the process is designed to serve. [P. 18]

This sounds nicely pragmatic or realistic, and it is true in some sense. I wish that Mandelbaum had given us a clearer comprehension of the ends graduate education as such is "designed to serve" and of the "standards" by which it should be evaluated, but, even if he had, I would be troubled by his approach, being more of a Platonist than he. I agree that one cannot work out a satisfactory view of what graduate education should be today without any reference to the social system in which it is to function. It is another thing to say that one's entire philosophy of graduate education is to be determined completely by the facts about the social system that prevails. To say that is to espouse a kind of conservatism and relativism that I find hard to accept. Mandelbaum does not say that. He even insists that he is against complacency, and I know he is; he believes one may even be "critical of existing social trends." Nevertheless, he proceeds as if all our thinking about what graduate education should be like were simply a function of the nature and beliefs of the society to which we belong. This seems to be the significance of his note 27.

My own belief is that if there is a place for criticism of existing society, then there is also a place for a part or kind of philosophy of graduate education that is independent of the facts about any given society. I would like to hear more about this part or kind of philosophy of graduate education. I agree, of course, that it should not be carried on "apart from the broader context" of a view about what society as a whole should be like. No doubt one's final conclusions about what to do practically in graduate education should depend partly on the facts about one's society and the rest of our educational system, but this does not mean that all of one's premises must rest on such facts. These may still rest on some Platonic vision of the ideal, or they may just be basic value judgments and ethical principles, possibly different from those prevailing in one's culture.

Reply to Frankena

Professor Mandelbaum: I take it that three major points are involved in Frankena's response to my paper; the third, I believe, is the most critical issue that divides us.

With respect to the first, I contended that there is no sharp line, and there probably should be none, between undergraduate and graduate education. Frankena asks whether I then think that graduate education should become more liberalized or should be vocational. If it is to be wholly vocational, where will the liberal, broadening element arise?

In a paper you will hear this afternoon, Vlastos argues eloquently for liberalization at the graduate school level, and I agree with him that a great deal of that can in fact be carried on. With regard to Frankena's point, I admit that there is not just one vocation to which graduate training leads, that there are teachers in different kinds of schools, and even, as I suggest, people who are going to do graduate work who are not going into teaching. I think that all of those distinct vocational missions could be accommodated within a single department if it also used the other facilities of any university. Graduate education which crosses departmental lines is implicit in some of what Vlastos will say, and I agree with him that our departmental lines are presently apt to be too impermeable. I doubt, however, whether graduate training can be as widely extended into other disciplines as he seems to suggest it should be. I think this is a practical problem which has to be worked out on an ad hoc basis, and different universities will doubtless differ as to the success they can achieve along these lines. But this is a far cry from the question Frankena raised as to whether there should be a common liberal core for all students in all graduate departments, regardless of their vocational interests. My answer to that question is negative, and I stick to my view that vocational education, even at the graduate level, need not necessarily be narrowing.

As to Frankena's second point, he raises a question about whether I commend the idea of a graduate school, such as arts and sciences, being a replica of the multiversity, that is, a mini-multiversity. Although I probably should not say so in this building, I must confess that I don't really know what a graduate school of arts and sciences is. My past association with this university has been relatively slight. My other associations with graduate schools have been with Harvard, Yale, and Johns Hopkins. So far as I can see from my experience with them, graduate education is not a unitary thing: it is largely departmentally regulated in all essential respects, though with some rather general, and not very precise overall quality control. I don't think that what I have been suggesting will greatly change the situation as it exists in the universities with which I am familiar.

But here the third and larger question arises. It involves what one might describe as my functionalism, using that term as anthropologists and sociologists use it. Functionalists have often been criticized for being conservative, for accepting the status quo rather than appealing to what ought to be. And this is somewhat true of what I have said. I am willing to face the charge. To defend myself I should like to say that although I am a contextualist or functionalist in my estimates of such institutions as our economic or educational institutions, or our forms of family life, I do not want to be interpreted as saying that I would hold the same thing with respect to all aspects of culture, such as art or science. In short, I draw a distinction between societal institutions and cultural phenomena, and I do not necessarily interpret art, science, or other cultural phenomena, which are not tied to specific institutions, in a wholly functional, contextualist manner.

I think the easiest way to answer Frankena is to admit that in those matters which concern us here, I have not drawn the distinction he would like me to draw between the *ought* and the *is*. I think I could perhaps suggest the difference that separates us, and perhaps the difference which separates me from Vlastos, by recalling to you the deep but friendly differences that separated Thomas Huxley and Matthew Arnold with respect to what constituted a liberal education. The tendency to criticize what is the case through comparing an institution as it exists today, and will presumably exist in the immediate future, with the same institution as it existed in the past is, to some extent, illegitimate. This is what I think Huxley refused to do, but which he and others, although not wholly justifiably, thought that Arnold did. Arnold, he thought, was looking back to a particular type of education which had a disguised vocational aim—training in those fields which had been regarded as important for a certain class of persons aspiring to political and moral leadership in their society. Huxley's interest in the polytechnic schools and in training in science was looking to what would be the function of liberal education in the present and the immediately impending future. In this debate I am to be judged a Huxleyite.

Questions and Answers

Q1: If students are to be admitted to doctoral humanities programs whose major concerns and inclinations are toward nonacademic careers, then isn't there a danger that precisely the sort of dilution of the quality of more traditionally oriented academic Ph.D. training may occur, as you suggest, with terminal M.A. programs in the humanities?

A: I have expressed my hope that there will be a widely recognized degree between the master's degree and the Ph.D., which unlike the M.A. would be entirely parasitic on the Ph.D. Both Columbia and Yale, and now NYU, have the degree of Master of Philosophy, which is the Ph.D. with all qualifying examinations, courses, etc., but without a dissertation.

On the basis of a survey conducted by Ernest May of Harvard and Dorothy Harrison of the New York State Education Department, there seems to be an increasing tendency in some fields in the humanities, particularly philosophy, for students to want to go beyond the A.B. degree. They want more rigorous training in philosophy for their own advancement and satisfaction, but are not interested in a career in teaching. I hope there will be such a degree, and that it would not only involve advanced training in philosophy, up to the predissertation level, but would also allow for courses taken outside the philosophy department—courses that would be relevant to whatever vocation the student may subsequently pursue. This would involve a cut down, not a watering down, of the extensiveness of the training within the discipline, but would permit students to get training in other things which may be of later vocational interest to them. With respect to philosophy, for example, courses in computer science, in systems-analysis, statistics, and the like, come immediately to mind. I also think that courses in medical ethics, and in other fields relevant to applied ethics, would be useful and would not in any way constitute a watering down of the philosophic training received.

Q2: Could what Newman and Mill say be accepted if one removed their class bias and if one assumed that liberal education will not necessarily precede professional vocational education? Do you not underrate the value and importance of liberal education as an essential part of professional education and practice?

A: I'd like to separate these two questions. To the first I would answer perhaps so, although I would have to know what sort of liberal education would then remain. I would also acknowledge that for those undergraduates who have no idea as to what subsequent careers they wish to follow, though these seem to get fewer in number with each passing year, what is generally thought of as a liberal education may be as good an option as any.

As to the second part of the question, whether I underrate the value and importance of a liberal education as an essential part of professional education and practice, my answer is no. I really don't want to draw this distinction between professional and liberal education. I think that if vocationally oriented courses are properly taught at both the undergraduate and graduate levels, some of the wider implications of these studies, which Passmore will be stressing, will be brought out. I also believe that throwing in courses that are supposedly liberalizing, but which are remote from careerist and vocationalist interests, aren't necessarily going to be effective, at least not on the graduate level.

The Philosophy of Graduate Education

John Passmore

An Australian university with which I am reasonably well acquainted, but out of a mixture of prudence, loyalty, and charity shall not name, recently set up a working party to reconsider its graduate education program. That committee has issued a preliminary document, inviting submissions, and, to facilitate such submissions, has "tentatively drawn up" a list of "the broad aims of graduate education." I propose to take that statement of aims as a starting point, not out of local pride, but because it illustrates in an admirably succinct fashion the confusions and cross-purposes to which discussions of graduate education are universally subject. The working party distinguishes three main aims:

1. To train graduate students in the conduct of research, thereby stimulating critical and creative thinking on questions of fundamental importance, and, by so doing, to throw light on the problems of contemporary society;

2. To provide such training at the graduate level as will meet the perceived needs of the community whether short-term or long-term;

3. To contribute to the general pool of scholarship and discovery.

I shall presume, in a Platonic spirit, that the philosophy of graduate education is an attempt to discover the "proper excellence" of graduate education, what, of the various things it can do, is particularly worth doing and it is peculiarly suited to do. The working party is suggesting, in these terms, that graduate education has not one single proper excellence but rather a conjoint set of proper excellences. We shall examine these supposed excellences separately, without taking it for granted that they are mutually consistent.

First, however, a point of explanation. The working party, in the passage I quoted, is talking only about the doctorate and, more narrowly, the doctorate awarded for advanced work in the humanities, the natural sciences, or the social sciences. Going on to discuss the

40

master's degree, it remarks that it "had some difficulty" in identifying any single "philosophy" for that degree. It therefore contented itself with distinguishing the different types of master's degrees and nominating the special excellence of each such type.

Did time and space permit, we might usefully follow its example, drawing up a more internationally-minded classification and including as master's degrees those Oxford postgraduate baccalaureates and diplomas which differ from what are elsewhere master's degrees only through an idiosyncracy of nomenclature. Any such list would range very widely, from the Oxford master's degree "in course," as it used to be called in the United States, awarded on no other ground than that the bachelor has grown older, can afford to pay the necessary fee, and has kept out of jail, through the Scottish master's degree awarded for completion of a four-year undergraduate course, then by way of remedial degrees, professional degrees, try-out degrees, further education degrees, consolatory degrees, interdisciplinary degrees, preparatory degrees, to what are substantially mini–doctoral degrees. Each such type of master's degree, one might say, has its own philosophy; something peculiar to it would be lost if it were to be abolished. But the degree as such marks nothing at all, not even that an education has been carried beyond the bachelor's level.

If the working party found some difficulty in discovering a single philosophy for the master's degree, it is for the good reason that there is no such single philosophy. We might envisage in fantasy a world in which Oxford and Scotland changed their ways, where professional master's degrees were everywhere converted into diplomas, where the master's degree universally signified the completion of substantial academic work beyond the bachelor's level, although not sufficient in research content to count as a doctorate. But, in reality, the degree is likely to continue to be polymorphous, even within a single university.

To return then to the doctorate. The working party puts research first. The object of the Ph.D., it says, is "to train graduate students in the conduct of research." There is nothing revolutionary in this. Indeed the emphasis on research-training is sometimes carried to startling extremes. Consider the following, the product of a Berkeley committee in 1966: "First and foremost [graduate education] is training and only as a by-product is it education. The graduate is viewed primarily as an initiate undergoing preparation for a defined vocation: historian, economist, or physicist. The task of the faculty is to ensure that the student acquires the qualifications and special skills appropriate to the particular vocation."[1]

On this view, graduate education has but one proper excellence, as, to cite the Berkeley statement further, a "specialized apprentice-ship" in research. No doubt the exceptionally uncompromising man-ner in which the Berkeley committee framed this philosophy of graduate education partly derives from its special character as a mili-tant response to student radicalism, with its characteristic hostility to vocations, training, specialization, apprenticeship. Obviously, the working party does not agree with the Berkeley committee; graduate training, it says, "stimulates critical and creative thinking on questions of fundamental importance." If it does this, it is educational in intent, not merely as a by-product.

Nonetheless the Berkeley statement fairly represents a leading tendency in graduate education: to identify it with specialized training to an extent which makes the use of the word "education" in relation to it something of a misnomer—at least if "education" is used in that evaluative sense which links it with the concept of an educated person. The graduate, to requote the Berkeley manifesto, "is viewed primarily as an initiate undergoing preparation for a defined vocation: histo-rian, economist, or physicist." The word initiate in this context is an interesting one. Philosophers of education have not uncommonly ar-gued that initiation into such forms of activity as history, economics, or physics is precisely what constitutes education in the eulogistic sense of that word. But now, in a German-influenced manner, history, physics, and economics are being thought of not primarily as critical and creative intellectual activities but as vocations, or, less grandly, as jobs for which graduates need to be trained much as a doctor or a mechanic is trained. Alternatively, it is being taken for granted that education, by its very nature, must be generalized and diffuse, so that the mere fact that doctoral training is specialized prevents it, except *per accidens,* from being educative.

With these alternatives in the back of our mind, let us ask three questions:

1. Why should there not be research training at the under-graduate level?
2. In what exactly does training consist?
3. Is training for research essential for every doctorate?

Not long ago I should have felt somewhat embarrassed, playing the role of a visitor from outer space, to ask in the United States the first of these questions—Why cannot research training be undertaken at the undergraduate level? The United States for long adhered to a three-tier educational system. To describe its functional divisions crudely, the high school was for socialization; the college was for liberalization; the graduate school was for specialization. And research was conceived of as something which only specialists would need to undertake.

But we are in search of a general philosophy of graduate education, not merely an American philosophy of American graduate education. Or at the very least—for in many European countries the distinction between graduate and undergraduate education does not exist—we are trying to formulate a philosophy of English-speaking graduate education. In other English-speaking countries, if to varying degrees, specialization has usually been introduced into the education system much earlier than in the United States. And even in subjects in which they are not specializing, students are already expected in the later stages of their high school, to say nothing of their undergraduate education, to engage in a considerable degree of independent work.

Whereas the Berkeley committee supposes apprenticeship to begin at the graduate level, the 1966 Oxford Commission of Inquiry into education at Oxford says of the Oxford tutorial: "If a few bore-holes are sunk in different types of territory and the *apprentice* learns to manage in that area, he may be left to carry out further exploration on these lines by himself" (§233, my italics). In such subjects as history, at least, high school students will have been weaned away from textbooks long before they finish that stage in their education. During an honors degree at the university they will already be undertaking what deserves to be called research, if on a necessarily modest scale.

To the regret of those who, like E. J. McGrath, blame the graduate schools for the decline in liberal education, the movement in the United States, at least in some of the better colleges, would appear to be in the English direction.[2] A professor of chemistry at Dartmouth is prepared to speak of "the spectrum of research and teaching activity as a continuum from the undergraduate through the postdoctoral."[3] The relationship between college and graduate school can no longer be symbolized, so Storr has argued, by a box on top of a box but rather by "two upright, somewhat overlapping wedges placed butt to edge."[4] "The wedge standing butt down," he goes on to explain, "represents the more general part of the student's higher education, tapering off toward the top; the other wedge is specialized education, occupying more and more space toward its upper end." Such American educational theorists as J. S. Bruner have carried to an extreme enthusiasm for discovery methods, which envisage every physics student, however elementary, as a young physicist. But if I read the situation correctly, few if any American educators would agree with an Australian professor of history, Professor R. M. Crawford, himself a product of Sydney and Oxford, when he wrote in 1956: "The undergraduate courses should bring the minority who go on to research to the point of being able to engage in it, not without supervision but without further training."[5] Yet, in the years before the Second World War, this, in Australia as in Oxford, would have been revolutionary in its supposition that a graduate in the humanities needed so much as *supervision* in order to embark upon research.

Then why does an Australian working party now speak of the doctorate degree as a training in research? Partly because times have changed. The expansion of knowledge was for long accommodated by stiffening and extending the high school and undergraduate course. More could be done to reconsider how much of that knowledge a person needs to learn as distinct from being in a position to find out, and how much detail he needs to be taught if he acquires a firm grasp of general principles. Even so, the compacting of high school and undergraduate courses has its obvious limits.

The more fundamental reason why the working party wrote as it did is that only as a doctoral student does the student undertake, or participate in, a large-scale investigation extending over three or four years. And such concentrated and extensive research will require some sort of further training. Perhaps, then, if we amend the working party's statement from "to train graduate students in research," to read "to train graduate students to carry out large-scale and systematic research" we shall have hit upon something which would generally be recognized as a proper excellence of doctoral work, inside as well as outside the United States. The statement, as amended, certainly has the virtue of being largely independent of any difference of opinion we might have about the proper excellence of the undergraduate years, the extent to which those years should include some measure of training in small-scale systematic research. For no one would suggest that large-scale research can be undertaken as part of an undergraduate degree. I should perhaps add, parenthetically, that I am not demanding a thesis of Cyclopean proportions. In philosophy, a thesis of thirty-thousand words should more than suffice to sum up the results of large-scale research. A thesis in history would be larger; a thesis in mathematics smaller.

Let us now turn to the second question: What counts as training? In the passage I quoted earlier, Professor Crawford sharply distinguished, by implication, between supervision and training. A graduate student, he said, will need supervision but not training. If this antithesis between supervision and training is accepted it will not, after all, be internationally true that graduate education offers a training in large-scale systematic research. For English-style graduate education—I say English-style rather than English to make it plain that this sort of graduate education is not confined to the land between the Channel, the Welsh borders, and the Tweed—still quite commonly consists, solely, in writing a research-based thesis under supervision. But even though it is certainly not schooling, why should supervision not count as training?

Admittedly, English-style supervision has sometimes been so nominal that it cannot plausibly be counted as such. The graduate student has then worked almost entirely by himself, officially allocated to a supervisor who might know very little indeed about the topic of his thesis, but would offer him, from time to time, a little polite conversation and a pale sherry. In quite a few English-style universities and especially, but not solely, in the humanities, that situation still holds. The old Humboldt ideal of "loneliness and freedom" is then carried to an extreme point. It has its virtues, as a means of encouraging maximum independence. But, not unnaturally, it leaves many students floundering.

If we agree then that graduate education is a training in research, we can rightly be interpreted as rejecting as insufficient such nominal supervision. The 1966 Oxford Commission of Inquiry substantially took this view. Indeed, the system of nominal supervision can more properly be described as graduate self-education than as graduate education. It differs only in respect to the standard required from the situation which prevailed before formal graduate work was introduced into the British educational tradition. A scholar or scientist could then obtain a doctorate only by submitting, at any stage in his life, his published writings to his university.

The story is very different when the candidate is subject to maximal supervision, in the manner of my own university and a good many other English-speaking universities. Then doctoral students are, in principle, not accepted unless they can work closely with a supervisor. The relation envisaged, as in the Berkeley statement, is that of master to apprentice. Students are selected very carefully, normally with at least a good first class honors bachelor's degree, not infrequently a master's degree. They are asked to attend and read papers to work-in-progress seminars; they have the opportunity to discuss their work with a good many visitors and members of the staff beyond their official supervisors; they may, more rarely, be called upon to fill out their education by taking special courses; they will see their supervisors regularly and are expected to submit drafts for their criticism. In short, English-style graduate education moves toward American-style graduate education, even if the gap is still considerable. Some students are reluctant to accept even this degree of supervision; they want to be left quite alone. But in the natural sciences it is often inevitable that graduate students will work as members of a research team; this is more and more often the case in the social sciences. Even in the natural sciences, so I am however told, the University of Cambridge offers a choice; some students, for whom this is adjudged to be the better course, work as team members, others as individuals. This conforms to my own experience; individuals differ so much that it is highly undesirable for graduate education to be of only a single pattern. At Oxford, similarly, some students take the B. Phil., with its examinations, other students the thesis-based doctorate.

But even if we count maximal supervision as one kind of training, it certainly is not, as I have already admitted, schooling. Indeed, the English-style doctoral student does not describe himself as going to graduate school; rather, he "does graduate work." In my own country, at least, he does not even call himself a graduate student, he calls himself a research student. The difference in nomenclature is significant. America's belief in the need for schooling, in every respect and up to the highest levels, is what especially links it with the German and dissociates it from the English tradition. It helps to explain why, as Mayhew and Ford have put it, "American universities tend to treat graduate students as though they were undergraduates and to organize their learning along custodial or protective lines."[6]

This American emphasis on schooling sometimes leads to absurdities. Practical knacks are then inflated into theoretical principles, what ought to be a few words of advice to apprentices is swollen into courses with fancy Greek names. But this objection by no means always applies. Their emphasis on schooling, indeed, may well do much to explain why the United States and Germany lead the world industrially, and why, in contrast, fundamental British discoveries so often run aground at the level of application.

At the scholarly-scientific level which is our more immediate concern, the virtues of schooling are equally marked. The American Ph.D. is often noticeably better schooled than his English or Australian analogues, less likely to fall into the traps of amateurism. The amount of schooling in the American system of graduate education is no doubt a product of the fact that America has a unique concept of undergraduate work and, beyond that, of high school work. But it would be quite wrong to see in it nothing more than an attempt to remedy, late in the day, what English-style educators would call the defects of the American high school and the run of American colleges. It is based on a firm belief that people need to be schooled in what they are going to do, taught in class, examined formally, instructed in techniques. And, furthermore, that not rigidly to insist on the application of these techniques is simply not to be the professional one ought to be.

It is interesting to observe how Flexner was torn on this point. The Oxford graduate, he begins by saying, is a "charming and intelligent young person, but essentially an amateur." A little later, however, he writes thus: "the type of instruction employed, the extent to which the honors student is thrown on his own resources . . . the avoidance of the spoon-feeding so prevalent in America—this type of instruction has, I say, much more in common with genuine university spirit than much of the work of the American graduate school."[7]

To reconcile the ideal of training for complete professionalism with an emphasis on the maximum independence for students, encouraging a willingness, as Australians put it, to "have a go," may be next to impossible. One thing must always be remembered. Graduate students are at what often turns out to be the most imaginative, the most audacious, the most fecund, period of their life. Overzealous instruction can abort their bolder concepts, convert an impetuous river into carefully controlled streams which at first appear to fertilize but finally render sterile, through salinity, the lands through which they flow. That is a high price to pay for professionalism.

The contrast between the English and the American tradition comes out in an objection raised by Bernard Berelson to American graduate education which precisely reverses the objections sometimes raised by good Australian students who have gone to the United States to take a doctorate and have been repelled by, and finally retreated from, the atmosphere of the graduate school. Berelson says:

> . . . I believe that from the sheer standpoint of learning the subject, there is a certain wastage in the [graduate] system that is now disguised as "independent work" and that the symbol is probably not worth its cost. After all the graduate faculty is (or should be) the source of doctoral training. The faculty knows (or should know) what training is best for students of different interests, specialties and capabilities. Some independent work may be profitable at some stage, typically on the dissertation, though even there, as most thesis advisors know, it is not characteristic of most students to demand or want a completely free hand. In

short I believe that the danger lies in giving too much independent work to too many students rather than too little to too few.[8]

Berelson makes a sharp contrast between "being trained" and
"doing independent work," in conflict with our earlier assumption
that graduate training is training in doing independent work. Learning to do independent work, in our view, is an acquired capacity; to
acquire it, one needs to engage in supervised doing. That entails
being taught, unless supervision does not count as teaching.

To rely on a distinction I have made elsewhere, the capacity to do
independent work is an open, not a closed, capacity. The student
cannot be drilled in it, as he can be drilled, say, in setting out bibliog-
raphies. But he can be encouraged, set an example to, criticized,
corrected, and to strike a balance between encouragement and criticism, a balance suited to a particular case, can be an exceptionally
delicate pedagogical task. Like the Berkeley committee, however, Berelson seems to think of graduate training as approximating to condi-
tioning, its success to be judged rather as the success of a drill sergeant
is judged, by the fact that its recruits will go through the right professional motions.

He goes on to suggest, in this spirit, that "the need of the times" is
"to make graduate training more efficient: more purposeful, more
directed, more compressed, less *beholden to the Ph.D. symbol* and more
dedicated to the actual task of training men in skill and knowledge."[9]
Note that phrase "less beholden to the Ph.D. symbol." Less beholden,
I suppose he means, to the traditional concept of the doctorate in the
humanities and sciences as being fundamentally a research degree, a
concept symbolically recognized in the fact that the American
graduate student is not officially a candidate for the Ph.D. until he
embarks on his dissertation. Berelson, then, is another example of the
pressure on American graduate education to make of it a professional
training course. So far, he is at one with those critics of graduate
education who unfavorably contrast graduate education with medical
and legal education "in which tightly-knit programs designed to produce definite intellectual results absorb the students' entire time and
offer few choices."[10]

This particular contrast is one which would not naturally occur to
anybody who works in the English tradition, where graduate education is not an alternative to medical and legal education. If any such
unfavorable contrast were made, it would be between a bachelor's
degree in arts and a bachelor's degree in law or medicine. At this
point, the fact that medicine and law are in American graduate

schools turns out to be of central importance in setting the tone of American controversies about graduate education. Inevitably, it establishes a frame of reference. It encourages the suggestion that if changes are to be made in the graduate schools of the humanities and the sciences they should be in the direction of making them more professional, so that they will more closely conform to a general pattern of graduate education, just as on the other side it encourages the suggestion that professional schools should be research centers. Yet, on the face of it, there are quite fundamental differences between doing advanced work in the sciences or the humanities and preparing oneself to offer expert guidance, in the manner of a doctor or a lawyer or a manager.

If we do think of graduate education as preparation for a vocation, the question naturally arises: for what vocation is training in research a preparation? Most medical graduates practice as doctors. In contrast, a Ph.D. in the sciences or the humanities may, to an extent which varies from subject to subject, become a researcher, a teacher, or enter employment in industry, government, or some other form of enterprise. Is training in research the best preparation for each and every one of these vocations?

Relatively little attention has been paid to the relevance of a research-centered degree as a preparation for vocations in industry or government. Yet, if we look at graduate education vocationally, the only hope, as matters stand, of maintaining graduate schools at anything like their present size would be to encourage Ph.D.'s to enter these areas and employers to accept them. In contrast there has been a great deal of discussion about the suitability of a research-based degree as a preparation for college teaching. The proper excellence of a graduate education, it is often argued, is to train college teachers, just as the proper excellence of a law school is to train lawyers. Why pretend otherwise? "If the retort be," writes Carmichael in this spirit, "that the graduate school is not a professional school and should not be compared with one, the answer is simple. It is the only agency engaged in the education of college and university teachers, and a substantial proportion of its products enter that profession. It cannot therefore disclaim responsibility in this professional area."[11] The preparation of college teachers, in other words, is what graduate education is indispensable for doing and should be what it does best. If, as is admittedly true, a certain proportion of graduate students become professional researchers rather than teachers, the obvious thing to do, one might naturally suppose, is to divide graduate students into two separate groups and offer them quite different educations, just as lawyers and business managers are separately trained. And this step has, of course, been taken by some American universities.

We are now well embarked on the third question I raised: Should every doctoral degree in the sciences and the humanities offer a training in large-scale research? The argument to the contrary is, as we have just seen, a quite straightforward one—that a graduate education should prepare those who embark upon it for the professional way of life in which they will later participate and a way of life which for the most part is teaching, not large-scale research. Their vocation is not to be a physicist, a chemist, an economist but to teach these subjects. True enough, the college teacher will often be expected to do research and to publish his results. But this requirement, it might very plausibly be argued, results from a defect in the present system of promoting college teachers, the emphasis being on research rather than teaching; it is not at all a good reason for insisting that the potential teacher must be trained to undertake research.

To make matters worse, the argument might continue, most of the resulting publication simply clutters up the worlds of science and scholarship, unread, unhonored, and uncited. Any education is absurd which encourages the college teacher to put his teaching second while he spends his time writing a meticulous essay on, to take a relatively serious example, Brown's reply to Smith's criticism of Jones' interpretation of Wittgenstein's use of the word "game." (And let us not pretend that the situation is any better in science; it is just that scientists are more expert in concealing their trivialities in "the decent obscurity of a learned language.") No doubt there can be disputes about what is and what is not trivial. "It has long been a maxim of mine," Sherlock Holmes once remarked, "that the little things are the most important." But on any conceivable criteria, there are now very many college teachers doing research in a narrow area whose time would be better employed reading, discussing, reflecting, or attending refresher courses, to the last of which university funds might profitably be redirected from the graduate school.

This line of argument is a very powerful one. Given that American emphasis on schooling to which I previously drew attention, it has led, almost inevitably, to the setting up of doctoral degrees for college teachers which incorporate such subjects as the history of the liberal arts college, educational psychology, and the like. But it might more fruitfully have led in a different direction, to a degree which would be genuinely philosophical. Not that it would necessarily include courses in philosophy. Philosophy has become yet another professional speciality, as much in need as any other speciality of being looked at philosophically, in the sense in which I am now using that term. What I have called the genuinely philosophical degree should enable and encourage the graduate to look critically at the subject he is going to teach, at its structure, its presumptions, its place in human culture. It should help him to understand it as a growing subject, to shake himself free from the notion that it must always be as it now is, to prepare him to spend the rest of his life learning more about it, as it progresses or retrogresses. Such a degree should concentrate at once on the frontiers of the chosen subject, as it advances into the darkness, and on its boundaries—its relationships, actual and potential, to other subjects. So it would at once prepare the teacher for future learning, by making it plain to him where the obscurities still lie, and enable him more readily to sympathize with the intellectual problems of his colleagues, to talk with them and with their students about problems which cross subject boundaries. Given the character of much American college education there is a quite peculiar absurdity in offering to potential college educators graduate work which is basically professional training in the research techniques of their subject rather than an attempt to get them more fully to comprehend the role of that subject in human culture.

I do not mean that this is all a graduate education can accomplish; the college teacher will also need to become more expert in his chosen subject especially if his undergraduate course hasn't been a specialized one. But I envisage a course of studies which would be of real value to those who simply want to advance their education, insofar as it will help them to understand more clearly the virtues and the limitations of their expertise. If there are no positions for them as researchers or college teachers, they will not feel that they have spent their graduate years in vain. At present it is a recurrent complaint of those who employ Ph.D.'s that they cannot look around a problem, following it up in its various aspects, trained as they have been to pick out that segment of the problem which lends itself to solution by a particular set of techniques. As one industrial scientist has written:

In the industrial scene people are used to solving problems . . . . Problems know nothing about the division into the disciplines of a subject, e.g., if the problem is about food preservation, then we start to employ some physics, some chemistry, some biochemistry, a lot of social behaviour, some psychology. The postgraduates generally coming into industry find this sort of situation very difficult to face. . . . Within the University department the problem may be looked at briefly as a whole, and then the bit which contains the discipline is taken up. The rest of the problem is thrown away.[12]

Isn't the encouragement of such cross-discipline thinking the proper function of the undergraduate level? I don't believe that such an emphasis is valuable at that stage. Only after obtaining a reasonable grasp of the ins and outs of a subject is anyone in a position to take a general look at its place in human culture, to see what it is all about, what humanity would lose did it not exist. At any earlier stage, to discuss such issues is to encourage journalistic woolliness.

Just because it might multiply these effects, let us take a second look at the picture I have just drawn of a possible doctoral degree for college teachers. It would be, I believe, a better degree than one which attempts to turn the graduate school into an advanced teachers' training college, with the notorious weaknesses of such institutions. My qualms about it remain: Is it possible to master a subject to the degree to which a college educator needs to have mastered it, without embarking on a reasonably large-scale piece of research?

In its 1954 report, the Committee of Fifteen made some interesting observations on this point, in the course of describing what it took to be the ideal dissertation for a college teacher. They wrote:

> We believe that the dissertation can, and should, be one of the most exciting intellectual experiences of the future college teacher. It should be *primarily a contribution to the knowledge of its author, an instrument of his intellectual growth,* and the result of an adventure, not necessarily into virgin territory, but into the world of ideas that are worth wrestling with.[13]

Now we have reached a moment of truth for every doctorate which demands the writing of a dissertation. For the Committee of Fifteen the dissertation is primarily a contribution to the knowledge of its author. On the traditional view, to which the Australian working party subscribes, its object, very differently, is to "contribute to the general pool of scholarship and discovery." Ideally, of course, the two coincide; the student then learns by discovering and what he discovers is a contribution to the general pool of knowledge. But the coincidence is far from being a necessary one. The dissertation which has most to contribute to the graduate's own knowledge, including his own self-knowledge, may not be the dissertation which has most to contribute to the world of learning. On the other hand, it may prepare him for writing a book which will be of interest to that class of persons we are supposedly turning out in very large numbers, liberally educated persons, whom the modern scientist and the modern humanist so strikingly neglect, leaving them to the ministrations of the charlatan, the sophist, and the more sensational sort of journalist. "The hungry sheep look up and are not fed." Or are these hungry sheep nonexistent? Is the whole apparatus of mass college education, therefore, an expensive farce?

From the point of view both of his own education and the future education of his students, the doctoral candidate, at least in the humanities, may do best to tackle a relatively familiar topic, to wrestle with ideas that are worth wrestling with, as the Committee of Fifteen puts it, rather than to venture into virgin territory. In philosophy, certainly, this is most often the case. There is in philosophy very little virgin territory. Graduate students show and discover the quality of their mind by tackling a familiar problem. Their thesis reveals whether they can cope with it, in the sense of understanding the issues, seeing clearly how certain plausible-looking ways of tackling the problem lead to impasses. No doubt, they will also try their hand at doing better. But only very rarely will the thesis be, in any substantial sense of the phrase, a contribution to the pool of learning. Although one has to be careful not to generalize from one's own subject, I do not believe that philosophy is, in this respect, unique. An English student will surely learn more by attempting to come closely to grips with Shakespeare's *Troilus and Cressida,* making his way through the network of commentators and the cruxes of scholars, than if he contributes to scholarship by writing the first thesis ever written on the minor writings of a properly forgotten author. In the mordant words of the poet-professor A. D. Hope:

> Is there a minor poet by others missed
> Dull sermoneer or maudlin novelist,
> Some corpse to build a reputation on?
> A thesis swallows them and they are gone.[14]

An A. E. Housman, no doubt, can demonstrate his scholarly dexterity on a Manilius, but a young student should not be encouraged to embark upon that sort of exercise.

The Ph.D. did not, of course, create pedantry. Goethe was already complaining about the minute scholars of his own time, adducing them as evidence that "the Germans cannot cease to be Philistines," as they disputed whether he or Schiller had written certain poems which both had included in their collected works or, in a manner that was to become a passion with German scholars, sought to trace influences. As if, Goethe says, "they were to ask the strong-man what beef, mutton and pork he had eaten in order to distinguish what part of his strength he owed to each."[15] Graduate education took over the minute scholars holus-bolus from already existing traditions and offered them a rigorous training, so that they would at least be accurate Philistines.

George Ticknor, a student at Göttingen some twenty years before Goethe delivered himself of these opinions, had hoped rather to import into America that other German tradition "of pursuing all literary studies philosophically—of making of scholarship as little of drudgery and mechanism as possible."[16] That tradition, too, has its dangers; if pedantry is the Scylla of the humanities, empty generalizations are its Charybdis. As a necessary constituent of every sound piece of research, there will be a measure of drudgery, of routine mechanical work. The future college teacher, as much as the professional researcher, needs to understand this. I am arguing only that the title of doctor of philosophy should not be awarded for work which is merely mechanical, mere drudgery, totally devoid of the philosophical spirit, whatever its claims as training. And, as well, that such pure drudge-work is the worst possible preparation for a college teacher. At one point, the Committee of Fifteen remarked that the dissertation should involve "vigor and care." This is admirable. But I suspect "vigor" is a misprint for "rigor."

Even in science, the graduate student who is a mere cog in a highly polished scientific machine, solving a minor problem in a research program which may well have lost its momentum by the time he enters it, can easily be led, in virtue of these facts, quite to misunderstand the nature of scientific research, except at its dreariest level. And in principle a similar situation could come to dominate the doctoral degree in the humanities. Indeed, according to Storr, it sometimes happens even now that students are asked to write dissertations on particular topics, not because inquiry into these topics will be peculiarly educative for them but because, as Storr puts it, they are "the next items on the agenda of the professor." If a student ends up writing a good thesis, Storr goes on to add, "he is often doing it in some degree against the current of the department in which he is working."[17] This is a really dreadful situation, if what Storr is saying has any truth in it.

The choice of a thesis topic for a potential science educator is a peculiarly difficult one, once the thesis is thought of as contributing to the education of the student, not as a mere training exercise with the student acting as an underpaid research assistant. But I should think it essential that the student's topic let him see how scientific problems lead on to one another. Yet not by being in an artificial sense interdisciplinary; the need to cross boundaries in order fully to explore a certain type of problem should become apparent in the course of trying to solve that sort of problem. But I am only too conscious of the great difficulties which attach to selecting such topics in a highly organized scientific research school.

In talking about graduate education, it is very tempting to proceed as if certain qualities were inevitably conjoined which may in fact be regularly disjoined. On the face of it, this is what the Australian working party has done. The objective of the doctoral degree, it says, is "to train graduates in the conduct of research, *thereby* stimulating critical and creative thinking on questions of fundamental importance and *by so doing,* to throw light on the problems of contemporary society." Read in the most natural way, with "thereby" and "by so doing" functioning as consequential expressions, this, I fear, can only be dismissed as humbug, the sort of humbug we have come to expect from educational committees. It is just not true that to train in research is thereby to stimulate creative and critical thinking. A research degree, while not failing to train, can turn out graduates who are rigid, uncritical, unimaginative pedants, and this in the sciences as well as in the humanities.

As for the working party's phrase "by so doing"—i.e., by training in research—"to throw light on the problems of contemporary society," in fact a research-training thesis normally concerns itself with those problems which are seen by some in-group as central to its inquiries at that particular time. Only very rarely do these coincide with the problems which beset contemporary society or, indeed, throw any light on them. This is so even in respect to the social sciences, let alone the natural sciences and the humanities.

Let us suppose, however, that the working party's statement should be interpreted rather differently, that "thereby" and "by so doing" should be interpreted as imposing limitations rather than as pointing to consequences. On such an interpretation, the working party is suggesting that graduates ought to be trained in that sort of research which stimulates critical and creative thinking on questions of fundamental social importance and results in a contribution to learning—not that every sort of research is automatically bound to be of this character. Then the objection that in fact graduate training is not for the most part like this will fail. The working party is saying simply that this is what it should be like.

There are those, as we have seen, who would react against this pronouncement by stopping the working party's statement at the end of the phrase "training in research," so that it reads "to train graduate students in the conduct of research." To demand that this research be critical and creative, should help to solve questions of social importance, should be a contribution to learning is, they would say, quite to misunderstand the nature of the Ph.D.

In this dispute, I should wish to mediate. I agree with the working party that the research topic should encourage critical and creative thinking, as against the view that it should be no more than the occasion for a technical exercise. This is true whether the graduate student is going on to be a researcher, a teacher, or to enter some other form of employment. The worst thing that can possibly happen is that the graduate student should take his Ph.D. no longer loving his subject, thinking of it either as a form of toil or as a game at which he happens to be good, not as a worthy object of devotion, a labor of love.[18] And either of these results is very likely to flow from the preparation of a technical-exercise dissertation. The dissertation should, of course, display a mastery of techniques but as applied to a demanding problem. So far I am with the working party.

I have questioned, in opposition to the working party, whether a good dissertation will necessarily be a contribution to learning. If contribution to learning is taken to be the first essential, there is a real risk that the student will be set a very minor topic, easily coped with by established methods, and will in the end be left with no conception whatever of the kind of travail involved in genuine discovery. The dullest of investigators can make innumerable contributions to learning by conducting a statistical analysis of the world's telephone books, comparing, let us say, the percentage of Scottish names in Kabul and Addis Ababa, their occupations, etc. So let us put the matter thus: compelled to select, we can properly select students who have some prospect of making a contribution to learning and should encourage them to choose problems where there are significant contributions to be made. But the factor to be maximized, all the same, is the educative value of writing the dissertation, at least, but not only, for those graduate students who will move into college teaching.

What about the working party's suggestion that the thesis should be a contribution to questions of public importance? That requirement is intended to rule out trivial theses. A similar position is very strongly argued by Carmichael, after citing a set of trivial doctoral topics, and by no means in a narrowly practicalist spirit. "What a gold mine of material for master's theses and Ph.D. dissertations," he writes, "is to be found in the excavation of the ideas that underlie the concepts of democracy, of inalienable rights, of the dignity of the individual, of justice, of freedom in all its forms, of the rights incorporated in our Bill of Rights, and many others that are the motivations of a free society."[19]

Such topics, however, have their problems even for educative dissertations. They are excessively difficult, largely because they are exceptionally amorphous. Unless they are discussed at a level of abstraction at which they become empty of all specific content or degenerate into a mere exercise in propaganda, they call upon a broad experience which the ordinary graduate student is unlikely to have at his disposal. His chance of making a real contribution to these "problems of public importance" is minimal. Graduate education, to be sure, should produce men and women who can contribute to the solution of problems of broad social importance as a partial consequence of their graduate education. That is one reason why the dissertation, whatever else it is, must be so designed as to be genuinely educative, not leaving students with the feeling that the only problems which are worth tackling are those which lend themselves to neat solutions by the application of professional techniques. But we cannot reasonably expect that contribution at the graduate level.

I have left myself no time to discuss the final observation of the working party, that graduate education should meet the perceived needs of the community whether short-term or long-term. I should like to end by saying an inadequate word or two about it. Its intention may be quantitative; it should then be read as suggesting that the number of graduate students should be restricted to the number the community is likely to be able to find suitable jobs for. If the doctorate is thought of in purely vocational terms, as a training either for research or for college teaching, this makes sense. But an educative degree retains its value, whatever the demand for professional researchers or teachers, to the person as such and as a participant in the creative work of his society. If the fact is made plain to potential graduate students that a graduate education is not a guarantee of specific sorts of employment, they should be free to enter upon it; as for support from public funds—and it must be remembered that outside the United States almost every graduate student is so supported—the case for flexibly educated persons is a strong one.

If, however, the working party's reference to the perceived needs of the community is meant qualitatively, rather than quantitatively, intending to suggest that the content of the Ph.D. should be determined by perceived needs, we have to ask "Needs perceived by whom?" We should not let ourselves be fobbed off by the answer "The community as a whole," for there is no such thing. What will be involved in practice is the needs as perceived by some particular government organization. Their record in perceiving needs is not such as to inspire confidence. No doubt, as the working party goes on to suggest, it is sensible to encourage Ph.D.'s to work in obviously central areas, as in Australia's case to encourage research which particularly bears upon Asia and the Pacific. But education and research continue to be the proper business of universities; they have the responsibility for perceiving needs and cannot fob that responsibility off on the community.

To sum up, then, I have stood by the conception of graduate education as having as its special excellence training in research. But I have argued that research needs to be broadly interpreted and need not issue in a contribution to learning, in any serious sense of that phrase. I have refused to accept the view that graduate education is improperly so called, that it is really training in the sense that is synonymous with drill. I have gone in search of a graduate education which opens up rather than closes down the mind.

I must not be taken to be hostile to specialization. I see no good reason why specialization should not begin relatively early in a student's career, provided only that the subject in which he is specializing interprets its responsibilities widely. To know more and more about less and less is not necessarily worse than to know less and less about more and more. What I am opposed to, rather, is an undue insistence on professional standards when that is carried so far as to discourage students from trying their hand at anything they have not been professionally trained to do. The English historian, A. J. P. Taylor, after a bachelor's degree in medieval history at Oxford, suddenly found himself plunged into the Austrian diplomatic archives. He had no training as a diplomatic historian; he wasted time, he made mistakes. But he came out of that experience with a quirky but still important book, *The Origins of the Second World War*. Had he gone to graduate school would he perhaps have said to himself, "I have not been trained to do this work; it would be unprofessional of me to attempt to do it?" I hope not; I fear so. Lacking a doctorate in education, should none of us be discussing our present topic?

Finally, I must confess to an old-fashioned prejudice. I like to see young men and women standing largely on their own feet as soon as possible, if not financially then at least intellectually. Any system of education in which young men and women are still under tutelage when they are a third of the way toward their death, needs, I feel, to be seriously reconsidered. Too many courses are given, and required, because it suits the teacher to give them rather than because, at this stage in their education, his pupils positively need them. Formal teaching ought not to be multiplied beyond necessity. Otherwise, there is a real risk that mediocrity will flourish and excellence decline.

NOTES

1. California University, Academic Senate, Select Committee on Education (The Muscatine Report), *Education at Berkeley* (University of California, Berkeley: March 1966), cited in L. B. Mayhew and P. J. Ford, *Reform in Graduate and Professional Education* (San Francisco, 1974), p. 219.

2. E. J. McGrath, *The Graduate School and the Decline of Liberal Education*, Teachers College, Columbia University (New York, 1959).

3. J. F. Horning, in *The Development of Doctoral Programmes by the Small Liberal Arts College*, Bowdoin College (Brunswick, Maine, 1967), p. 53.

4. Richard J. Storr, *The Beginning of the Future: A Historical Approach to Graduate Education in the Arts and Sciences* (New York, 1973), p. 64.

5. R. M. Crawford, "Postgraduate Training in the Nonscience Faculties," in *A Symposium on the Place of the Australian University in the Community,* (Melbourne, n.d.).

6. L. B. Mayhew and P. J. Ford, *Reform in Graduate and Professional Education,* pp. 233–34.

7. Abraham Flexner, *Universities: American, English, German* (New York, 1930), p. 277.

8. Bernard Berelson, *Graduate Education in the United States* (New York, 1960), p. 236.

9. Ibid., p. 260, my italics.

10. Referred to by the trustees of the Carnegie Corporation, quoted in ibid., p. 87.

11. Oliver C. Carmichael, *Graduate Education: A Critique and a Program* (New York, 1961), p. 36.

12. K. L. Sutherland, "The Responsibilities and Needs of Industry," in *Australia's Needs in Postgraduate Education,* Melbourne University Research Students Association (Melbourne, 1969), p. 33.

13. F. W. Strothmann on behalf of the Committee of Fifteen, *The Graduate School Today and Tomorrow* (New York, 1954), p. 27, my italics.

14. A. D. Hope, *Dunciad Minor III* (Melbourne, 1970), p. 35, ll. 191–94.

15. J. P. Eckermann, *Conversations with Goethe,* December 16, 1828.

16. Quoted in R. J. Storr, *The Beginnings of Graduate Education in America* (Chicago, 1953), p. 16.

17. Ibid., p. 138.

18. I am relying at this point on distinctions I made in *The Perfectibility of Man* (London, 1970; New York, 1971).

19. *Graduate Education,* p. 26.

Comments by William K. Frankena

Again, I shall limit myself as indicated in the first paragraph of my earlier comments. Doing this entails less injustice on my part now than it did then, since Passmore more nearly limits himself in a similar way. In general, Passmore's approach is more to my liking than Mandelbaum's; it is explicitly more Platonic, and involves denying, more than Mandelbaum's does, that the job of general education is to "meet the perceived needs of the community whether short-term or long-term," as the Australian working party says it is. Passmore's conclusions are also more to my liking.

We find again in Passmore the contention that there should be no sharp difference in kind between undergraduate education and graduate education, either in aim or in method, one being liberal, general, or educative, the other vocational, specialized, or a matter of training. Once more, even if we agree, and I am inclined not to, our question is: What are the implications for graduate education? We are to conclude that undergraduate education should be, at least in part, specialized, vocational, and a matter of training. Are we also to conclude that graduate education should be, at least partly, liberal, general, and educative? Most of the time Passmore is concerned about the vocational aims of graduate education, which like Mandelbaum and myself, he takes to be of several different kinds. Thus he says three times, "If we think of graduate education vocationally (as the Berkeley committee did), then . . ." But are we to think of graduate education in purely vocational terms, i.e., should graduate education be wholly vocational in its aims, methods, etc., concerned only to prepare people for some vocation or other? Here Passmore is not so clear as I should like, though more explicit than Mandelbaum. He is very much interested that graduate education include a course or kind of study that will be of value to individuals "who simply want to advance their education" or who may end up finding no vocational use or need for what they learned in graduate school. This I can only applaud.

Passmore seems to think, however, that such individuals will be well served by courses or studies of a special vocational kind, namely, by courses that are designed to prepare people to teach but which are nevertheless "genuinely philosophical" because they "enable and encourage the graduate to look critically at the subject he is going to teach, at its structure, its presumptions, its place in human culture." These studies would then, for him, be a part of graduate education only because they make the graduate better at his vocation of teaching; they would indeed have a nonvocational value or reward, but this would not be the reason they are there or take the form they do. As I said, I applaud Passmore's concern that such studies be a part of graduate education, but I wonder if they ought not to be more frankly nonvocational in spirit and purpose or just plain liberal.

Otherwise I find myself very much attracted by Passmore's view of what graduate education should be like, including his conception of two kinds of dissertation, an idea that has been around in one form or other for some time, and which he argues for most persuasively. But, if one accepts this idea, how should it be carried out? Should there be two distinct, though possibly overlapping, doctoral programs, besides M.A. programs of whatever sort? Or should the difference between the two sorts of students be mainly a matter of advice and choice within one and the same program, some students being informally guided in one way and some in the other?

More generally, Passmore begins by presuming, in a Platonic spirit, that the philosophy of graduate education is an attempt to discover the proper excellence of graduate education and ends by concluding that the special excellence of graduate education is training in research, or independent work, where "research" is broadly interpreted and "training" is taken in its best sense. This is persuasive but I have three questions. First, does this mean that graduate education is not to include any training in teaching other than training in research? Second, can all of the study and learning involved in good graduate education be accurately thought of as training in research? Is not some of it simply the mastery of a tool or the learning of a body of material? Third, just how does a training in research help to prepare students for vocations other than teaching and research itself? Passmore complains that "relatively little attention has been paid to the relevance of a research-centered degree as a preparation for vocations in industry or government." But then he too proceeds to pay relatively little attention to it. I do not really doubt that training in research of the broader of his two kinds is relevant as a preparation for vocations in industry or government that do not themselves consist of teaching or research. But I should like to see this spelled out and supported.

Reply to Frankena

In my article I certainly directed too much attention to preparation for research and for college teaching, and too little attention to graduate education as a preparation for other modes of life or as a form of liberal education with no vocational implications. It is hard to free oneself from the assumptions of a period in which the products of graduate schools have almost invariably become either researchers or teachers. Let me now look at Frankena's questions in turn. First, like so many others who have been subjected to them, I am very skeptical about the value of courses of lectures on teaching. But we have been too reluctant to comment on the papers our students deliver from a pedagogical point of view rather than as contributions to learning. This sort of individualized advice can be of great help to a potential teacher. It can be extended further by attending classes which are taken by graduate students and commenting critically on them. This can be done by a third person, with a special interest in teaching, if we are too conscious of our own defects as teachers to do it ourselves. On the second point, the degree to which graduate education is training in research, in order to universalize my topic I devoted my attention to that sort of graduate work which is common to the Anglo-Saxon world, the conduct of research under supervision. This has a bearing on the answer to his third question about the way in which training in research can help to prepare students for vocations in industry and government. Insofar as an American graduate school substantially undertakes the sort of work which is elsewhere undertaken at the honors undergraduate level, then it prepares in exactly the same way as such a degree does, and can constitute a liberal education precisely as that education does. It is only insofar as it is a research degree that special questions arise about its suitability. I believe that the experience of undertaking an inquiry in depth can offer a form of education which is highly suitable as a preparation for careers outside academic life or for rounding off a liberal education. The fact that it is specialized does not mean that it is educational only for specialists. There is no antithesis between doing specialized work and having a broad education if the specialized work is conducted in a way which brings out the connection between the specialized work and broader problems.

Questions and Answers

Q1: Can you make any suggestions about how to raise the level of significance of research?

A: As I remarked in my paper, this is a particularly acute problem in science, when the graduate student inevitably finds himself participating in a research program. In the humanities, if we concentrate the student's attention on major problems and major writers, and think of the thesis as educating the student rather than as contributing to learning, I do not think that we need have any fear of triviality. Triviality arises out of the determination that the thesis shall contribute to learning. I don't think that the best way of avoiding triviality is to put large social problems before students. That way leads, inevitably, to superficiality. One of the things that worries me, incidentally, is the suggestion that the B.A. is no longer enough, so that everyone needs the Ph.D., and then scientists need a postdoctoral fellowship after that because the Ph.D. doesn't suffice. Where is this going to end? I do believe that some of those who go to graduate school would do better to return to university life in later life for refresher courses especially if their undergraduate education is tightened up.

Q2: There are trivial dissertations which might benefit the author and trivial dissertations which might not. In my experience, people who have written trivial dissertations can go on to write good books, perhaps because they have written trivial dissertations.

A: Here the judgment and the character of the supervisor is all important. A topic can sound trivial to an outsider and yet open up questions of great importance. To do a quite minor piece of work in the laboratory of a great scientist can be an enormously rewarding experience. Doing exactly the same kind of thing in a laboratory where the research program has lost its momentum and its leader his enthusiasm can be quite stultifying. Something similar is true in the area of scholarship.

Graduate Education in the Humanities: Reflections and Proposals

Gregory Vlastos

By the word *philosophy* I shall understand what it is used to mean in present-day idiomatic speech, not by philosophers but by practical people, lawyers, businessmen, politicians—i.e., a statement of the overall purpose of an enterprise by reference to which its practices may be appraised and criticized. Because my approach will be intensely practical it will have to be personal—regrettably so, but unavoidably, for the convictions I shall be sharing with you spring out of personal experience and have little beyond the authority of that experience to recommend them. Let me then start by identifying the area of experience from which I speak.

I have taught both undergraduates and graduates, only undergraduates in the first seventeen years of my working life, both undergraduates and graduates thereafter. I have also taken part in those quasi-administrative jobs which sometimes fall to the lot of the teacher-scholar. For nine years I served as departmental chairman. For six I served on a faculty Committee Advisory to the President on University Policy, for seven on a faculty Committee on Appointments and Advancements which was, among other things, the bottleneck for all determinations of academic salary. On those committees I represented the humanities. I must serve this conference in the same capacity, and no other. It would be a presumption on my part even to formulate, let alone try to solve, the problems of the natural scientists. I shall not even attempt such a thing for the social scientists. Their world impinges on mine; I know something about it, but not nearly enough to enable me to speak about it with the assurance of firsthand knowledge. At any rate, to speak for the humanists will give me not only all I can decently cover in this address, but a good deal more. Forced to select among the problems I would have confronted had I been writing a hundred-page monograph instead of an hour-long address, I shall give much the higher priority to those besetting our graduate students. Not that we, their teachers, lack problems of our own. But theirs are so much more urgent that they have the greater claim to our attention.

I am content to formulate the purpose of graduate education in the familiar phrase, the advancement and communication of knowledge: advancement through research, communication through teaching under the special conditions of the American graduate school, whose professors, with few exceptions, must teach not only graduate students but undergraduates as well, their graduate students being themselves prospective teachers of undergraduates. Let me speak to the first phrase in that statement of purpose, "the advancement of knowledge through research." That "research" should now be used, both in and outside the university, to apply to inquiry in the humanities no less than in the sciences, is something new—postwar, indeed post-Sputnik. Is this a questionable development, as some humanists still feel it to be? Does the word belong of right to the scientists, so that for humanists to claim it is to betray a readiness to ape aims and methodologies alien to their own? I want to argue that there is no warrant for such a feeling—certainly none in etymology or in history. From the word itself all we get is "search" with an intensifying prefix. What could be more to the humanist's purpose? "Careful search, close scrutiny," the primary sense of research in Webster's, is what the humanist does when setting himself to advance knowledge in his own domain by whatever methods and in whatever styles seem appropriate to him.

What do humanists search for? Sometimes for particular facts, as when editing a text (Is this the right choice from the variant manuscript readings of a verse in Aeschylus?) or seeking to determine authorship (Was that curious document, "The Donation of Constantine?", really the work of its titular author, or the outright forgery that Lorenzo Valla, the Italian humanist, proved it to be in the fifteenth century, after it had fooled popes and emperors and their wise men for many centuries). As my second example shows, so far from being foreign to the humanists, those from whom the word derives, it was they who made research the scholar's business and got spectacular results from it when research in the natural sciences was barely getting started. Or again a humanist may be searching for the explanation of some previously unnoticed, or insufficiently noticed, general fact. Thus: Why is it that while the British nineteenth century novel is so heavily preoccupied with the relations of men to women and of women to men, its American counterpart largely bypasses this theme, spurning it altogether in those towering works of fiction—*Moby Dick* and *Huckleberry Finn*—which are most indigenously and characteristically American? Why in the world should anyone hesitate to apply the word "research" to what Leslie Fiedler did in trying to make sense of this extraordinary fact in his *Life and Death in the American Novel*?

Nor is the humanist's searching less appropriately termed research if, as sometimes happens, he records its results in poetic, even lyrical, language, as in these lines from an essay by Geoffrey Hartman:

> If Romance is an eternal rather than archaic portion of the human mind and poetry its purification, then every poem will be an act of resistance, of negative creation—a flight from one enchantment into another. ("False Themes and Gentle Minds," *Philological Quarterly* 47 [1968]: 60.)

The verse of Coleridge connects with the strain of romance that had lived throughout the centuries in the folktale and balladry of the British Isles. The connection takes that special form which Hartman, compounding metaphors, chooses to call "purified enchantment"— where "purification" stands for enlightening and demystifying the dark, demonic, spooky elements in its source materials. It also connects with antecedent or contemporary verse, Blake's or Wordsworth's, as does each of these with his predecessors, each being thought of by Hartman as displacing those before him by "negative creation," negating not by attacking but by "fleeing" into new creations in the same mode of "purified enchantment." To say all this in just this way is to succeed admirably in setting down for us how the author has come to understand sequential products of British poetic imagination from Spenser and Milton down to Blake, Wordsworth, and Coleridge. Are we to doubt the genuineness of search which had this outcome? If so, why scruple to call it "research"?

There is one general feature which all forms of humanistic inquiry share with one another and with research in the social sciences, on one hand, and with works of the imagination, on the other, setting apart the searching which goes on in each of these three domains from that of the natural sciences. In all three of these the advancement of our knowledge changes us, the knowers, in that peculiarly intimate way we call our sensibility—our sensitiveness to what we experience, our openness to our world and our resonance to it. Though this, of course, affects our intellectual, discursive, cognition, it strikes at something still more elemental in us, for its core is not in how we conceive our world, but in how we perceive it—how we see and hear and feel its facts and possibilities. If the advancement of knowledge does have this power, its importance for humanity individually and corporately is incalculable. What changes our perceptions affects the very core of our being—our soul, our individual self. What is the self except that unique center of perceptual and imaginative awareness which determines how we shall feel, think, and act from hour to hour and from day to day? And there are critical periods of history, ours among them, when a widespread change in forms of awareness becomes a sufficient condition of massive institutional change.

The most profound changes in American society within our lifetime have come about in this way. Let me enumerate them:

the Welfare State.
racial desegregation and the upgrading of the dignity of ethnic minorities,
the sexual revolution, and
the movement for the liberation of women.

Each of these changes had multiple, complex causes. But could anyone doubt that crucial among them had been the altered sensibility resulting from advances in knowledge, occurring either by themselves or in conjunction with the impact of new poetic visions of reality? A propos of the first two changes let me mention just two titles: J. M. Keynes, *The General Theory of Employment, Interest and Money* (1936); and Gunnar Myrdal, *An American Dilemma* (1944). For many readers of these two books, a Great Depression which left one in three of the working force workless and a system of segregation that made two nations out of one, heretofore felt to be unavoidable, became unthinkable. As to the third great change, one thinks not only of the works of Freud and of collateral studies like those of Havelock Ellis, but also of the effect of writers like Walt Whitman, Proust, Gide, Thomas Mann, D. H. Lawrence, Joyce along with the numerous critics, largely academic, who interpreted for us the high seriousness of that explicit confrontation of the turbulence of sex in works of great literary power. In the case of the liberation of women one title should suffice, Simone de Beauvoir's *The Second Sex.* No one can read that book and continue to live comfortably with the inherited status of women.

Let me recall the closing lines of Whitehead's *Science and the Modern World,* well-known though they are:

The great conquerors, from Alexander to Caesar, and from Caesar to Napoleon, influenced profoundly the lives of subsequent generations. But the total effect of their influence shrinks to insignificance, if compared to the entire transformation of human habits and human mentality produced by the long line of men of thought from Thales to the present day, men individually powerless, but ultimately the rulers of the world.

Whitehead's vision is elitist. He sees giants standing on the shoulders of giants. He does not see the multitudes of searchers of varying dimensions, most of them of quite ordinary stature, cooperating in diverse ways, to produce in the aggregate those epochal changes in understanding and in feeling which alter the course of history. But when we have entered this correction in the quotation and adjusted it to the contemporary time frame, we are left with the momentous fact that the power to effect long-range changes in our society's perception of its own values, and hence the power to effect changes in those values themselves, has now passed into the keeping of the humanist, the social scientist, and the imaginative artist. Clerical thought still contributes, though with decreasing effect, conservative influence. But its power to refresh and renew our values has now passed into other hands. The secular student of man and of the works of man, and the creative artist, are now the transvaluers of our values, and will remain so irreversibly as long as the framework of our Western civilization survives intact. For the scholar this is an awesome responsibility. The moral and spiritual health of his society depends on his work being done well.

I may now turn to the second component of the purpose of graduate education: the communication of knowledge. By virtue of our employment as teacher-scholars we are called upon to communicate with no less than five distinct groups, each with its distinctive interests, needs, and capabilities:

fellow specialists in our field of research,
graduate students,
undergraduates,
colleagues in other fields, and
the public at large.

If time permitted I would run through that list, trying to indicate *seriatim* the various ways in which communication with each of those groups pertains to the purposes of graduate education which each of us is pledged to further. But time does not permit. In any case, to so distribute my attention would not be consonant with that special concern I indicated at the start for one of those five groups: our graduate students. To them we have an altogether unique relation. Many of them become our personal friends. In our professional capacity we are not only their teachers but, for all practical purposes, their academic employment agency as well. Moreover, we have a say in determining whether or not the kind of education they get while they are with us will enhance or impair their chances of finding and keeping the employment which will make optimal use of their talents throughout their life. Everything I shall be saying through most of the rest of this address will be dominated by that concern.

I start with the teacher-scholar's communication with fellow specialists by way of publication in media addressed to them. That we should have such access to fellow searchers is a great blessing in our life. But publication, however useful for research, cannot be identified with it. The identity fails on both sides. On one hand, there is research which never gets into print because its sale would not meet the dollar-cost of its production. This creates problems which are real, but not nearly so urgent as those arising from the converse fact that a great mass of work passing for research gets into print which does not advance knowledge and clogs channels of communication with work which is dull, repetitive, trivial, pedantic. It is writing which no one wants to read but keeps nonetheless being written at a feverish pace in response to publish-or-perish pressures.

This prospect looms large in our graduate students' view of their own immediate future, should they be lucky enough to get their first appointment as assistant professors. They are well aware of the administrative dogma that the *sine qua non* for the achievement of tenure is the completion of a certain quantity of published or publishable work—a policy now virtually universal not only in the major, research-oriented universities, but even in institutions at the other end of the spectrum, whose self-proclaimed *raison d'etre* is to educate undergraduates. From the start of their new life as teachers, Ph.D.'s must start thinking how to turn out publishable work at a time when they are engrossed in new tasks, extremely demanding of both time and energy: teaching three or even four courses each term; and even when it is only two, as it is now in some of the best institutions, it is still a full-time job, a heavy one, all by itself. In those intervals of release from the day-to-day demands of teaching, they will be working against time producing work that stands a chance of being accepted in one of the refereed journals of their tribe. So, pressed as they are for time, they look at what others have done to get theirs accepted and rush to do more of the same. The results are masses of dreary work, well known to those who referee papers for the journals: minute variations on formulae which have worked in the recent past and may be expected to work again if given a slightly new twist; copies, or copies of copies, of established models; emendations upon emendations of fashionable answers to fashionable problems. Nor is such recycling and repackaging likely to be avoided by cannibalizing the dissertation, for that too often suffers from the same disease.

I have sometimes wondered what would have become of me if I had started teaching under such conditions. The first item of substantial scholarship I managed to publish appeared in my ninth year of teaching. Under present practices I would have been fired for sterility long before that. Let me then raise two questions: (1) Should we keep the six-year probationary term for promotion to tenure? (2) How highly should we rate publication in estimating merit for this or any other graduate school appointment or advancement? To the first question my answer should be already clear. Well aware of the weighty reasons against any prolongation of the period of personal insecurity and political vulnerability at the start of one's career, I would still want to argue that the six-year term is much too short. If kept at all, it should be made more flexible, so that it can be stretched by three or even four more years to meet special needs. As to the second question, much the larger of the two, here too my answer is unequivocal. Once we have sorted out publication from research in our minds, publication as such should merit no positive recognition. The mere filling up of pages in books or journals, so far from being meritorious in itself, should rather be counted a demerit if what it offers is quantity in lieu of quality.

Here again I beg leave to refer to a personal experience, which, I dare say, many others could duplicate. By mid-career the hankerings after visible reputability had got into my blood. So when a year's leave came to me I resolved that this time around I would produce at last that book I had so far failed to write. I kept the resolution. Month after month successive chapters of a book on Socrates came out of my typewriter, and by June 1 a book-length manuscript had been finished, and would have got into print—there was a market for it—if the institute where I had done the work, or my university, had put the slightest pressure on me to show results. I cannot be too grateful that there was none of that. For half-way through that year's writing I began to realize that I had not yet solved the deeper problems of that work and that, short of that, all I could offer in that book would be a copiously footnoted rehash of what was already known. I persisted doggedly nonetheless, hoping for a miracle which never came, and when I read over the finished work and saw how secondhand it all was, how uninspired an account of one of the most inspiring philosophers who ever lived, I put it into a file where it has rested ever since. Looking back on that event a quarter of a century later, it is a great relief to me that the typescript never got into print. It would have been bad both for others, since inferior work in circulation cheapens the currency of the realm, and for me since the persona in which a scholar meets his peers in published work cannot be kept distinct in their minds or in his from his real self. Vexing though that year was—there is torment in executing day after day a program one knows to be foredoomed to mediocrity—it was one of the most salutary experiences of my life. By doing the wrong thing that year I learned what not to do thereafter.

The moral of this tale, for whose sake I trust its self-dramatization may be excused, is very clear. If what I expounded in the first part of my address is true—if the scholar's glory is in whatever increment given him to bring to the advancement of knowledge—then he must spare no effort to keep the offering pure, to save it from vulgarization. And the word he should be getting from those who judge his work for purposes of appointment or promotion should not be "publish or perish" but "publish *and* perish."

But where does that take us in answering the second of those questions I raised above. Let me rephrase it, replacing now "publication" by "published research," where "research" has its true, nonquantitative and antiquantitative force, and making the question more definite by comparing excellence in its communication to peers through publication with excellence in its communication to students through teaching. Which of these excellences should be rated first when taking the measure of a teacher-scholar's worth to his employer? The usual formula, which pervades the rhetoric of university presidents and deans, is that these two criteria are of equal standing. This fudges the issue. The fact is that for different purposes they are of unequal standing. For the purposes of the graduate school as such, research comes first. For the purposes of undergraduate education it is a poor second to good teaching. To say this is not to contradict the prevailing slogans. Many administrators would say that they agree, that this is what we all believe anyhow. Certainly it is what governs a part of our practice. But if it governed all of it, a good undergraduate education would not be the rarity it has now come to be in this country.

I had not meant to speak of this when I first planned this talk, but two things happened to change my mind.

First, further reflection on what we owe our graduate students. All of them will be teaching undergraduates at their first academic job, and most of them will be teaching only undergraduates throughout their working life. It would be a cruel irony if what they get while they are with us would be more likely to make them unfit for that vocation.

Then I caught up with an excellent book, *The Academic Revolution*, by Christopher Jencks and David Riesman (1968), whose indictment of the graduate school's relation to the undergraduate college crystallized similar thoughts in my own mind. The indictment is that the needs of undergraduates are being sacrificed to the concerns of the research-oriented faculty, whose influence in the university gives it de facto control of its policies:

> It is only a small exaggeration to say that undergraduate education in most universities and university colleges is simply a cut-rate, mass-produced, version of graduate education. [P. 248]

They picture the graduate school's relation to the college as an imperium over an undeveloped territory:

> First the graduate schools import the colleges' most valuable "raw material," i.e., the gifted B.A.s. They train these as scholars. The best of them they keep for themselves; the rest they export to the colleges whence they come, to become teachers. Like all imperial powers, the graduate schools believe they are doing their empire a favor by keeping order and maintaining standards in it. [P. 515]

The worst of what is done to the undergraduates is that they are used as course fodder to swell enrollments and strengthen departmental claims to more FTEs and more TAs, without being given due service in return. And what is that? Certainly not to be fed diluted versions of graduate courses, sugared and warmed up. To do this to them is to rob them of their birthright of cultural treasure.

When this happens, why does it? Chiefly, because good undergraduate teaching cannot be a mere by-product of successful research, as good graduate teaching often can. Between research and graduate teaching there is a happy symbiosis. By the start of their second year our best graduate students have moved up to the frontier of knowledge, can meet us there, can not only understand the searches going on there, but judge them, bringing a fresh vision that can improve and correct ours. Many of us can testify that we have often received better criticism from students in our seminars than from peers at professional meetings. How different is our relation to undergraduates. Taken by the large, they are nowhere near the frontier and would be only disoriented if parachuted to it. Not only would they not know what is going on there—they have not learned its idiolect, are not abreast of its literature, cannot see the rationale of its projects—but, more importantly, they have no particular desire to come to know any of this. Why should they? They have no professional commitment to our subject and only the vaguest notion of what there might be in it for them if they were to come to know it. It is for us, then, to cross the gap, to go over to their side of it, to see our subject through their eyes—how it would look from their point of view, if it were connected up with their present intellectual and emotional concerns.

Can this be done? I submit that it can, *if* we were willing to meet its great cost of labor to the teacher. This "if" does not mean changes in the curriculum. A course on Western Civilization or on the Nature of Man, like those at Columbia or Harvard, would be useful, but hardly indispensable. Virtually any course in the humanities and social sciences could be its vehicle. Let me speculate on what lines the design of such a course might take in the subject I know best—Plato. What is there in Plato's thought that speaks to one or another of those problems our undergraduates may have already run into, argued over, dogmatized about? Perhaps one or more of the following:

He has a concept of psychic health—a vision of nonrepressive harmony of reason, sentiment, and physical appetite, which is so much more optimistic than Freud's because, but not only because, it antedates the discovery of the unconscious.

He invents a new form of erotic love, homosexual in his case, yet anticipating the earliest version of romantic love in western Europe from the ballads of the troubadours to Dante's *Vita Nuova.*

In social theory he blends radicalism with conservatism: he would stand with Marx against Adam Smith on public control of the economy, with Hegel against Marx on class-stratification, with Mill against Hegel on the emancipation of women.

In metaphysics his transcendentalism has much in common with the otherworldliness of classical Christian dogma, yet no less also with secular recoils from it, such as the rationalistic mysticism of Spinoza and the aesthetic mysticism of Proust.

His epistemology, harshly antiempirical, despising sensory observation as a source of knowledge, has nonetheless, paradoxically, a benign effect on the natural sciences of his time, particularly on astronomy.

To implement such a course would call for lectures whose style, tonality, and use of imaginative and expository tropes would be drastically different from the idiom of graduate instruction. Expertise in any of those other subjects with which Plato's thought was to be linked up would not be necessary. What would be necessary would be a certain breadth of general knowledge. If a Platonic scholar had not cultivated, concurrently with his research on Plato, an interest in the main currents of European culture, he couldn't teach such a course successfully.

Are we now giving our Ph.D.'s the resources to do this kind of teaching? We are not even trying. Our leading graduate schools do not see, do not care to see, this problem. They ignore the fact that many of the B.A.'s who come to our humanistic departments for graduate work are already well advanced in their own specialty, but poorly educated, at times almost uneducated, in other things. A philosophy department may admit a student whose college career had contained a heavy battery of courses in analytical philosophy, logic, the philosophy of language, mathematics, statistics, but little history, less of political or social science, perhaps not even a single substantial course in English or European literature. We may get students who have not read a single one of those books which figured in my description, earlier on, of the impact of the advance of knowledge on the consciousness of post-war America—students to whom *American Dilemma* and *The Second Sex* are only names; who moreover have not read the classics, Homer, Thucydides, Pascal nor *Walden, The Education of Henry Adams, The Theory of the Leisure Class;* have read nothing of Proust, Kafka, Thomas Mann, Eliot, Yeats. How can a student who has been so victimized himself, culturally so disinherited and pauperized, be expected to command the resources needed to make a humanistic subject alive to undergraduates?

Is it then crying over spilt milk to ruminate over this fact? Must we assume that the harm done in a defective undergraduate education cannot be undone in graduate school? I would say not, judging from my own experience, if I may be permitted to refer to it once again. One of the best things that happened to me while toiling for the Ph.D. at Harvard was Irving Babbitt's famous undergraduate course where Rousseau was flayed for subverting the tradition of decorum and restraint dear to Babbitt's heart. Three of us in philosophy would wander over to Sever from Emerson Hall in the middle of the afternoon, as to a higher form of coffeebreak, laying bets along the way on how many times poor Rousseau would be vilified in the lecture we were about to hear. But though pretending to go to Babbitt not for instruction but recreation, his vast knowledge of his subject and his passionate involvement in it disarmed our condescension. He drew us, in spite of ourselves, into Rousseau's world, brought us into the presence of the people in it—Voltaire, Diderot, d'Alembert, Grimm, Madame d'Epinay, and the rest. And the whole of the French Enlightenment came alive in our imagination more than any period to which our courses in philosophy had introduced us. A few years later I made excursions of the same sort, first in Oxford, listening to Cyril Bailey on the *Clouds* of Aristophanes, then back at Harvard, hearing W. S. Ferguson on Athenian History, MacIlwain on Medieval Constitutional Theories, Schumpeter on the Utopian Socialists and Marx. Still more salutary for the better-late-than-never part of my education were those forays into French literature I took on my own a few years later, picking one author at a time for a summer's reading, getting in that way into Baudelaire, Flaubert, Rimbaud, Proust. Nothing that happened to me in the course of my adult life did more to improve my power to communicate with undergraduates and colleagues in other departments. In a better undergraduate education much of this would have been anticipated in my late teens, but having missed it then, I now wish I could have made up as much of it as possible during my years of graduate study.

It is along such lines as these that we should rethink the shape of our graduate programs in the humanities. What is now their greatest strength—the high gloss of technical polish which it enables good graduate students to achieve—is also its gravest weakness. For the production of specialists who could reproduce their kind, our leading graduate schools are now probably unsurpassed anywhere in the world. But for the production of teachers of undergraduates our graduate education is a failure. Its shortcomings could not possibly be remedied, as some people appear to think, by either adding courses on teaching methods, which would be useless except for inculcating mechanics and cosmetics, nor yet by so-called supervised teaching (who would supervise supervisors who are themselves bored and boring teachers?). The only answer I can see is to change the content of our graduate education—to diversify and enrich it.

A step in that direction would be interdepartmental programs, such as those in classical philosophy or in political philosophy, which have got under way in some schools in recent years, or revive an older pattern, much the same thing under another name, of an extra-departmental minor for the Ph.D., which still exists in some schools today. But I do not believe that either of these moves would go far enough in meeting the need. For that purpose nothing less will do than a systematic attack on the rigidities of departmental require-ments which now make it often so difficult for a student to take work outside of his own department on the same campus. I happen to know of a student who came some years ago to a leading graduate school to study classical philosophy and then, having enrolled in the depart-ment of classics, found things so rigged there that he was unable to take, all the way to his Ph.D., even a single course or seminar in the highly reputed department of philosophy on his campus. How many such horror stories there are to tell, how much of such extreme disci-plinary self-segregation still prevails, I do not know. But even in its milder form it is still a reproach to American graduate education. In many respects ours is now a model for other countries. But in this our colleagues in Britain and in Europe find our system bizarre, almost a joke. They marvel at its affront to *Lernfreiheit.*

To remedy this fault without impairment of the professional ex-cellence we certainly wish to keep, we need to permit and foster a fanning out into extra-departmental courses, mainly but not exclu-sively, after the departmental requirements have been met by passing the predoctoral examination. Thus a graduate student going for his Ph.D. in the optimal four-year stretch of full-time study, passing his preliminary examinations at the end of the second, would be advised to devote the better part of his third year to branching operations in other fields, taking courses or seminars which may, but need not, tie into his dissertation topic. Thus suppose he was to write a thesis on the political philosophy of David Hume. Here is a menu from which he might select fare to enrich what he had been fed so far by his depart-ment:

A course on the history of eighteenth-century England and Scot-land, especially on British constitutional and economic history, or, if there were such a thing, a course in which manners and morals in England and Scotland were studied by comparison with those of France, where Hume had lived as a stranger, when com-posing his masterpiece, as a very young man.

A course in the English department on the satire, essay, and novel of the eighteenth century, and in the department of French on the Enlightenment or, better still, on Rousseau and on Romanticism generally with which Hume's own concept of sentiment, so fundamental in all branches of his thought, has such ambiguous affinities.

Courses in the politics department, not necessarily only the usual one on the seventeenth-century contractarians, to study ancient, or, still better, medieval and renaissance political theory—Aquinas, Marsilio, Calvin, Hooker, Machiavelli—or post-eighteenth century thinkers, like Hegel, De Maistre, De Tocqueville, might do more for him in widening his horizons.

A course on the history of economic theory, especially if it took seriously, as such courses rarely do, the earlier phases, the physiocrats and Hume's contemporary, Adam Smith.

A course on the classics of historiography, where he might have the chance to see why Hume's own work in this area compares with, yet falls far short of, peak achievements like those of Thucydides and Gibbon.

This menu has stressed relevance to the thesis topic. But I would not wish him to be so tied. A course on Dante, Shakespeare, Frederic the Great, Freud, contemporary literary criticism, any of these might do more for him, depending on who taught them. And if there are great humanistic teachers on the campus, the stature of the teacher would be reason enough for going to him, whatever his subject. If our aspirant for the Ph.D. on Hume is to be himself a vital teacher of undergraduates, nothing is better fitted to show him what this is and to inspire him to do it than to give him the chance to see its craft and magic enacted before his eyes. I speak of magic because the teacher's artistry at its best transcends all rules and rubrics, so that to come to know it one has to see it. Think of a man like Christian Gauss of whom Edmund Wilson was to say for himself and for his close friends, Scott Fitzgerald and John Peale Bishop:

> He made us all want to write something in which every word, every cadence, every detail, should perform a definite function in producing an intense effect.

And Judge Medina was to testify,

> He led and guided with so gentle a touch that one began to think almost despite oneself . . . . He continued in such fashion as to

instil into my very soul the determination to be a seeker after truth—the elusive, perhaps never to be attained, complete and utter truth, no matter where it led or whom it hurt. [Both quotations are from Edmund Wilson's essay on Christian Gauss in *Shores of Light.*]

Or think of a man like William Ellery Leonard, of whom Leslie Fiedler was to write:

> It was he who first not merely told but showed me—showed in the rich, tragic, quality of his own being as well as by the excitement he engendered in the classroom—that literature is more than what one learns to read in schools and libraries, more even than a grace of life; that it is the record of those elusive moments at which life is alone fully itself, fulfilled in consciousness and form. No one who has been his student can regard literary criticism as anything less than an act of total moral engagement. [Op. cit., rev. ed. (1966), p. 15]

Are there Gausses and Leonards on American campuses today? They are few and far between, but they exist. And we can render our graduate students no greater service than to do what we can to bring them into live contact with the wizardry of such teaching. If I knew what was ahead of me when I was a graduate student, I would gladly have traveled from Cambridge to Princeton or Madison to spend at least one term there under such a teacher; and the fact that his subject was literature, not philosophy, should have been no deterrent but, if anything, an added attraction.

This gives me the opening to make my last plea on behalf of our graduate students, continuing my plea for *Lernfreiheit* and now proceeding to widen its scope, pleading for ways that will make more accessible to graduate students throughout the nation the wealth of both scholarship and teaching now concentrated in the most fortunate schools. The concentration, inevitable in the free academic labor market in which we all believe, results in the vast enrichment of a few elite institutions, to the impoverishment of the rest. When scrambling for moveable talent as department chairman, well aware that it was a form of predation, I never felt happy over the fact that talent so captured should be sequestered in one academic preserve, made its employer's property, as closed to students elsewhere as the Rembrandts and Matisses in a multimillionaire's private collection are closed to everyone except his own handpicked guests. Is this consonant with our sense of equity? Suppose James, Royce, and Santayana were now lecturing in Emerson Hall at Harvard, as they were three-quarters of a century ago, and you and I were graduate students on some other American campus. Would we not labor under a rankling sense of unfairness at the fact that our enrollment in some other school deprived us of any chance of sustained personal access to these great men whose writings we were studying and whose thoughts were in our minds day and night? Whether or not such giants exist now, and, if so, where, is a question which prudence and charity forbid me to press. But no one would doubt that today in every humanistic discipline figures of world renown hold forth on particular campuses, their ideas being the ones which are discussed and argued over in scores of seminars from coast to coast and are made the topics of graduate theses. Is it just to deprive totally anyone but a privileged handful to be the students, for even a brief time, of these scholars?

Granting that the sheer numbers of those desiring and deserving access must be a harsh constraint, even so I see no moral justification for allowing the present exclusionary system to persist intact. Surely partial remedies are possible, and we are derelict in our duty to our graduate students if we fail to explore them.

As a first possibility, that third year of cultural enrichment which I suggested a moment ago—the year after the predoctoral examination has been passed at the student's own university—should be made one of free mobility, within reasonable limits, from campus to campus. When the demand exceeds the facilities of the host institution, as it frequently will, preference would be given to those making the stronger case for special benefits to their particular research or teaching derivable from a visiting-residence for a term or for a year on a given campus.

Also, since it is certain that this first proposal would not begin to match the need, the summer could be used to similar purpose, as it is now being used in an extraordinarily valuable program of summer seminars for college teachers in humanistic disciplines under the auspices of the National Endowment for the Humanities. A parallel program for graduate students would be as feasible and no less valuable. It would involve bringing together every summer leading scholars in each discipline to a few centers, different ones from summer to summer, to give instruction there, in lectures and seminars, in their own subject—instruction to which qualified graduate students from any school in the country would have free access. One of the incidental benefits to the summer migrants would be that students from different departments would mix and find out how the views which dominate in their own department differ from those prevailing elsewhere and hammer out such differences in those endless self-managed, unstructured discussions in which graduate students educate one another. The program should also include on its faculty outstanding teachers of undergraduates from whose performance the visiting graduate students might learn by example how good teaching is done.

Neither of these projects would be cheap. They could not be implemented without substantial funding. But the entailed expense would be amply justified in opening up access to the finest quality of scholarship and teaching throughout the country to those who are now deprived of it—in sharing this great wealth on a more equitable basis within a population of graduate students now held captive in the schools where the accidents of admission procedures have cast them.

I warned you from the start that the problems of our graduate students would have first claim on my attention throughout this address. I have so acted. All the remedial measures I have proposed have been addressed to their special needs. But I don't have the heart to close without so much as mentioning either of the two great problems we, their teachers, now face:

First, is the question of time. To do our own research would be of itself a full-time job, and a job of the highest importance to our society whose perception of its own values is being molded by our collective work. Yet in addition to that, under the terms of our employment, not at research institutes, but at American universities, we must also engage in a radically different form of work, demanding a different, and very costly, outlay of imaginative energy: we must make our subject alive to undergraduates. When we face up honestly to both of these tasks, instead of giving the second poor leftovers from the first, the demands on our time and energy are cruel. No group in the population is more hardworked than ours. To survive we need desperately not only breaks in teaching schedules which come in the course of the academic calendar, but extended periods of release from all teaching duties to pursue single-minded, whole-hearted research.

Second, research, of necessity highly specialized, pushes us into intellectual isolation even from colleagues in our own department, to say nothing of colleagues in other fields. For humanists this is a mortal peril, for when we cannot communicate with fellow humanists, our own work becomes dessicated, overpreoccupied with formalisms and techniques, we lose the sense of its human importance and this impairs our ability to do work which has human importance. To maintain a vital and sane *problematik* in our own specialty we must decline to be the slave of territorial imperatives. We owe it to our own discipline to be venturesomely interdisciplinary. We need facilities for this outreach. Today more than ever we need centers of intercommunication among humanists. Graduate education in America will be the richer and healthier for them.

Comments by Annette Baier

Vlastos emphasizes one grave fault of graduate education in the humanities, particularly philosophy: it fails to help graduate students equip themselves to do the thing most of them want to be hired to do—teaching undergraduates. Graduate education is aimed too narrowly at reproducing the sort of skills graduate teachers need and too little at allowing graduate students to prepare themselves for undergraduate teaching. Whether it prepares them for nonacademic employment is an issue he does not discuss.

The emphasis on research is due in large measure to the criteria in current use for awarding tenure and promotion. The emphasis on published research present in the reward structure of academic institutions spreads into and distorts the education given to future job seekers in universities and colleges. We turn out people adept at getting an article published by a journal because that is the ability they will need to be kept on in any university job. But Vlastos claims that this ability should be esteemed less than the ability to refrain from publishing, and he says that, for purposes of undergraduate teaching, the demand should be for good teaching rather than for any research, published or unpublished.

No one could quarrel with the claim that the current emphasis on published research as a criterion for success as a professor is exaggerated and harmful. Because of the publish-or-perish policy, journals proliferate and the point of publication is lost. Publications become an obstacle to the very goal they should attain—a shared common tradition, a dialogue between minds. When so much is published no one can reasonably expect colleagues, even in the same area, to have happened to read the same articles, not even those which discuss their own views. We get metajournals and journals of abstracts to help us pick our way among other journals, and the point of publishing, namely making something public to those with common interests, is increasingly difficult to attain even for those whose work merits general attention.

That wise and public spirited philosopher, Leibniz, gave us, some three hundred years ago, this timely advice in his *Memoir for Enlightened Persons of Good Intention:*

And as for those intellectuals capable of contributing to the increase of knowledge, they should think of projects which not only serve to get them known and applauded but also to produce new knowledge . . . for to write for writing's sake is only a bad habit, and to write merely to make people talk about us is a wicked vanity, which even does harm to others by making them lose their time in useless reading.[1]

What we are currently doing to our graduate students, by example and by training, is to encourage what Leibniz calls bad habits and wicked vanity. It is not only wicked, but futile, since however much they will publish, few will succeed in getting the attention of others, except perhaps for those important others who sit on tenure committees.

But if we are to put right this fault in graduate education we must first correct its sustaining cause—the disproportionate reward for research rather than good teaching. To do this we need a reliable way of judging which teachers are good teachers, and we are a long way from having that. Vlastos wants imaginative undergraduate courses which place a text, like Plato's *Republic* or Hume's *Treatise,* in a broad cultural context, not merely a narrow philosophical one. But the typical vice of courses which aim at this undoubted excellence is superficiality and lack of depth. How do we tell when we have a good rather than a bad undergraduate course on Plato, Freud, and the health of the soul? Popularity with students, while they are taking the course, is an inadequate measure. Ideally one should consult them several years or decades later, to discover which entertaining courses were instantly forgotten, which irritating or boring courses left something of lasting value.

How does Vlastos propose that we modify graduate education so as to help graduate students become good undergraduate teachers? He wants them to work in their field with graduate teachers selected primarily for excellence in research, but also to have time to take "a higher form of coffee break" by attending exemplary undergraduate courses in any field. He also proposes that means be found to enable them to move from university to university, seeking out good teachers and good scholars, and to seek out one another's company in summer schools taught by the most sought-after graduate teachers and the most respected scholars. I think the summer school idea has more chance of acceptable implementation than the idea that third-year

---

1. Included in *The Political Writings of Leibniz,* translated and edited by Patrick Riley (Cambridge University Press, 1972), pp. 108–9.

students be given a free pass to visit any graduate program. But I agree with Vlastos that we should encourage, at the graduate level, any practicable means of breaking down the barriers between one department and another within one university, and between graduate programs in the same subject in different universities.

What worries me most about Vlastos's recommendations for changing emphases in graduate education is the hidden assumption that, although good undergraduate teachers need not be productive scholars, good scholars will be good graduate teachers. He says that "for the purposes of the graduate school as such, research comes first." But there is no necessary correlation between excellence in research and excellence in imparting the scholar's research skills, let alone in imparting the sort of attitude to one's subject which will help anyone give an undergraduate course that will catch the imagination of the students. So it would seem that the only way one could ensure that graduate teachers, appointed for research excellence, help graduate students become good undergraduate teachers, is by ensuring that they not hinder them, that they not monopolize their time, but allow them freedom to observe good undergraduate teaching, and to think about their subject in ways which may help their teaching more than their research. This seems too negative a contribution from a graduate teacher. A graduate program ought to do more than refrain from obstructing the majority of its students from finding out for themselves how to become good teachers while launching the rare creative few on their scholarly careers. At the very least the dissertation requirements could be altered, to allow it to exhibit the sort of knowledgeable and imaginative thinking about a subject which promotes good teaching. But if we had dissertations of that type we would need graduate faculty who could direct them, who could give help not merely with original research but with the sort of thinking good teaching requires. I think Vlastos must suppose that anyone who has the research excellence which he wants as a prerequisite for graduate teaching will also have the other excellence which is to be imparted to graduate students and which is the most one should demand of an undergraduate teacher. But that is an overoptimistic estimate of the unity of a graduate teacher's virtue. One teacher is unlikely to combine creative ability, discrimination needed to judge what is worth writing, worth attacking, worth commenting on, the ability to transmit those abilities to others, and in addition help students think about their subject in ways which will help them become good undergraduate teachers. I think we must expect members of graduate faculties to show different excellences, and to reward all the needed excellences. Only thus can we expect those faculties to help their students prepare for a profession in which those distinct excellences, of good teaching and creative research, are each recognized and given their proper place.

Reflections on the Graduate School

Anthony Quinton

I am going to begin my consideration of the future of graduate education with a short and selective survey of its past. In its first medieval beginnings the university was a place of graduate education. The earliest universities were wholly graduate schools. Salerno was a school of medicine, Bologna a school of law. With Paris and Oxford in the twelfth century something more stable, and more recognizable as a university, came into being. In both there is a clearly marked distinction between the basic, preliminary studies in arts and the higher studies in theology, medicine, and canon and civil law for which alone doctorates were granted. The basic arts course of study was the liberal aspect of the whole undertaking. Its components, after all, are the original liberal arts: logic, grammar, rhetoric, mathematics, and astronomy. The higher studies for which a master's degree in arts was a required condition were all vocational. They trained men for the professions of lawyer, medical man, and ecclesiastic. Most students who matriculated in the medieval university failed to graduate in arts and only a minority of those who did went on to work for a higher degree.

The graduate aspect of the university was one of the casualties of the decline of universities in the early modern period. Doctorates were still awarded, but in an honorary or virtually honorary fashion. That process of decline is most clearly observed in England, the most progressive country of the epoch. The extraordinary intellectual vitality of Oxford in the thirteenth and fourteenth centuries was severely reduced by the Black Death. But it was not finally extinguished until early in the fifteenth century with official suppression of the Wycliffite heresy. The advancement of knowledge then ceased at the university, to be carried on for the next four or five hundred years almost exclusively by private individuals working outside any learned institution. What the great English thinkers of the seventeenth century acquired from their universities was a settled hostility to the Aristotelian system they had been subjected to there. Bacon, Hobbes, and Locke were all in self-conscious revolt against the type of learning with which the university seemed to them to be indissolubly identified.

Bacon supported his mature studies by his successes as lawyer, politician, and judge. Hobbes and Locke had earls as patrons. Where the new learning had an institutional connection it was comparatively informal and unrelated to the university. The Royal Society may have been conceived in Wadham College, Oxford, during the Cromwellian interregnum. It came to fruition only in Restoration London as a club for intellectual gentlemen.

The universities conveyed to their students the old mixture of inert medieval lore, lightened here and there with a little Renaissance polish put on by way of the reading and imitation of classical authors. The undergraduate body consisted in part of well-born young men with no practical reason to bother themselves with degree getting and, in larger but less conspicuous part, of future clergy, now more usually the younger sons of gentry, than the socially humbler scholars of the middle ages. The end result of the process was the Oxford of Edward Gibbon, a kind of academic Sodom in which it would have been hard to find half a dozen intellectually active and distinguished men among the permanent residents. Attention should be given to the time scale of university history. Oxford had two and a half centuries of vigor between its mid-twelfth century beginnings and the onset of stagnation in the early fifteenth century. Four hundred years of torpor then ensued until at the beginning of the nineteenth century various signs of life began to emerge.

The reformers of the mid-nineteenth century were more interested in ensuring that the university earned its endowment income by the effective teaching of properly selected students by properly qualified teachers than in its revival as a place for the advancement of knowledge. Jowett's conception of the university as the finishing school for the ruling class of the chief imperial nation of the age prevailed. Another reforming point of view was that of Mark Pattison, who wanted the university to concentrate on pure scholarship, the accumulation of knowledge, and the fostering of truly learned men. That policy, which had none of the public appeal of Jowett's scheme of a training camp for philosopher-kings, was, of course, inspired by the nineteenth-century triumph of the German universities.

The universities of Germany had also had their period of decadence. Their historian, Friedrich Paulsen, points out that by the late eighteenth century they were ignored by such intellectually distinguished figures as Leibniz and Lessing. But they revived much sooner than the universities of England. In the late eighteenth century, with Halle, the first Prussian university, and Göttingen leading the way, they had developed the distinctive qualities that made the German universities of the nineteenth century so productive and so much admired. The principles of *Lehrfreiheit* and *Lernfreiheit* encouraged scholarly specialization by both teachers and pupils. Emphasized in the university of Berlin, founded by Humboldt in 1810, they soon came to permeate the entire German-speaking university system. The double freedom in question meant that the studies of the university were not subordinated to any externally determined principles of social usefulness, whether liberal and general or vocational and particular. The freedom was not abused. Germany in the nineteenth century had the benefit of universal recognition of the fact that its universities were the best in the world. Much more original and substantial work came from them than from the universities of Britain and America. Their graduates were altogether more learned than graduates anywhere else.

It was the conception of the university exemplified in nineteenth century Germany that inspired the development of a university system really deserving the name in the United States. Before the 1870s and the Johns Hopkins of Gilman, the American college had been a kind of demure and conventional high school. In much the same way as the revived but not yet truly reformed universities of early nineteenth-century England, American colleges were staffed by young men of no great expertise who taught all the subjects offered and were ruled by clergymen more concerned with orthodoxy and decorum than with learning. Gilman's conception of the university as a graduate school on German lines linked up with the element of *Lernfreiheit* embodied in the elective system, the development of serious professional schools and a generally widespread secularization to establish the vast American university of the present age, with its undergraduate college, its academic and professional graduate schools, its research institutes, and the various kinds of socially purposive educational institutions that are attached to it.

English universities have increasingly come to follow the American pattern, within limits set by poverty and insular complacency. That is particularly true of the urban universities founded in the late nineteenth century, the "Redbricks," whose theorist, "Bruce Truscot," claimed were more genuine universities than Oxford and Cambridge on the ground that a university is possible without undergraduates but not without research, which, in his view, the urban universities emphasized. Now all English universities have more or less plausible arrangements for graduate study. In the last few years the possession of advanced degrees, which has for a long time characterized all recruits to the academic profession from the natural sciences, has, for the first time, come to be true of most recruits from the humanities.

The reform of the older English universities in the middle and late nineteenth century does seem to show that organized graduate study is not an indispensable condition of academic respectability. If the private Carlyle and Macaulay, Mill and Spencer gave way to the professorial Stubbs and Maitland, Bradley and Sidgwick, the latter did not have doctorates until encumbered with them *honoris causa* at an advanced age. By English-speaking standards the German universities have for the last two centuries been almost wholly graduate schools. It was by the addition of the graduate school, particularly the academic graduate school of arts and sciences, to the old undergraduate college that the modern American university was brought into being out of comparatively unpromising raw material. Even if the old English universities revived without any perceptible emphasis on graduate studies, they have in the course of this century come to accord almost as important a place to them as they are given in all but the most insistently graduate-oriented American universities.

So far I have done nothing to define graduate education explicitly, but have assumed that the phrase will be uniformly interpreted. An obvious criterion might be the directing of a course of study toward a doctorate. Unfortunately there are many bachelor's and master's degrees that are earned only by what is clearly graduate work such as bachelor's degrees in law, medicine, and divinity, and master's of arts degrees where that is not, as in Scotland, the first degree or, as in Oxford and Cambridge, an automatic sequel to the Bachelor of Arts. A more serious difficulty is that being directed toward a doctorate, even if proposed only as a sufficient condition of the graduate character of a course of study, is defectively superficial in relying on a convention of naming. It is reasonable to award a doctorate for the successful completion of a course only if that course is in its nature of the graduate kind. It is worth noting in this connection that the main degree of the German university is the doctorate. Matthew Arnold and Abraham Flexner were not simply bewitched by a word when they took the completion of the course at the traditional German gymnasium to be equivalent to a first degree in the English-speaking world. The nature of the German university student's work from the outset was such as to make the doctorate an appropriate reward for bringing it to completion.

The idea of independent study has some attractions as a criterion, but the relativeness of the concept of independence makes the idea vague. In comparison to the drilled note-takers whose main academic work is attending lectures and memorizing the contents of textbooks, the essay-writing undergraduate of the Oxford tutorial system, sent off with a topic and a reading list to come back with an essay a week later, is studying independently. Yet this kind of tutorial procedure is to be found in the sixth forms where the pupils in the better British secondary schools spend their last two or three years before going to the university at all. On the other hand, most graduate programs involve course work of a more or less authoritatively instructional kind, at least in their earlier phases, and in graduate professional schools such course work bulks very large indeed.

To move back toward a more formal and conventional indication of graduate character, there is the matter of a central part being played by the thesis or dissertation. The distinguishing power of this feature is weakened by such things as the American undergraduate's term paper or the long essays British undergraduates are now often allowed to offer in place of a timed and invigilated examination script in their final examinations, although such papers and essays will ordinarily be a good deal shorter than anything acceptable for a master's or, even more, a doctor's degree.

A further suggestion comes from etymology and history. One who has successfully completed a course of graduate study is a doctor, or, at least, a master, and both of these terms imply being qualified to teach others. The master is one who has mastered a craft or art, who knows how to exercise a skill and is thus fit to be imitated by apprentices. The doctor is one who has mastered a science, is the possessor of knowledge that certain things are the case, and is qualified to convey that knowledge to others, a capacity that involves understanding the grounds on which the knowledge rests. This notion of graduate study as directed toward a qualification to teach applies more neatly to academic than to professional graduate work. The latter is concerned to produce qualified practitioners rather than theory builders.

Etymology is, of course, a questionable witness in this kind of case. But its suggestions may survive the tests they have to be given. I think what is suggested here has one very solid virtue. In the universities of the English-speaking world, academic graduate schools, graduate schools of arts and sciences, are now professional schools for intending entrants to the academic profession. Almost all students of academic graduate schools intended, when they started, to become professional academics. That is no doubt more true of the humanities than of the natural and social sciences. Natural scientists may enter graduate school intending to follow the careers in scientific research for government or industry that they actually go into. Intending diplomats or journalists may well seek doctorates in political science or international relations, intending investment analysts in economics. There are no noneducational professional openings of that degree of closeness to graduate work in philosophy, history, or literature.

In what follows I shall assume that our main concern is with the academic graduate school. There are reasonably clearly demarcated bodies of knowledge and levels of competence in applying them which can be used to define professional qualifications in medicine, law, engineering, accountancy, architecture, even social work and school teaching. And the professions in question serve definite, persisting, and fairly uncontroversial needs. These factors make the graduate school for professionals comparatively unproblematic. Neither applies in the case of the academic graduate school. Every profession ought to take stock of itself from time to time. What has made this particularly urgent for the academic profession is the increasing disparity between the numbers of those who seek such a career and of the occupational places open to them. The practical problem that lies behind our presence here is the way in which various factors, most substantially demographic ones, have reduced the demand for academic professionals.

There are two main ways in which the training of professionals generally is and has been carried on. The first is, in effect, on-the-job training, made necessary by the incapacity of the higher faculties of the universities to serve the purpose for which they were apparently designed. Lawyers in England have for centuries received their training in the Inns of Court in the form of apprenticeship to a practicing master. Doctors have been trained in hospitals and where these are near enough to universities to be associated institutionally with them the association is often of a very formal nature. The degree of connection between professional training generally and the universities varies between these two limiting cases, both of them pretty remote, at least in every profession except the academic. But for the academic, of course, to be trained at the university is to be trained on the job to the extent that the academic's job is that of being a university teacher.

The alternative, American, method is to have professional schools as genuinely included parts of universities. The actual difference between the two modes of proceeding should not be exaggerated. What makes it a little less profound than might at first appear is that in British undergraduate courses a good deal of the curriculum of an American law school or medical school is to be found. The difference is, nevertheless, a real one.

The point of drawing attention to the difference is that nonacademic professional training, which is now such a very large statistical part of the American graduate school as a whole, stands in no very close or necessary relation to the university. There could well be, as there largely are in Britain, wholly separate schools for the training of entrants into the nonacademic professions. It is not even necessary that such schools should require their students to have obtained a first degree at a university. In England there is no such requirement and many people entering the legal and medical professions there even today have not come to them from undergraduate university study.

If there are academic graduate schools attached to universities, it is natural that other nonacademic professional schools should cluster around them. Both types of institution give further instruction to the products of undergraduate colleges, even in England, both are concerned with the maintenance of standards. There are also considerations of convenience. Where the interests of academic and strictly professional school overlap, there can be a sharing of such expensive things as libraries, visiting experts, and ancillary courses. A liberal arts college can afford a Bach choir or a rock-climbing society, but for a consort of ancient musical instruments or a stilt-walking group you probably need something on the scale of the modern multiversity.

Let us turn, then, to the academic graduate school proper, the graduate school of arts and sciences. These are, of course, usually associated with undergraduate colleges in universities. As I said earlier, if we assume that the purpose of academic graduate schools is to train university teachers, then that association makes such schools instances of on-the-job training of the English type. Indeed, given the extent to which the teaching of undergraduates is put in the hands of graduate students, that is not just a matter of institutional form. The student as apprentice engages fully in the firsthand work of the profession. But, continuing with the assumption, the comparatively sequestered, more American option is a possible one. Academic graduate schools could be, as a very few of them actually are, altogether independent of undergraduate colleges. If that arrangement became general it might compel the recognition of a possible infinite regress of academic professionalism. There would then be two rather clearly distinct kinds of academic teacher: the teacher of undergraduates, employed by a college, and the teacher of future college teachers, employed by a graduate school. Where, it might now be asked, should the latter be equipped for their special function of professor-training and by whom? In fact the regress could be stopped quite painlessly by allowing the academic graduate school to replenish its own staff. In any educational system of finite complexity there must be a highest kind of teacher whose final training is received from teachers of his own kind and not a higher one.

There can be no doubt that, in actual practice, the main work of most of those who successfully complete their courses at academic graduate schools is university teaching of undergraduates and often of graduates as well. It is equally evident that the courses followed in academic graduate schools contain no formal instruction in the technique of university teaching. What is supplied in abundance is practical experience of the humbler varieties of such teaching. It is often so amply provided that, by absorbing so much of the energy that should be applied to the more central aspects of the course, it causes its completion to be seriously delayed. So, even if university teaching is what those who emerge successfully from graduate schools actually do, it is not what they are directly and explicitly prepared for. We should then examine the assumption that what academic graduate schools are intended to produce is university teachers.

As we all know, academic graduate schools devote themselves to producing scholars, learned men, or, to be quite precise about the present state of things, researchers, advancers of knowledge. That final, Baconian aim is enshrined in the formula defining the appropriate quality of the doctoral dissertation that is the crucial element of the graduate's pursuit of his doctorate, that it should make an original contribution to knowledge.

I argued a little while ago against the assumption that the training of university teachers is the intended or acknowledged purpose of the academic graduate school, that such schools give no instruction in the technique of university teaching. To see some force in that argument is not to suppose that an instruction in those techniques alone would be sufficient to qualify someone for teaching in a university. The technique of communicating knowledge and understanding is empty, without some content to communicate. The trained university teacher must be a scholar, in the sense of being an appropriately informed or learned person, as well as an instructor. But does that mean that he has to be a researcher, to be equipped with the capacity to add to knowledge? I do not think it does.

I touched earlier on a point about the nature of knowledge from which it follows that one who possesses knowledge or reasonable belief, in the self-conscious or self-critical way it must be possessed if it is to be authoritatively communicated, cannot be just a repository of truths and of well-grounded beliefs. He must understand that what he is communicating is knowledge or reasonable belief and why it is so. It could be held that the main point of the propositions and theories he puts across is the service they give as examples, through attention to which the power of critically assessing beliefs can be developed.

The scholar or learned person, I maintain, must have not just knowledge but, rather, a critical understanding of the extent to which what he believes in his particular field of study is knowledge. A scholar on this view is not simply a person who knows a great deal. But to insist that he is more than that is not to hold that he must be a researcher in the full, Baconian understanding of the term. He needs to have a critical mastery of the current state of discussion and should not see it as a steady accumulation of uncontroversial truths. He must be familiar, not just with the results of past discussion, but with the way in which those results were supported and the way in which they succeeded in displacing alternative views. The crucial point is that although playing a game may be a good way of acquiring a critical understanding of it, it is by no means the only or the usual way. Every interesting game has many more skilled and critical spectators than it has really gifted players.

The issue I am concerned with is often presented as a problem about the proper relation between teaching and research in the academic career. On the whole it is success in research that is esteemed and rewarded, so it is not surprising that it is research rather than teaching that academics want, or think or say that they want, to do. But the community at large is more ready to pay them for teaching. The received doctrine on this topic is that the two activities are necessary to each other, so that the community cannot have teaching of the quality it wants unless it allows and encourages its university teachers to engage in research. More particularly, it is maintained that teaching without research is flat, lifeless, and uninspired; while research without teaching, which is less painful for the academic mind to contemplate, may become precious, overspecialized, out of touch with life.

I do not think that anyone takes the argument against research without teaching very seriously. Governments and industry, as well as intellectual philanthropy, often set up research institutes and employ highly intelligent people in full-time research but they are not criticized on these sort of grounds. What is commonly objected to about research institutes is the morally or socially deficient character of their objects, such as chemical weapons or cheaper and nastier foodstuffs. Even where the objects of research are criticized for excessive inwardness, refinement, or hyperacademic triviality, it is not suggested that the best way to divert attention to more valuable objects of study is the introduction of some teaching work into the researcher's program. But resistance to research without teaching is really only there for the sake of symmetry. It is the alleged necessity of research to teaching that is the important case.

Is teaching without research inevitably defective? It seems to me that this constantly affirmed principle is bluff. It is, of course, exciting and generally splendid when a really original contributor to the advancement of knowledge in some field is a gifted and willing teacher of it as well. There are such people. Who were our own most effective teachers, and, of those whom we encountered in our undergraduate years, who were the most creative advancers of knowledge? Were they generally the same? In my own case there was rather little overlap and for an intelligible reason. Those active in research tended to use their teaching as ancillary to what they saw as their main business. They generally managed to ensure that the instruction they gave was confined to the area of their current preoccupation. That is at any rate to be preferred to a not uncommon alternative: the perfunctory and more or less exasperated discharge by a researcher of his teaching duties.

The claim that teaching, on the scale required for present-day undergraduate populations, is best carried on without requirement or expectation of research from those who give it is hard to support with familiar examples of great, nonresearching teachers. Teaching prowess on its own tends to secure only a local fame. It would not be all that relevant to produce such instances if they were available, since the material consideration is good teaching, not great teaching. But some indirect support is surely given by the large and superfluous mass of low-grade academic publication that is generated by the requirement, ordinarily crucial for tenure and promotion, that the university teacher should be a researcher.

To deny the necessity of the research requirement is not to deny something with which, I suspect, it is quite often confused by those who take it to be a precondition of lively and stimulating teaching. That is the entirely different requirement that the teacher should be "abreast of his subject," that he should have a good idea of what is going on in the areas of growth within it. I suspect that this condition is not important for its own sake but more as a symptom of a live interest in his subject on the part of the teacher. Research, it must be said, is often hostile to it. The most creatively productive academics are often ill-informed about what is going on in the rest of their discipline.

Research, I am arguing, is not necessary to preserve the life and freshness of a university teacher's teaching work. But, even if that is correct, there may well be other good reasons for combining the two functions in one profession. There are indeed reasons for the different principle of combining teachers and researchers in the same institution. The chief of these, perhaps, is that the two groups provide, respectively, critical and constructive environments for each other that are valuable. That is simply an institutional version of the arguments I have questioned which affirm the necessity to each other of teaching and research in each academic individual. But it is, I think, more plausible than they are. However, what I am concerned with at the moment is the individual version of the principle.

There are two somewhat pedestrian considerations of a practical kind which may be brought forward in support of it. The first is that the kind of intellectual creativeness that is needed in research work is in various ways fitful and unpredictable. Early signs of originality may turn out to have been deceptive. Bouts of inspiration may be separated from one another by relatively stagnant periods. Something that is irresistibly obvious in mathematics may be more widely diffused in a less unmistakable way through all the fields of higher study: the tendency of creativeness to die away with age. The combination of the two academic functions smooths out the ups and downs of intellectual creativeness by extorting the appearances of research in various forms from the more or less uncreative while providing steady teaching jobs for the creative to fall back on as and when their creative powers dry up. This strategy, at the very least, avoids embarrassment, getting around the problem of the academic counterpart of the superannuated sports star.

A second practical reason for the combination is that it is a convenient device for getting fundamental research paid for. Governments and business firms are anxious to support research for what seem straightforwardly advantageous purposes. But the institutional consumers of knowledge who are in a position to pay for it do not take the same view of the questions which research should be directed to answering as the intellectually creative producers of knowledge do themselves. That is not to say that official and commercial funding of research is always or, even predominantly, philistine. It is remarkable how much unpractical-looking academic inquiry government and business do endorse in one way or another. But as institutions they are accountable, formally to the electorate or the shareholders, more realistically to politicians and finance directors and that sets limits to the possibilities of intellectual philanthropy open to them.

How else is comparatively unpractical, comparatively academic research to be supported? The founders of the colleges of Oxford and Cambridge handed over large chunks of often questionably accumulated wealth to the colleges, for, among other things, the pursuit of learning for its own sake. It must be acknowledged that in this respect they did not get value for their money. The misuse of endowments during the four to five centuries of torpor entirely justified the principle of ultimate control by public legislation that underlay the highly fruitful reforms of the nineteenth century.

This is really more of a problem for the humanities than for the natural and social sciences. For the latter there are numerous research institutes in every advanced country which, while certainly carrying on some research of a practical and directly usable kind, are not confined to it. Staff of the highest quality is attracted to such places by the opportunity they give for the pursuit of research interests with the best equipment and without the hindrance of teaching duties. It is not fanciful to imagine that all research in the natural and social sciences should be carried on in such establishments. Future researchers, furthermore, could be trained as apprentices in them, coming directly on from undergraduate courses. But that does not seem a plausible solution for the problem of supporting research in the humanities.

An old device that I alluded to when I mentioned the great nonacademic thinkers of seventeenth century England is patronage. That is insecure, as shown by the relations between Bertrand Russell and Dr. Albert C. Barnes, and increasingly thin on the ground in an epoch of confiscatory taxation. There is also the marketplace, which by way of his bestselling history of philosophy, supported Russell for the rest of his life, relying while he wrote it on money Dr. Barnes had to pay him for unjust dismissal. The trouble here is that the crucial things do not get supported. The great works of mathematical philosophy Russell wrote in the first decade of this century may not yet have covered the cost of their production.

What in fact happens is that research is subsidized, particularly in the humanities, out of the general income of the universities in which academics, conceived, unless they are administrators, as both teachers and researchers, are employed. It must, therefore, depend to some extent on the income derived from student fees. If the endowment income were not spent on sabbaticals, study leave, travel grants, research assistants, and other expensive instrumentalities of the non-teaching roles of academics, it could be used to reduce student fees in general or to supply more scholarships. In a way, then, the student helps to subsidize the research that is supposed, in my view questionably, to improve the quality of the teaching that he receives.

Before jumping to that conclusion, let me reconsider a proposal I dismissed as implausible a little while ago: that of research institutes in the humanities. Things going by that name exist and serve respectable purposes, such as the institute of historical research attached to the University of London. But the phrase is misleading. What are called research institutes in the humanities are not comparable in size or autonomy to research institutes in the natural and social sciences. In general, research in the humanities does not offer the same kind of return to cooperation as it does in the sciences, nor does it rely on physical equipment, apart from books and documents, to any marked extent.

A much more fundamental point, however, is that what is called research in the humanities is a very different thing from what is done under that name in the sciences. Of course original thinking has its place in the development of the humane disciplines, but the maintenance of the tradition of the discipline has an importance to which nothing corresponds in the sciences. A civilized physicist or economist will know something about the history of his discipline. But he does not need to be a civilized physicist or economist to be a good one. The humanities are to a great extent textual disciplines, in which a traditional set of major articulations of human experience is kept alive. It is more appropriate to call them fields of learning than of research. Dr. Johnson's engaging definition of scholarship as preserving the remains of ancient literature applies to them, if allowance is made for a certain archaism of phrase. This is true of philosophy considered in a historical manner, of the more familiar and less scientistic kinds of history and, obviously, of literature. It would be possible to study philosophy without ever meeting the names or reading the words of the major philosophers of the past, but it would be an absurd tour de force, since in any adequate presentation of the subject they would be present but hidden. The ideas, arguments, and points of view that the student of philosophy studies are all rooted in some text. I should argue that history ought to have a historiographical component, not just as in classical history for lack of other evidence than what is to be found in the pages of Thucydides and Herodotus, Livy and Tacitus, but because to understand an age one must find out what its historical consciousness of itself was. The raw, unreflective, practical documents are too raw to yield enlightenment on their own.

This kind of scholarly, textual apprehension of a tradition of thought and expression, at a fairly simple level, makes up the background of general knowledge, or, in an older idiom, of polite learning, that many feel has so nearly evaporated in our own age through the abandonment of widespread study of the Bible and classical literature and then of the literature of our own language, or other current languages, before the present century. An undergraduate course in the humanities does not ordinarily allow for sufficient specialized attention to the acquisition of scholarly competence of this kind to qualify a person for teaching it to other undergraduates. But it is something that is obviously needed by university teachers of the humanities in a way that a research potential, which in this area is both hard to define and hard to discern, is not. It is something that a graduate school, consciously devoted to the training of university teachers as its main task, should continue to perform. The curriculum for it, while more specialized than that of an elective undergraduate course, need not lay the kind of stress that is now usual on the dissertation.

Of course the study of the humanities is not exclusively textual in the way I have described, although I believe that most of it should be, certainly more than usually is now. To some extent the subject matter of the humanities is absorbed into other, more scientifically methodical disciplines. Beyond its elements logic is a part of mathematics, social history (for example, family studies) is a kind of retrospective sociology, some part of the study of literature is contained in linguistics. Of more interest and importance, however, is the kind of really substantial innovation to be found in the work of philosophers like Russell and Wittgenstein, historians like Namier, critics like Leavis. Of these four only Leavis was a full-time academic for most of his adult life and even then it was in a marginal and rather angrily detached way. The others had only fitful and more or less idiosyncratic university connections.

That suggests something that is independently altogether credible: true innovation in the humanities, as distinguished from the preservation of a tradition of scholarly understanding, is rare, unpredictable and not an object that can be institutionally planned for or cultivated. But our present conception of the academic profession, and so of the way in which new entrants ought to be prepared for it, rests on a different assumption, which is that the ideal academic is a creative virtuoso in his field. From that the requirement follows that in order to qualify, a candidate must, in his graduate work, make an original contribution to knowledge in his field. A further result is the rather large number of academics who do not really compensate for a certain barbarousness of specialization in the their fields by the capacity to make a real addition to them. We should shift the emphasis from pioneering to cultivation.

I am inclined to suspect, furthermore, that what is true of the humanities is at least partially applicable to the natural and social sciences. Direct involvement, in the manner of an apprentice, in research work in natural or social science is essential for those who are going to be researchers proper in those fields. But a fairly advanced understanding of science is needed by many whose careers will not consist in directly enlarging its scope. The management of science-based industries and such jobs as journalism, banking, and public administration come to mind in this connection. If the work of conveying understanding of the sciences appropriate to these purposes is carried on under the same institutional umbrella as the fostering of original research in them, the two activities should be recognized to be as different as they are.

Reality is perhaps closer to what I have said ought to be the case than might at first appear. Plenty of respected academics, after a ritual obeisance to the virtuoso principle with their Ph.D.'s, publish nothing much more afterward. But the principle does take its toll, particularly on candidates for entrance to the academic profession. The painfully long interval between B.A. and Ph.D. in most cases provides a pool of inexpensive teaching labor for universities at the cost of a good deal of distress to those who supply it. For the graduate student in the humanities who is aiming at an academic career, or in the sciences, aiming either at an academic career or at a science-related one, the style of dissertation ordinarily exacted, which is what drags out the length of the course, is really irrelevant.

Invited to talk about the philosophy of graduate education I have allowed myself the indulgence of unpracticality. I have argued that the main role of the academic graduate school is and ought to be the training of university teachers, and that there is no compelling reason why the nonacademic professional school should be associated with it in the university. I have argued that it is indeed the university teacher, and not the advancer of knowledge through research, with whom the academic graduate school should concern itself. Research proper could well be carried on, as it increasingly is, in separate institutes, which would train their new entrants as apprentices. The aim of the academic graduate school should not be the production of virtuosos, since all that is achieved if that goal is pursued is for the most part anxious and hollow imitations of the rare and gifted ideal. What can be trained is the person equipped with a lively understanding of the current state of discussion in an intellectual domain and where, as particularly in the humanities, it is appropriate, of the way in which it arrived at the position it now occupies. Starting from a rather narrowly vocational conception of the immediate aims of the academic graduate school, I hope I have arrived at a liberal conclusion about the manner in which it should pursue it.

Comments by Annette Baier

Should we, as Quinton recommends, not merely recognize that teaching and research are distinct capacities, so that they need not be expected to be combined in one person, but also give up the expectation that one university department or one graduate program will have both sorts of persons among its faculty? Should we separate the scholars from the teachers and the teachers of teachers? In my comment on Vlastos' paper I agreed that the two skills are distinct, and I argued that they can diverge as much when the teaching skill in question is teaching graduates as when it is teaching undergraduates. But the thought of the segregation of the few creative thinkers in separate humanities institutes is a very depressing one. However much the creative thinkers might welcome it, those who teach must resist it. If necessary they must drag their creative excolleagues back to the cave and insist that they keep company with their less creative fellows, whose teaching will otherwise become an increasingly dreary and pointless activity. Quinton says "research proper could well be carried on in research institutes which would train their new entrants as apprentices. The aim of the academic graduate school should not be the production of virtuosos, since all that is achieved if that goal is pursued is for the most part anxious and hollow imitations of the rare and gifted ideal." I agree with the last sentence, but I am very concerned about the way the nonvirtuosos are to be trained, how and by whom they are to acquire "a lively understanding of the current state of discussion in an intellectual domain" if neither they nor their teachers are to be in direct communication with those rare gifted ones who are to be nurtured in the research institutes.

Whether or not the creative thinker gains from the discipline of teaching, the teacher gains from discussion with the creative thinker. A lively understanding of one's own field and its current borders and boundaries is best and most enjoyably obtained by talking and working with those who are extending those boundaries, redrawing those borders, or reinterpreting the great texts. I think the ideal conditions for the flourishing of excellence in teaching are ones in which the teacher has close contact with creative thinkers but is under no pressure to publish anxious and hollow imitations of their creative contributions.

Quinton says that it is mere bluff to claim that teaching without research is inevitably defective. That may be true at the individual level, although even there I doubt whether excellence in teaching will often be found unless there is at least the occasional attempt at research. Certainly good graduate teaching is unlikely from someone who has no research ambitions. But ambition without significant attainment may be sufficient, and we should perhaps ask with Vlastos what original work a person has written but refrained from publishing in promotion and tenure decisions. At the departmental level, however, I think teaching without research is defective, certainly in a graduate program. The good teachers need the company of the researchers, and the researchers may sometimes benefit from the comments of their less creative colleagues. Even if they do not, their commitment to the preservation and transmission, as well as the enrichment and perhaps revision of a tradition of thought should be enough to motivate them not to segregate themselves from those who teach in their field. An occasional sabbatical in a research institute is a good thing, but permanent tenure in one is the worst form of ivory-tower isolation, and ought to be prevented. For the sake of the teachers and the students in a graduate school, and for the sake of the undergraduates taught by both, we must keep the scholars and original thinkers among us.

There is no reason why, in deciding tenure and promotion, we should not give consideration to more than teaching and published research. Not only should we look at those suppressed manuscripts Vlastos spoke of, but we could look also at written comment on the work of others, which the commenter at no point intended for publication. We might encourage people to emulate that prolific letter writer Leibniz, whose advice on publication I invoked in my reply to Vlastos. Letters make thoughts public enough to further discussion, without clogging the channels of fully public communication. The dangers of sycophancy would be no greater than they are at present, when publishing a comment or an attack upon an established thinker is a standard way to try to get noticed. Tenure committees could consider and reward that indirect support for creative research given by those whose semiprivate comment and discussion help more creative colleagues. If we are to discourage the vanity of publication Leibniz deplored we must find ways to reward modesty. But even this sort of modest indirect contribution to research cannot easily be made if the creative few are closed off in special humanities institutes. I think we should keep something like the present system of mixing research with teaching, giving proper weight to each.

Passmore suggested that the proper time for reflection on the relation of one's narrow field of interest to a wider context is during graduate study. If that is so, then such reflection will need both the assistance of those graduate teachers who can give the brilliant undergraduate courses which both Vlastos and Quinton rightly value, and also of those graduate teachers whose own original work advances the internal dialectic in the graduate student's special area. If writing only for writing's sake is vanity, teaching only for teaching's sake is equally vain—in the humanities we need writing worth preserving, teaching, and reinterpreting, and we need teaching from those close enough to the writing to transmit the excitement of a living tradition.

Reply to Baier

I do not know if it is decent for me to refer back to things said by Passmore and Vlastos. At first sight, I suppose, what I have said is more extreme than anything they have said. But I would suggest that it is not wholly at odds with what they have said. Passmore claimed that the proper excellence of graduate study is independent work by the graduate student. He opposed that to the docile, obedient, passive participation in authoritatively instructional courses which was, I think, in his view the main depressing feature of graduate study. Now the word research is available here to apply to the sort of independent work he had in mind. Yet I do not feel that this adds up to a direct, head-on clash between us. No doubt there is a disagreement of emphasis here, but the research he is defending is not necessarily the kind of thing I have been opposing. The kind of thing I am opposing was also, I think, pretty much what Vlastos was opposing. There is quite a lot of overlap between what he and I say. But it seems to me that there were two aims struggling within him, with one of which I could wholly associate myself, while I was not so sure about the other. He held that a prime responsibility of the teacher is to his undergraduate pupils and an important way in which that responsibility is discharged is through preparing his graduate students to be good teachers of undergraduates. What he was emphasizing in particular was an aspect of what I thought appropriate to the preparation of teachers of undergraduates: namely, supplying them with a certain generality of culture to enable them to relate comparatively narrow topics to a wide set of issues, to put them in their proper places in the total geography of a culture. Now that is not something that is very successfully pursued through close involvement with research. So far we are in agreement.

But there is another thing which I am rather more doubtful about. That is the "band of brothers" picture that Vlastos has painted of the researcher, the highly skilled advancer of knowledge, surrounded by gifted young graduate students with whom he discusses the problems he is engaged with in a state of perfect intellectual equality. They watch what he is doing; they make suggestions; he criticizes those suggestions and rejects them; or he takes them up and develops them. Now there is no question that there is a place for that kind of thing. But it does seem to me that it is inevitably going to be something exceptional. Let me finish with a last remark that is related to these matters. Some very polite gestures have been made to the fact that I have come here from dear old Oxford. One of them was Passmore's praise of the Oxford tutorial system for its encouragement of independent work. I must confess that that system has always seemed to me slightly like the life of an officer in the Italian army in the Western Desert around 1940. An enormous amount of sword brandishing goes on, but what in fact happens is that the tutor asks a question, the pupil looks back at him in a kind of frozen condition, and if he goes on long enough, the tutor, in order to avoid embarrassment, then answers the question himself. It is like the officers trying to stimulate the discouraged troops to make a fight of it. Now that is not to say that the genuinely cooperative ideal is never realized. But, to make a parochial point, I think that in Oxford we are far too extravagant with individual tuition. It is a valuable substance that should be a bit more thinly spread than it is. What I am suggesting is that quite often it turns into something pretty instructional or doctrine-conveying and is not at all that free, open, equal flow between teacher and student that it is supposed to be. It is much more like an actual Socratic dialogue as recorded by Plato than the Socratic dialogue of legend. Naturally every activity of this kind has its best, its most splendid and rewarding moments. We all know that can happen with teaching graduates, occasions where something really rather exciting takes place. You are excited in what he is finding; it fits in with some preoccupation of your own. In just the same way there can be an exciting exchange at the undergraduate level. But that is not the sort of thing one can base planning on. One has to plan for the ordinary and not for the exceptional.

I thought from something Baier said earlier that I was going to meet a fiercer assault. As it turned out, the one point she mainly took issue with was something I was prepared to admit. In one perhaps rather congested passage of my remarks I said something about two versions of a principle, to only one of which I was hostile. That was the individual version which holds that the ideal academic is both a teacher and a scholar. The other is that the ideal academic institution is one in which both teachers and researchers are to be found. And I said of the latter, collective principle that I thought it an entirely reasonable one. In so far as I was prepared to envisage its abandonment, I was carrying out an intellectual experiment to heighten what I take to be the correct view that there really is not all that close a connection between the two functions. I quite agree that there is no need to disturb existing arrangements where both kinds of persons happen to be together. The reason I gave for that is that they create a valuable critical and constructive environment for each other and I think that is entirely acceptable.

Now looming behind our whole discussion here is the problem that arises from demographic decline, later retirement, the general expense and reduced popularity of universities. There are enough academics already in jobs from which they cannot reasonably be extruded to provide for the teaching of everybody for the foreseeable future. That is, of course, a very discouraging state of affairs for those who are currently in graduate schools. The consequential question which we ought to consider, surely, is whether we ought not to cut down graduate schools a great deal, whether they are not the relics of a departed period of extreme prosperity, like the vast hotels of Florida put up in the 1920s. In the 1950s and 1960s, under the influence of post-Sputnik emotions, great sums of public money were poured into the academic system. Perhaps the community did not get all that marvellous a return on its investment, in particular, from the enormous expansion of graduate schools. What we are considering today is not wholly unpractical. Practical decisions turn on conclusions as to just how important graduate schools are. My position is that they are primarily places where the teachers of undergraduates are taught and that this should determine both their nature and their size.

Questions and Answers

Comment from floor (Vlastos): Quinton said, and I think also Baier, when it comes to recruitment, to deciding who deserves to be on the faculty of a graduate school, that we have to judge them in terms of their contribution to the subject. That's what we all do anyhow, unless we're hypocritical—get the best contributor to the subject, taking a chance on other things; you want the person who advances knowledge. Now the connection with published research, is that that's where you find who is the best contributor to the subject. I don't yield on making that first. The problem which then arises for a university like this one, Princeton, Harvard, Berkeley, etc., which want to be both great graduate schools and good undergraduate institutions, is a real one. I have really no answer as to how to combine the two. But I think that desideratum must be kept first; it is first, the good graduate schools are doing that. Now, with respect to the last remark Quinton made as to whether we've spent too much money on this as we have on hotels in some parts of Florida, I don't agree with that. I do think, however, and this is extremely difficult to implement, that the uniform expansion of graduate education scattered all over the country is something that really needs to be looked at. I know for example in philosophy, three or four years ago Harvard cut back its admissions, very drastically, something like less than half of what it used to be. Now, has the same been true in Nebraska and Tennessee and Louisiana, and so on, or has there been a pressure of self-protection for the departments in many of these places to keep, and of those that haven't had the Ph.D. program to try to introduce it, on the chance that by introducing it they will benefit their own department to some degree? If we were in the position of dictators dictating what ought to happen in the future, I believe that the rational plan would be to introduce a certain amount of restriction in this country, where the proliferation of graduate programs has been so great, trying to restrict them to a smaller number than we have now. That certainly is the problem of the graduate student who is disadvantaged because it happens that the offer of an assistantship or something like that makes him a permanent fixture in a graduate school where he is not getting the best kind of teaching he should be getting.

Q1 (Sussman): Before the recess of a philosopher, I think it would be a shame if we addressed simply the quantitative issues that you have raised in your last remark about the diminishing numbers of graduate students alone. I would like to address a question that Mandelbaum raised and it's a more qualitative subject; it relates to something he hit glancingly. What is the role in the minds of the philosophers of terminal master's degree programs? For example, in graduate schools, should those be encouraged in institutions like ours, or should there be a segregation of those perhaps less desirable types of programs in respect to the energy they may draw from the typical Ph.D. program, or not? That's a set of issues that afflicts graduate schools particularly now as we witness the decline you called attention to in the Harvards and elsewhere. I think the only alternative is not diminished size in terms of the number of Ph.D. students; one is this qualitative shift to which I've referred.

A: What about courses for graduate schools other than the standard Ph.D. program, programs of less magnitude, length, difficulty?

Should we favor them? Mandelbaum was very worried about the extent the standard doctoral program of a graduate school might be diluted by having a lot of people do M.A. degrees of a less demanding and exigent kind. He thought that would somehow destroy the intrinsic and traditional values of the doctoral program. At the same time he was much concerned with the problem of placing the products of the graduate school, and that is something for which the traditionally conceived graduate school is not very well adjusted in the present climate. So there is a bit of tension there. I do not have much direct experience of this problem, but I can say something about the teaching of philosophy. In Oxford, after the war, the genial, avuncular dictator of Oxford philosophy, the late Gilbert Ryle, introduced a degree with the desperately humble name of the B.Phil., Bachelor of Philosophy. It is a two-year graduate degree and people typically do complete it in two years, unless they start it having done little philosophy as undergraduates or have nervous breakdowns and other such extraneous delayers. But the only academic cause of delay is sheer ignorance, so it is quite commonly completed in two years. There is a course element and a short dissertation of, at the most 30,000 words. Ryle's idea was that this should be regarded as a perfectly adequate qualification for a university teacher, whereas the standard, Teutonic doctoral dissertation, heavy with footnotes and bibliography, was really beside the point. Ryle was a man of fairly definite opinions and, as far as he was concerned, the old D.Phil. was worse than useless, a sack of coal on the back of the applicant, having no conceivable relation to his employability as a teacher of philosophy. We do not have to share that very extreme view of the traditional doctorate to favor his preferred alternative. In fact, the standard of the B.Phil., which has been extended to many other subjects, has been kept very high, but then it is acceptable in England as a qualification for university teaching. Now when you talk about these other uses for master's programs, I am not quite sure what kind of output they are going to have. What are the people trained in them going to do? Are they going to be high school teachers, for example, heads of departments of math or history or social studies in high school?

Sussman: In that connection we are told frequently that the educated public, we have after all produced an unprecedented number of people with baccalaureate degrees and education begets more education, will be asking for more graduate work. If that is the case, and it seems to be the case in some respects, then these people may not wish to have this enrichment in graduate schools in terms of more degrees perhaps, or in research degrees, but may wish learning for learning's sake. That is one set of persons to whom this question has been addressed. Another is the student who wishes to get some enrichment before going to a professional school. There are still others, so I'm speaking about a diversity of types of persons and not suggesting that any one school should take on all responsibilities, but asking whether it is seemly for a school like ours to consider the possibilities.

Comment on Sussman's comment (Passmore): It seems to me that there are certain areas in which some type of master's degree is completely desirable. One master's degree we had was in formal logic; a person could do a great massive amount of advanced logic, more than a doctoral candidate would want to do. Again, there are a great many areas where a person wants to do a slightly applied version of the subjects he has already studied. He may, for example, study sociology but want to do some special work on urban planning or something of that sort, and again the one-year course seems to me absolutely admirable for this purpose. It takes the pressure off, I think, in the American situation in which you don't have a specialized honors degree during the undergraduate course. An extra year can in fact fulfill a function rather like an honors degree in the English or Australian system, with a person specializing in one subject and nothing else for the year and bringing himself up to something like the honors degree level.

The Antinomies of Higher Education

Sterling M. McMurrin

Every effort to construct a philosophy of education that can prescribe for American educational policy confronts contradictions, paradoxes, and dilemmas which produce confusion in both theory and practice. I will comment on four difficulties which I will loosely refer to as antinomies. Although they are in logical opposition, they are not in every instance contradictories and are not antinomies in the classical sense. I will call them practical antinomies because they involve oppositions in actual practice rather than in theory. These practical antinomies are basic to the persistent task of defining the purposes of education for our culture and society:

1. The practical antinomy of the Absolute and the Relative;
2. The practical antinomy of the Useless and the Useful;
3. The practical antinomy of the Liberal and the Technical; and
4. The practical antinomy of Elitism and Egalitarianism.

The discussion of the purposes of education must first raise the question of where those purposes are grounded, of what are the proper determinants of educational theory, policy, and practice, and of where we must look for the guiding principles on which ultimately to base our educational decisions. Because of its essentially normative character, education cannot be treated as a science and therefore there can be no scientific statement of the purposes and goals to be pursued by the schools and universities. Education is not a science; it is an art, a fine and practical art. The sciences can provide much of its substance, and can contribute much to its design and methods, as they do for any technology, but the determination of the meanings, purposes, and worth of education is a philosophical enterprise. It is a much neglected and often misguided normative task that properly builds wherever possible on the sciences of human behavior and the human condition. But its purposes issue from the elemental human drives and interests and in its better forms it is concerned with the things that matter most in our experience.

I believe that much confusion has been produced in educational thought by the efforts of those who have attempted to deduce educational theories from premises established in metaphysics, the theory of knowledge, or even value theory. While I doubt that anyone has successfully constructed an effective philosophy of education as a logical entailment of a metaphysical system, the attempt to do so persists. To search for the roots of educational theory in speculative philosophy seems to invert the proper order of things in a vain attempt to find absolutes that will simplify educational thought and deliver it from the transient facts of personal and social existence. But it is precisely these facts that provide the occasion and set the conditions for education which should define both its purposes and substance.

The determination of the meaning and purposes of education must be grounded in a phenomenology of the culture, where nothing of central importance in the life of the individual and society escapes description and analysis, but where whatever is essential and crucial to the distinctive character and quality of the culture is clearly identified and appropriated. The substance of the educational enterprise is composed of the facts of life.

This means that education is properly conceived as a function of the culture, that its character depends upon the nature of the culture and that radical variations in the culture mean consequent variations in education. This is the case whether we consider education in its totality, involving the whole experience of the individual, or partial education concerned with more specific ends. To have practical worth, an educational philosophy must be grounded in the culture of which it is a vital element. It is not an implicate of some philosophical system or systems, a derivative of premises established ultimately by speculative thought and guaranteed by logic.

The obvious objection here, of course, is that anchoring educational philosophy in social and cultural facts subjects education to a thoroughgoing relativism, even a subcultural relativism, whereas the traditional ideal of education has commonly been some kind of universalism or at least a high degree of generality that can transcend large cultural differences, overcome particularity and parochialism, and bring us into the promised land of value absolutes.

To this objection there are two replies: first, that cultural relativism is not in itself something to be avoided or overcome; indeed in many ways it is a very good thing, something to be preserved and even cultivated, for there can be a kind of intrinsic value in difference. But we are so committed to absolutism in education that we tend to make absolutes even of our relative values. Social and cultural relativism in the philosophy of education can translate into relevance in educational policy and practice. The education that is most irrelevant to the life of the individual and society is education that is fashioned to fit absolutes or pseudoabsolutes that are defined by abstract thought, often in indifference to the facts of life.

Second, to describe education as an ingredient of the culture, as a function of the culture which changes appropriately with changes in the culture, does not at all mean that educational policies and practices have no vitality of their own and are entirely at the mercy of other cultural determinants. Quite the contrary. University education should be the cutting edge of the culture, the base of its creative initiative and energy. Education is not something that should be dragged along by other social and cultural forces that have less sensitive awareness and are less capable of providing the requisites for intelligent judgment. Whatever degree of critical reasonableness has been reached in a culture is in a sense invested in its educational processes, where the analytic and rational capabilities of a society are best nurtured and expressed and where they most effectively contribute to social and cultural advancement.

In saying these things, of course, I exhibit the fact that my own conception of education is a cultural function, that it is a product of the primacy of reason and cognition which is a distinctive bias of our intellectually and scientifically oriented culture. But to suppose that we should construct a philosophy of education that transcends cultural differences is in itself a kind of intellectual arrogance. Far from being an ideal guide for educational policy, such a philosophy would detach educational practice from the firm ground of experience and expose it to the errors and evils which absolutisms quite commonly generate.

To say that education is a function of the culture is not to say that it is necessarily culture-bound in some parochial or chauvinistic sense. For an ecumenical or cosmopolitan perspective can be an indigenous ingredient of a culture; a search for absolutes can be deeply ingrained in its intellectual life, as it is in ours, and a sense of community with mankind can be built firmly into its moral structure, as it is at least in our idealism and our growing universalism. Indeed, there is no limit on the extent to which the development of a culture may produce ideas and ideals that reach beyond the boundaries which commonly constrain the thought and attitude of a people within narrow confines and restraints. But here the philosophy of education, however much it may reach for absolutes, is grounded in the life of the society and the soil of the culture and does not lose itself in a quest for roots in metaphysical ideas that are detached from the material facts, interests, and values that describe and characterize the people who are involved in the educational process. The thirst for absolutes, which is a deeply ingrained property of our intellectual and moral culture, is more than anything else a desire for full commitment to whatever has proved its practical worth, not to whatever makes a powerful logical claim and appeal.

That we have absolutes in education is obvious, as in our commitment to intellectual honesty. This is a high virtue which underwrites the integrity of our entire educational enterprise. But it is the cornerstone of our intellectual morality not because it is a prominent element in a metaphysical system or even in the structure of a theory of value, but rather because in the long history of morality it has emerged, quite probably for pragmatic causes, as a *sine qua non* of an acceptable intellectual life, a value that is constantly celebrated, protected, and nourished by the university, but which is never secure from the possibility of violation even by those who profess to prize it most.

The culture is not composed simply of social, economic, political, or artistic facts, though these are prominent in our consciousness and experience. It is equally the forms of thought and art and the methods of knowledge and argument, the interests and satisfactions of individuals and groups, their conceptions of value, both immediate and ultimate, the reliance upon sensory data, reason, or intuition, the quest for universals, respect for particulars, the commitment to truth, and the demand for evidence. Indeed, there is nothing of importance in our experience, thought, or aspiration that is not an ingredient of the culture, that is not entitled to make its claim somewhere at some time on education.

But formal education in the schools, colleges, and universities is necessarily a specialized enterprise. It cannot be concerned with the total task of education and must therefore commit its energies to matters that are inappropriate to the capabilities and disposition of other social agencies and that both merit and demand expert and specialized treatment because of their fundamental and central importance. Accordingly, in our culture the primary task of formal education, beyond the elementary charge of providing the skills of literacy, is the cultivation of reason and the pursuit of knowledge. Whatever other obligations or prerogatives are appropriate to a school or university follow from its central purpose of knowledge and rationality. Nowhere else in our society are these prized, protected, and nourished as they are in the processes of formal education.

Our commitment to reason and reasonableness and our demand

for knowledge were not originally the product of the universities; the universities were produced by them. It is in this sense that education is a function of the culture. This is true even though the universities now are the chief source and nurture of our intellectual virtues and values. Today the universities are basic elements of the culture itself and are powerful social institutions, and for anything to be fully consonant with the main constituents of our culture in its maturity, considering especially its intellectualistic character and its intense scientific disposition and technological structure, it must be compatible with the meaning of a university.

To say that education is a function of the culture, therefore, is not to deny that it is an immensely important force native to the culture. It is to say, rather, that it embodies the burden, conscience, and creative energy of the intellectual life of the people. It is determined by the character of the culture and the social institutions and conditions, but it is at the same time a powerful determinant of that character.

Now my point in all of this is not to argue against the pursuit of a high idealism in education or to suggest that we should not aspire beyond our actual reach. Rather, I have wanted simply to provide a theoretical justification for maintaining a close relevance of the university to the facts of individual, social, and cultural life, to ensure that it has whatever measure of tractability is necessary to enable it to respond effectively to the rightful claims which may be made upon it, while yet preserving for it that idealism that has issued from the cultural process and is, indeed, a quality of its own life, the idealism of reason and knowledge and their cognate values.

Much has been said and written in recent years relating to the question of the utility of a college or university education, especially of its practical worth as a preparation for a career. This has become a problem of serious proportions for colleges and universities which are faced with the possibility of a decline in educational resources, and therefore of quality, as student patronage declines in favor of increased enrollment in technical schools and colleges whose goals and curricula are now so commonly regarded as having more practical relevance and value than those of a liberal arts college or university. I would not for a moment disparage the worth to individuals and society of the recent increase in financial support for technical colleges, the marked improvement in the character of their curricula and the quality of their instruction, or especially the improved esteem which they now command in the opinion of the public. Notwithstanding that they commonly offer at best only a partial and deficient education, they are an immensely important element of our instructional establishment whether viewed from the standpoint of the student or the community. They clearly have very real economic value and economic values are of fundamental importance.

But I do want to reply to those who now so often support technical instruction by disparaging the practical worth of the authentic liberal education that is available in at least our better liberal arts colleges and universities and the advanced specialized education that is provided by our graduate and professional schools. By referring to practical worth I do not mean that there is not great intrinsic value in much that is sometimes described as useless in education, that the evaluation of a person's education should be simply in terms of its utility. It should be a necessary postulate of any serious discussion on education that both the arts and the sciences have an imponderable intrinsic worth that is not subject to any measurement but is quintessential to not only a genuinely humane quality of life for the individual, but as well for the effective criticism and strengthening of the social institutions and the sustenance and vitalization of the culture. Those who attack the university for its singular pursuit of knowledge and reason make themselves enemies of the most civilizing force that has yet been created, and those within the university who betray that purpose violate their professional duty and moral trust.

But to treat the immeasurable but vitally requisite and indispensable value of liberal education as if it were not a practical value is to sanction a dichotomy in the structure of value that not only distorts the very meaning of valuation but brings confusion into our thought and conduct, in this instance into our educational policy and practice. The distinction between the useful and useless in education has been encouraged by those elements of our society who are such complete captives of the sensate and material that they reduce human beings to a low denominator, treating them essentially as economic animals, simply as producers and consumers, perhaps also as voters. It is this apparently growing element in our society, who measure the worth of education primarily in terms of productive skills mastered and prospective dollars earned, who are becoming the most vocal critics of university education and whose irresponsible criticism should be vigorously opposed. But, strangely, the idea that a liberal education is useless is also all too commonly and sometimes seriously encouraged even within the university by those who find a special satisfaction in disparaging the material elements of our civilization and attempting to cultivate the virtues of the mind and spirit as if they could be perfected in some kind of rarified intellectual atmosphere that has no concern for the practical affairs of the world.

I will pass over the simple and obvious fact that virtually all preparation for the advanced professions is obtained through universities, most of whose students are enrolled in professional schools working toward degrees which will equip them for the professions, and will not dwell on the fact that university departments other than those in professional schools all prepare students for vocational activity. Here we need only ask where we get our physicists, chemists, historians, anthropologists, writers, and the host of others whose education is commonly referred to as academic rather than professional. Academic it may well be, but it is vocational—just as vocational as law, medicine, engineering, teaching, social work, or business. And it is education that makes the world go 'round just as much as, and indeed far more than, any vocational training that can be obtained outside a university. One wonders where the critics are looking who comment so vigorously on the failures of the universities to prepare their students for life's work. Which failures belong to the universities, and which to the employers who fail to recognize the real practical worth of an applicant's college or university education?

Of course the critics of the university fix their attention upon the liberal learning that must occupy so much of a university student's time and attention as contrasted with the average investment in liberal pursuits of a student in a typical technical school. But leave aside for the moment other possible values of a liberal education and consider only its vocational worth. It seems strange, indeed, that anyone should suppose that a liberal education that is devoted to the cultivation of the intellectual life, giving attention to the ways of knowing, the structure of science, some knowledge of the structure of contemporary society and how our society came to be where it is, with an appreciation of literature and art and the great philosophical discussions, in its better forms an education which attempts to induct a person into the culture of which he is a part—it is strange that this would not be seen as an essential and necessary preparation for any life's work that calls for judgment, intelligent decision, a capacity for critical thought, an understanding of human relationships, and some grasp of what the world is like. Why such an education should not be seen as genuinely useful, not simply as an enrichment of the quality of personality and life, but as a factor in the pursuit of one's vocation, is one of the mysteries of our society's perverse temperament.

Perhaps only a fraction of those who have come out strongly for career education over the last few years have been indifferent to the intrinsic values of a liberal education or opposed to the nation's large investment in liberal learning, and no doubt only a fraction have been oblivious to the overwhelming importance of the liberal arts college and university in preparing persons for successful careers. But there can be little doubt that the campaign for career education, whatever its values, has caused a large segment of our people to doubt the value of a liberal education, or, indeed, of a university education of any kind. I personally believe that we are involved here, in the antinomy of the useless and the useful, of the liberal and the technological, in an entirely artificial and unjustified distinction that has done serious violence to our culture in general and in particular to our educational policies and practices.

At best the distinction between the liberal and the practical is always blurred; no clear differentiating line can be drawn. Education is all of one piece; it is a continuous spectrum, granted that it moves from the theoretic to the actual, from abstract intellection to physical manipulation. The meaning of education is too closely tied to the generative powers of the intellect, the foundations of human personality, and the forces that ultimately move society, to entitle us to endorse this destructive distinction. All education, if it is authentic education that incites the mind, excites the spirit, and cultivates the moral character, is useful; all education is in fact both the preparation for and the pursuit of vocation, vocation in the fullest sense that embraces both economic productivity and the intellectual, artistic, moral, and spiritual life. Until we bring the generality of our people to an understanding and appreciation of this basic unity that should prevail in the analysis and assessment of education, we can expect to find the patrons of our colleges and universities increasingly confused about their value. We cannot afford to permit those who regard the worth of education simply in terms of the immediate economic value of training to continue their inroads upon the integrity of the educational enterprise any more than we can tolerate the all too common pretensions to superiority of those academics who refuse to acknowledge the concrete worth of technological training to large masses of our people as well as its necessity for the processes of our economy. This internal warfare that continues not only in educational theory and policy but even among educators themselves exacerbates the antagonism of the public toward colleges and universities.

The nature and value of liberal education in its relation to other facets of education have been labored endlessly, sometimes brilliantly and with real excitement, as in the Hutchins-Hook hassle, yet all too often with a boring pedantry that discourages interest in educational thought and discussion. I am not disposed to contribute further to that boredom, but I must risk a few comments on the matter of the relation of liberal education to advanced graduate work, for this is one of the large problems which confront us when we raise questions on the future of the doctorate.

It is a simple problem. How are we to preserve and enhance the quality and character of the doctorate as a specialized degree while at the same time providing for the liberal education of those who receive that degree. We need more, not less liberal education, not only for those who may pursue the liberal arts as their vocation or avocation, but for everyone who is capable of profiting from it in their careers, in their pursuit of personal ends, and in their preparation for intelligent participation in the life of society. Certainly those who achieve the advanced levels of graduate degrees are as much in need as the student in the vocational school whose education is commonly distorted and sometimes even intentionally prejudiced against liberal learning. Too often our Ph.D. candidates and our candidates for the professional doctorates are so completely specialized in their education that only in the narrowest sense can they be described as educated, an immeasurable loss to themselves and to society. This is a loss that our increasingly technological society can ill afford, the failure to cultivate a crucially important segment of our best intellectual talent in those directions that we all recognize as the meaning of a liberal education, the kind of education upon which the humane character of our society ultimately depends.

For the past quarter century we have indulged generously in a rhetoric of caveat, a dual warning against the approach of the apocalyptic judgment that our own technology has made possible as an imminent and permanent threat to survival, and a menacing deterioration of the character and quality of our culture as our society moves almost inevitably toward a technological order where the processes of mechanization, automation, cybernation, and bureaucratization threaten to vanquish the countervailing intellectual, moral, and spiritual forces which must sustain and strengthen the personal quality of life. Perhaps at times we have engaged excessively in this self-flagellation; it is difficult to achieve and maintain a perspective on these matters that does not distort the facts, produce a kind of self-deception, or even unconsciously conform our perceptions and thought to an unarticulated conception of history as an impending doom. Having abandoned the doctrine of progress under the weight of the massive human failures of this century, those of us who have refused to take refuge in an irrational faith have been confronted continuously by intimations of an almost-fated total disaster.

Whether and when the destruction will come upon us is largely a matter of statesmanship. Whether we are engaged in a final denouement of our culture is principally a question of our education, for it is especially in our educational processes, processes in large part affected by graduate education, that our interests are generated, our values formed, and our ideals fashioned and secured.

Here I can only say that it is what we usually mean by liberal education that is decisive, and that is why the decline in the liberality of education has such a portentous meaning for our culture and our civilization. By liberal education I do not mean general education as this term is sometimes employed in our curricular arrangements. To suggest that generality in a student's curriculum in some way ensures liberality in his education has been a source of much confusion and frustration. I frankly wish that the term generalist had never been invented. Generality in learning has its virtues and its satisfactions, but too often in our society it is a delusion that becomes on the one hand an impediment to true intellectual achievement and on the other a pseudosophisticated disguise for authentic education. With the demand for highly specialized competence increasing almost as rapidly as the fields of specialized knowledge are expanding, it is futile for us to suppose that we can in some way provide in a truly general education a depth adequate to convert it into a genuinely liberal education. I mean, rather, by liberal, that which liberates a person, that frees his mind from ignorance, superstition, bigotry, irrationality, and the frustrations of distorted perspectives and limited vision. If liberal education was once conceived as the education that is appropriate for a free person, it should now be defined as the education that cultivates the authentic freedom of the person.

How this is to be done, through what instrumentalities and by what instructional substance and process, is a complex problem for which there may be no solution. Certainly there is no single or comprehensive answer to this question. The substantive meaning of liberality in education is both ambiguous and diverse and the design for liberal education must be highly flexible, diversified, individualized, and relevant to the current structure of the culture and the basic problems of society. A course of study appropriate for one may not be appropriate for another. A curriculum that was effective prior to Hiroshima or Sputnik may not be effective today. No hard and fast prescriptions can be imposed on the program of liberal education.

Only its defining meanings can be described with any kind of conclusiveness, meanings which will roughly set its boundaries and, however ambiguously, express and explicate its purposes, and even those meanings have no finality. They are found not so much in knowledge, scholarship, and erudition as in the condition of the mind and the spirit, the recognition of and commitment to qualities and virtues of the mind that are symbolized by the passion for reliable knowledge, intellectual honesty, the love of truth, and their cognate values, and the cultivation of the spirit of intellectual adventure, artistic appreciation and creativity, and a general enthusiasm for life. However central and basic reason and knowledge are to a university education, cognitive values do not exhaust the objectives that are proper to that education, for these include both the cultivation of the affective life of the individual and society and the discipline of the will, the nourishment of the sense of moral responsibility and the development of an effective capacity for decision and action.

Now I mention these matters here because they are relevant to the purposes and substance of advanced graduate education. The Ph.D. attracts a not unimportant segment of the most highly qualified persons intellectually in the nation. Not all of these will prove to be leaders in the society or molders of the culture. But all are persons of uncommon abilities and together they should constitute a potential for powerful influence and leadership of the highest order. Of the highest order, that is, if they have the advantage of genuine liberal education as well as education for the doctorate. Fortunately, many of them have this advantage; unfortunately, both for them and society, many of them at this point are quite disadvantaged—they are culturally illiterate.

It is my contention that any doctorate, whether academic or professional, should be in itself a guarantee and symbol of a liberally educated person. This end is clearly difficult to achieve, but unless we move firmly in that direction we may fail to do something that should have been done and could have been done to contribute importantly to the forces necessary to stay an impending decline of our culture. Too many of our best and most highly trained minds, which could be sources of competent criticism and creativity for the improvement of the quality of life generally, are in effect incompetent, because of their educational deficiencies, to satisfy the demand for the measure of leadership which we are justified in expecting from them—a justification that follows from their capabilities, the investment that has been made in their education, and the positions of prominence and potential influence which they occupy in their professions.

I am not suggesting that time and energy be stolen from the doctoral programs for investment in liberal education. Far from it. The current demands in many fields for an increased commitment of the student's time to highly specialized work makes this quite unthinkable and certainly impossible. What I am proposing is that at this point graduate and professional schools be more exacting in their admissions and retention policies, ensuring that every student admitted to study for the doctorate or its equivalent give adequate evidence of having achieved the ends for which a genuinely high quality liberal education is designed. This can be done only by a careful assessment of the student's capabilities and experience, both academic and nonacademic, and acquaintance with the attitudes, temperament, dispositions, and values that have gone into the making of the student's intellectual character.

The liberal education that is our concern is not something that can be wrapped up and completed through the satisfaction of designated course and credit requirements. We can no longer treat liberal education as literary education or something of that sort. The sciences are as important to liberal education as are the humanities, and such disciplines as engineering and business are now not to be bypassed in the name of liberality. A liberal education is in a sense a state of mind that will carry the student through a lifetime of enriching intellectual experience. Achieving genuine liberality is an endless process.

I cannot consider the value of liberal education apart from a deep-seated fear that our society and culture, whatever their successes and triumphs, are moving slowly but steadily toward a deadening mediocrity. It is one of the virtues of our social order that we have been progressively committed to equality, first as an abstract moral ideal, but now, although falteringly, in actual practice. But we have not been able either in theory or practice to reconcile equality with difference, and this has meant that the pursuit of equality is moving us progressively toward the devitalizing mediocrity that must inevitably accompany the failure to prize genuine excellence. We have been too much attracted to the general and common, but excellence is an uncommon commodity and now too often it embarrasses rather than inspires us.

In our society it is now a delicate matter to raise questions about equality, but the meanings of equality are still up for discussion and certainly within the context of education what is to be meant by equality and the conditions upon which it depends is a complex question and one for which the answers are not all in. The definition of a value inevitably encounters problems in relation to other values, and the meaning of equality is no exception. My point is the simple one of insisting that while we recognize the equal intrinsic worth of every individual and wherever possible provide for that level of opportunity that will enable every person to advance educationally as far as his or her abilities, motivations, and interests permit, we should not allow that leveling of the character and quality of education generally that an extreme egalitarianism sometimes demands to satisfy a numerical conception of democracy. I do not agree with those who hold that education for all is education for none. But I very much agree that the same education for all must mean eventually educational mediocrity for all. The differences that obtain among us, whatever their causes, are a necessary factor in fashioning the educational structure. I believe that this means that there must be elements of elitism in education, that to ban elitism as an evil in education would be to violate the best meaning of democracy. More than that, it would deny our society the cultivation of intellectual and artistic talents at the highest level, a society which is already starved for greatness and despite its remarkable scientific and technological achievements seems almost propelled toward the commonplace in its statesmanship, its materialistic interests, its aesthetic judgments and tastes, its anti-intellectualism, its irrationalism, and its loss of ideal aspiration. Of course, I use the term elitism here in its best meaning and egalitarianism in its worst. But those meanings should be obvious.

I have the impression that as a general rule our colleges and universities have become confused in this matter. That confusion arises from the milieu of idealism, minority aspiration, protest, government regulation, the judicialization of the campus, the growth of litigation, court decisions, and the loss of faculty integrity. Its result is a softening of academic standards, a lowering of the demand for high intellectual achievement, and in general a loss of institutional nerve.

All of this places a large burden of responsibility on the graduate schools and professional schools. For it is in their advanced work that the universities can in some way overcome the antinomy of the elite and the equal. Here better than anywhere else in higher education, the meaning of equality in education can be worked through, albeit with the assistance of the courts, and policies and practices can be developed that conform to the best accepted meanings. This is not to say that the numerous social problems relating to equality can be solved by the universities; it is not the responsibility of our educational institutions to find a cure for every social ill. Already the social burdens that have been imposed on the schools have been a serious impediment to good education. At least the graduate schools can do as well or better in this matter than can be done in any other sector of education, and it is especially here, on a democratic base, that we can develop the intellectual elite that is essential to the strengthening of our culture by establishing standards of knowledge, reason, and critical intelligence that can be, as they sometimes are, powerful and ideal motivating forces in the intellectual life of the nation and the world.

I will conclude these comments by returning to my original thesis, that education is a function of the culture. Certainly the work of a university has value in itself; there is intrinsic worth in knowledge, in reason, in imaginative and creative thought. These are the humanizing and liberalizing elements of the culture. But, to speak metaphorically, they also serve the culture. In a sense they both exhibit its character and provide the foundations for its genius.

The genius of our culture, its characteristic achievement, its spirit and symbol, is the individual. Ours is the culture and society of the individual person. Whatever contributes to the integrity of the person, to the creation of an authentic individualism, contributes as well to the strength and lasting power of the culture. Whatever conspires to violate human personality and weaken individualism contributes to the disintegration of the culture and the destruction of the social institutions which are its material base. Now, as we are threatened with a dehumanizing mechanization of the person, with bureaucratization that endlessly regiments the individual, and collectivization that abolishes him, it is a central task of education to build new strength into our culture and our social institutions by preserving and enhancing the ideals of knowledge and rationality which have been major forces in shaping and securing the individualism that is the culture's chief foundation. It would be an inadmissible conception of the purposes of education, and certainly of advanced higher education, to hold that it should be indifferent to the task of criticizing, strengthening, and perpetuating the culture of which it is a part.

Comments by Ernest Bartell

As a relative newcomer to the world of American federal bureaucracy in Washington, I was impressed and greatly stimulated by the general premise of McMurrin's paper, that indeed higher education is functionally related to our culture. What I would like to do is to read a brief statement of my own impressions on the way in which federal policy demonstrates that functional relationship, and some of the concerns that that raises for those of us involved at the federal level, and save some of my more specific comments until after Miller's paper, when some common elements in the two papers can be addressed together.

At least since World War II, American graduate education has engaged the attention of those concerned with national policy and higher education. During World War II, enlistment of the scientific community for national purposes by the Department of Defense and by the Atomic Energy Commission, established a modern precedent for support of scientific research in graduate education that affected not only future federal policy, but the policies of admission and growth within our nation's colleges and universities. Later, the launching of Sputnik stimulated a national consciousness to a greater awareness of the importance of advanced, basic, and applied research, while rapid population growth was defining a need for instructional personnel with advanced training at all levels of American education. During the late 1950s and 1960s the growth of such agencies as the National Institute of Health, the National Science Foundation, and the National Endowments for the Arts and for the Humanities, provided direct and indirect aid to graduate education, in support of scholarly research. Grants and loans to students under various public programs further linked graduate education to national priorities.

More recently, higher education has been supported in federal policy, and McMurrin adverted to this point, as a vehicle for attainment of social goals of equality of opportunity for all citizens regardless of age, race, or sex. This link between higher education and equal opportunity has been largely grounded on the now-familiar premise of the increased economic productivity and social mobility associated with additional increments in levels of educational attainment. And it has led to an implicit acceptance in our country of the right of all citizens to higher education, not only for national purposes, but presumably also in order to uncover the latent excellence in the previously educationally disenfranchised sectors of our society. This does not imply, of course, the equal and same education for all citizens. And it does not deny the importance of the role of graduate education in maintaining a significant elite in our society and the contributions that such elite contribute to our society. But it does raise the question as to what responsibility graduate education has to this larger goal of contributing to social justice or finding appropriate models of education for all sectors of the society, including those previously disenfranchised from higher educational opportunities.

Unfortunately, the changing relationships between demand and supply in the labor markets have, as we are all well aware, recently weakened the force of the premise of the economic and social purposes of higher education as routes for economic and social mobility in the public consciousness. Moreover, graduate education itself has been especially noticeable as a victim of the weakened employment opportunities for those entering the work force with advanced degrees. There is then a corresponding danger that federal policy, focusing not on education itself but on its own social agenda, will begin to overlook the contemporary needs of a social asset, graduate education, that for half a century has been so closely linked to national purposes. Such a blind eye could have disproportionatly drastic effects at a time when internal policies of many colleges and universities are reordering institutional priorities in the interests of administrative stability and financial solvency. Several studies of graduate education in recent years have broken the necessary ground for development of appropriate policies, both within colleges and universities and within external agencies, public and private, for the future of graduate education. And yet the response from public and private sector policymakers has until now remained relatively muted.

Nevertheless, graduate education is in many respects a locus for the sharp definition of many of the very policy issues whose resolution will determine, not only the future of graduate education itself, but the future of all of higher education. I think that point has been made in several of the papers. I would like to cite a few current examples of concern in public policy in education with which we are preoccupied these days, in which graduate education plays a significant role and must bridge some of the antinomies which McMurrin has mentioned and which I think operationally identify education, again, as functionally related to our culture. For example, there is a continuing concern that as higher education depends more and more on public aid, and the regulation that accompanies it, the integrity of the enterprise may be jeopardized by that dependence. I think there's very real concern in government about this point. The modern history of graduate education in the United States, perhaps especially in the sciences, should yield some valuable lessons about the costs and benefits of educational activities that are driven, at least in part, by public funds in pursuit of national purposes.

At another level, the imposition of employment quotas of women and minorities in colleges and universities does little more than reallocate existing pools of candidates among the highest bidders until more effective provision can be made in graduate education itself for increasing the pool of qualified candidates. Thus, we at the Fund for Improvement of Post-Secondary Education, have supported the creation of a national Chicano-Research network which is based at the University of Michigan, to provide services that we hope will enhance the retention of young minority scholars in graduate programs and in entry-level faculty appointments. The academic legitimacy and effectiveness of adventures like these may ultimately help determine the extent to which colleges and universities can and should serve social goals of equal opportunity.

Meanwhile, one can sense some uneasiness within the educational community over the possibility of conflict between traditional standards of quality and excellence within disciplines and expanded access to higher educational opportunities. I happen to believe, as I indicated, that there is no inherent conflict of these goals. However, in an educational climate favoring experimentation to meet the needs of new students, such as minorities, adults, and the handicapped, the renewed interest in the definition of standards of educational quality is surely a timely expression of the need for absolute standards while education seeks to respond to contemporary cultural needs.

But I see it more as a tension than a contradiction, and so we do observe heightened discussion these days of the nature and purposes of general education, and renewed interest in establishment of more demanding undergraduate core curricula. It is, however, at the level of graduate education that the challenge may be felt most acutely to devise strategies for integrating policies of opportunity and access along with the traditionally high regard for standards of quality in research and scholarship. We are very probably going to launch a national conference on curriculum in higher education sometime within the next half year. It is my hope that these are some of the very issues that can be taken up in that context so that we can perhaps focus in a bit more directly on the role of the education community through its abilities to design academic programs to cope with these tensions.

On still another front, there has long been perceived within the higher-education community a tension felt by many faculty members between the demands of scholarship and the demands of instruction. Whether such tension need exist in principle may be debated. However, professional and institutional standards and strategies for appointments, promotions, and tenure can clearly affect the extent and nature of that tension, and so we at the Fund have felt it important, not only to support interesting initiatives in faculty development at the level of the individual college or university, but also to support within the academic disciplines inquiry and experiment in professional recognition of achievement in teaching appropriate to the individual discipline. Still, initiatives such as these suggest that a third and perhaps most appropriate locus of inquiry into the proper relationships of teaching and research in individual disciplines is within the graduate programs themselves, which inevitably act as transmitters of the priorities of the disciplines from generation to generation of faculties.

I fear that, particularly in this era of no growth, we may lose an entire generation of young scholar-teachers in that transmittal process. In effect the possibilities for graduate education acting as a source of fertility and vitality in recognizing the instructional needs of dealing with a larger clientele in higher education may well be constrained by the absence of job opportunities for that lost generation, which we hope somehow will not be lost. These are just a few of the examples of the practical concerns that are currently expressed by policymakers in the town where I am currently living and who are concerned with the future of education, but I hope that they can also illustrate the continuing importance of appropriate graduate educational policy to all of higher education. And I look forward to some more specific comments after Miller's paper.

Question and Answer

Q: Perhaps we should think seriously of developing alternatives to the university.

A: Yes. I'm inclined to think that the most important alternative to a university in this country is to be found in the so-called research parks associated with the universities. This, of course, is not an alternative in any full sense, but it does indicate the tendency of universities to depart from what you might call a standardized form of the university, and to work more in a close relationship with private business and industry. We see it developing elsewhere. The ties of the universities with the government are becoming more and more obvious. I'm referring to such things as internships in government, and business, such as White House fellows. This has been very common in the case of medicine and social work, but now we are seeing more of it in connection with schools of engineering and business, and in departments of political science that bring in people from government who are not strictly academic. I think that if you were thinking of this country and the foreseeable future, what we're likely to have is not a real alternative to the university but rather the universities developing along lines which are somewhat nontraditional, as in the present continuing education movements. I think there is nothing sacred about the structure of an institution, and it conforms to my earlier argument that education should serve a culture of which it is a part in various ways. Institutions should be flexible enough to adapt themselves to the evident needs of society. There may be better ways. I don't agree with those who have held that the schools are likely to be abandoned in favor of some other kind of educational technology. On the contrary, I think the schools and the colleges and the universities are very secure. I do believe that in the future we're going to see some very real modifications in their structure, in the directions which I have indicated. This is all to the good. It gets away from the tendency for educational institutions to isolate themselves.

Past, Present, and Future
in Graduate Education

Eugen Pusic

My contribution is likely to seem a little distant from this rather specific discussion of the problems of American graduate education. I felt one striking feature in this presentation: the frequent repetition of the confrontation of opposites. Should graduate education be the creation of knowledge or the diffusion of knowledge? Should we be in favor of a research orientation or of a professional and vocational orientation? Is education at the higher level necessarily elitist or should it be true to the democratic ideal, and how? Is education at our universities conservative or is science and graduate education progressive and revolutionary by implication? A number of such opposites seem to crop up in every paper we have listened to. There is an interesting problem with these opposites—are they dialectic in nature? There are so many platitudes about this subject told and written in eastern Europe that I somehow feel the necessity to clarify for my own use what I would mean by dialectic and nondialectic opposition. It seems to me there are opposites which pose the following problem: in the language of the mathematician, to maximize two criteria for the same function at the same time. I do not know if satisfactory mathematical methods exist for doing this. The real problem requires not a compromise, not a halfway between one and the other, not the domination of one by the other, but maximizing both is some way which will do justice to both. Along with the opposites which can be treated in this way, there are many that are simply contradictions, opposites you have to choose between or avoid the question altogether.

I would like to start with another one of these confronted concepts—the concept of past and future in graduate education, and in education generally, in the pursuit of science. Graduate education is the highest level formal education reaches in any one system. European systems are different from American in this respect. This highest level of education has an inbuilt critical intent which is necessary and independent of the progressive or conservative orientation of the individual scientist. Did you notice how often we consider stability an

129

ideal? We speak of a stable family, a stable individual character, a stable economic system, a stable political system, using all of these as terms of commendation. Is it not extraordinary that science is the only systematic and organized human endeavor where the opposite of stability is the ideal? To subvert existing truth is the highest aim in science. This is highly exceptional, and it is inbuilt in the activity. If we are true to our profession, we simply have to do this, whatever our political or ideological preconceptions may be. On the other hand, the institutions of graduate education in which we pursue science, the universities, are some of the most conservative institutions that exist, and are so necessarily and independently of the intentions of the radicals or conservatives who teach in them. In teaching you have acquired a special fund of knowledge, a special expertise, and you live by it, you are paid for it, therefore you are highly unwilling to relinquish it. You will do everything in order to preserve this specialty and this knowledge as being your monopoly, which is just the opposite of the aim of science, of what the logic of knowledge itself bids you to do. Mr. Smith has invented, if he's very good, something which is called the Smith's syndrome, or comrade Pavlov has found the Pavlov effect. Now Smith and Pavlov want to live the rest of their lives on this effect and on this syndrome. They do not want to see this changed, not because of any kind of personal political or social conservatism, but simply from the logic of the run of time. After a certain time in our career, we all see the end of the tunnel. At that time it is too late for any radical change of our own concepts. I may see that they do not hold very well, but to now take a completely different perspective, to familiarize myself with completely different methods which I have not learned in my formative years is not only extremely difficult, extremely risky, it is sometimes simply impossible because of the factor of time. I will be retired and dead before I have reached anything. Therefore somewhere in midcareer, I have to stick with what I have reached. This is a deep-seated reason for the institutional conservatism of the universities, and these people who are in midcareer and beyond are usually holding all the positions of power. It seems that this contradiction, this opposition, really does define the problem of graduate education as I see it. Graduate education is growing out of the past, a past which it neglects neccessarily, which it opposes, which it tries to improve upon, and develops from the present toward the future, a future which is made possible by the results of its work, but which is also constraining its present possibilities. The purposes of education have been mentioned several times here: the transmission or diffusion of knowledge, and I would say by implication in much that was said, the maturing of personality. Further along this line, when we reach graduate education, a more recent development in the field of education, work is aiming at a point, without neccessarily ever reaching it, where the dividing line between creation and transmission of knowledge disappears, where the discipline and the identity of the professional role merge with the freedom and the playfulness of the undiscovered. No matter how narrowly specialized and professional the programs of actual graduate education, how modest its achievements, the most advanced form of institutionalized education can never completely avoid the challenge of this double aim, or forget the ideal of creativity. This ideal, however, raises a very serious question: is creativity only a matter of freedom, of being unfettered by dogma, released from orthodoxy, untrammelled by any of the many limitations currently inhibiting the free working of the mind? Is this freedom, in principle, within the reach of all? Or is it also a matter of ability, and therefore unequally distributed, scattered along a Gaussian curve, broad at the base and narrow at the top? To get into graduate school today does depend in principle, in part, on a certain very narrow type of ability—the ability to pass tests and examinations. But this restriction might be a consequence of present-day organizations built on yesterday's values and so not binding for all eternity.

Let us come to the central problem, a problem that gives color and meaning to this and every other question in the area, the problem of the social context of education. The purposes of individuals, groups, or institutions in a complex social field can be assessed, their true weight estimated, only in relation to the structure of the field, to the forces present in it, to the character of the society in which they operate, to the social reality on which their own reality depends.

There is a restriction of resources for graduate education, for the time being, and a possible restriction of careers, speaking particularly, of course, of the American scene. I think that this problem has to be seen in a larger social context, a context I will try to sketch in three main dimensions. I will maintain, and submit this statement first of all to your criticism and critical scrutiny, that this holds practically everywhere; East and West, North and South, wherever we have a formal institutionalized activity which we call graduate education.

The first dimension is a condition of scarcity. Rewards and satisfactions, incomes and positions available to people, are insufficient to cover all existing needs, to satisfy all interests actually operative in the social field. This implies, of course, the full range from the most extreme physical want to the most preposterous hankering after luxuries as advertised on television. It is not justification that is considered now, but psychological and social reality that really moves people. Scarcity implies, among other things, that people have to work for a living, and that they study to learn how to work. It implies also, that whatever is done, education included, has to be done in a way which will give the maximum output for a given input, usually measured on an economic, quantifiable criterion.

The second dimension is the condition of division of labor. Division of labor is as old as humanity and almost as continuous as biological evolution. In its course differences develop that have significant implications for the interests and positions of groups in the network of social relations. Consider the differentiation of the military as a separate activity, the appropriation of the transcendental by the priest or medicine man, the identification of managing as different from the activity managed, the separation of thinking from doing, planning from implementation, white-collar from blue-collar work. But there is an additional and very important dimension to the division of work. In industrial or industrializing societies, the division of labor evolves a specific variant: the systematic fragmentation of the work process. A complex task is divided into progressively simpler and narrower assignments down to quite elementary performances, called work operations, to be integrated in a hierarchical arrangement of jobs, corresponding to the various assignments, toward the unity of the original task as a whole. This form of division of labor has the important implication that most of the work in classical industry is fairly simple, demanding little education beyond elementary, and offering little reward beyond the socially defined minimum.

And now the third dimension of the social context, the condition of stratification. It is a fact of life in all societies beyond the very simplest that some people get continuously more of what is considered desirable than others. The operative word in this definition is "continuously." Because differences in chances of interest-satisfaction that appear occasionally are virtually impossible to avoid where many interests face scarce opportunities for satisfaction, stratification appears only when individuals or groups have succeeded in cementing a position of privilege for themselves that neutralizes the essential randomness of the process and assures their interests of prevailing in all or a significant majority of cases. As interest-confrontations are always in a sense zero-sum games, privilege necessarily entails exploitation, that is, somebody else getting less than a random share. Now what is the significance of these three dimensions of the social context, scarcity, division of labor, and stratification, for graduate education?

Under conditions of scarcity, education is a scarce commodity and graduate education more scarce than other forms. There are limits to the amount that can be supplied and to the number of people to whom it can be supplied. The criterion of choice, indicated by the principle of efficiency, which still prevails whatever we might wish, is governed by the requirements of production in the widest sense, by the demand for labor. All education has, first and foremost, to produce a labor force. It cannot leave out skills that are in demand; the question is, should it educate for knowledge that is not in demand.

Under the still-dominant form of division of labor the demand is for a labor force with low education for a majority of jobs and a decreasing elite of professional and managerial positions toward the top. The educational system cannot help mirroring, at least to an extent, this demand structure, and making higher levels of education accessible under increasingly restrictive conditions even where this selectivity is not inherent in the educational process itself. Anything else would not only fly in the face of efficiency but would also intensify beyond endurance the frustration from the simple repetitive routine work that prevails on the bottom of the hierarchical pyramid, in proportion to the amount and level of education received. Education has to fashion personalities ready to accept heirarchy, specialization, and subordination, which, under the existing technology, will be the fate of most people anyway. Note that I am speaking of technology and not of the social and economic system.

Under conditions of stratification all education tends to fit the existing criteria of stratification. People do more or less important work and because of that get more or less of the existing store of scarce goods. Higher education gives access to more rewarding, in a socially defined sense, work. The access to higher education, consequently, must be made selective on a clearly understood principle. This is the source of the dominant one-dimensional concept of ability, where the main concern is not to match existing individual potentials with work at which they will have the best chance for maximum development, but simply to establish an acceptable reason for excluding almost everybody from elite positions to which their chances of acceding are statistically almost nil anyway. Stratification, however, being the tendency to perpetuate privilege, to reserve dominant positions for a group, is largely mirrored in the actual processes of educational selection. Offspring of those in positions of privilege have significantly better chances to satisfy the criterion as applied, owing to the greater wealth or power of their families. Education in this way tends to reproduce the strata that exist. Hierarchy, as the general structure of work organization, limits the places at the top; it is a pyramid.

Education fulfills the ambivalent role of motivation on one hand, by the expectation of upward social mobility through educational achievement, and frustration by having necessarily to disappoint most of these expectations on the other.

Under these circumstances, to sum up, graduate education in its social context is the production of the highly paid, highly situated, highly specialized elite in the labor force. The less developed the social system, and here we get beyond the American system, the poorer the country, the simpler the context, the more pronounced is the elite character of graduate education, the less important its content of actual knowledge and skill. The positions to be reached through graduate education are more desirable the less attractive the alternatives, but also their number is proportional to the level of wealth in a community. Thus, both stabilizing and unstabilizing features of graduate education become more pronounced in the poorer countries. The possibility of advancing to the top, even if a mirage, induces many to accept the system, until disappointment breeds an even more virulent disaffection. Think of the third world countries. Graduate education is the place where social change is hatched not only through questioning existing doctrines, from physics to ethics, but also by providing emotional reasons for believing the existing state of affairs not to be necessarily superior to all alternatives.

In the light of social realities, the ideals of graduate education— creativity in freedom, freedom to create for all who feel the urge— look as distant as the Holy Grail. Nevertheless they do remain ideals, that is, representations to inspire striving, to orient action, and potentially to take hold of the imagination of a sufficient number of people to move into existence. In the meantime, two possible positions merit warning: One is the belief that everything can be changed provided there is sufficient determination, seeing one grand reform as ushering in the educational millenium. Equally pointless is the other extreme, that nothing can be changed, that the ideal has to be abandoned as utopian and the existing state of affairs accepted.

The point is, actually, to see clearly the social setting of education, the social transformations that are probable and upon which educational change is predicated and which, in turn, education can influence. And also to see with gradually increasing clarity what can be done now, or at any other moment, in order to ease and help along both parallel processes, social transformation and educational change.

Now, the first condition, the reduction of scarcity, is so much the central goal of people everywhere that it needs no proclaiming. Rather, it is important to assess its prospects and also to weigh the impact that achieved levels of affluence are presently exercising upon education.

Technologically, freedom from poverty seems within reach. In the most affluent countries, people begin to give serious consideration to such institutional innovations as a guaranteed annual income. Other countries, so-called Second World countries, by changing their economic system, are actually providing, though at a more modest level and at a political price, economic security for practically the total population. In a large part of the world, however, the immediate problems are hunger and disease, lack of the fundamentals of existence, not to speak of education and science, or of increasing inequalities and stratificational differences within countries. The problem here seems to be a possible confrontation between the highly developed minority and the underdeveloped majority of the world, which at the present state of the population is a relationship of one to five. Of the one-fifth who live in developed countries, only a part actually enjoy all the advantages of the development of the country. Therefore, if the elimination of scarcity is technologically within view, the outlook is uncertain because of present differences in development levels and because of possible overall limits of the planet's capacity to sustain a population.

What about the second dimension, the division of labor? The transcending of the specific form of division of labor characteristic of classical industrialization, the fragmentation of the work process, the crumbling of work as Georges Friedmann put it, is not only in view, it is actually under way. Hierarchical organization was the object of increasingly severe criticism for the past forty years as being inhuman, stultifying, and, eventually, inefficient. In the last twenty years, through automation and the informational revolution, an alternative to hierarchy has begun to appear. If most routine operations in industrial production and in other work can, in principle, be transferred to machines, then people are left mostly with nonroutine, information-rich, knowledge-dependent tasks. Human cooperation on this new technological base cannot be regulated by hierarchical command and supervision but only by processes, still imperfectly understood, of mutual adjustment and self-management. The traditional job of the administrator—to plan, organize, staff, direct, coordinate, report, and budget—is either disappearing as an individual assignment, is collectivized in a group of specialists, delegated to many persons in turn, or it is being transformed into a service activity no longer implying relationships of subordination and superordination.

The transcending of stratification, the third dimension, seems the most elusive of the three lines of development we are considering. It has been wished for, proclaimed in programs, commanded in religious texts, heralded by movements, and even declared to have been achieved in reality, and up to now all these expectations have been disappointed. Societies have somehow always rediscovered that some are more equal than others. Prevailing bases of inequality among humans have changed from physical strength and cunning to persuasiveness, power, wealth, or organization. They might change to knowledge and still inequality would be the outcome.

On the other hand, however, let us not be fatalistic about it. Nothing human is necessarily forever. With progressing differentiation in societies, stratification seems to have become less clear-cut. At least there are different standings in different social hierarchies. We have come to understand better the role of property, the rule of class, the right of position, the rise of merit as sources of inequality. If we so desire, we are better able than ever to guide developments toward greater equality, in the economic sense, and also to effect quicker rates of change. Societies are more vulnerable to violence but also have greater resources of self-repair. As traditional institutions of power wither away the political process, what you call politics, should become ubiquitous.

What is the place of graduate education in these processes? By its very nature and apart from any conscious engagement of the people involved in it, graduate education is a future-oriented activity. It is most interested, in a way, in new facts, new paradigms, new points of view, the extrapolation of trends, the possible surprises waiting along much-frequented paths. At the same time graduate education as an institutional activity is tied, by its institutional framework, to the present, and through it to the past. It has its share of pride and prejudice, its stereotypes, its vested interests, but also its responsibility to the day, that is, its hardheaded tasks, its proven methods without which the play of the imagination is not creative but mere daydreaming.

This situation itself is a program: to build upon the foundations of existing reality, choosing what is solid among the materials found and discarding what is not, in order to liberate the future contained in the present.

There is, first, this question of ability. On any of the aptitudes of mind and body, people are unequal. This is a fact. High ability in anything is as rare as any freak. Some abilities are more relevant to given types of activity than others. The ideal goal of graduate education, it seems to me, is not to insist on a particular form of talent to the exclusion of everything else, but to expand the span of interest in

human possibilities, to match an increasing variety of gifts to a growing assortment of academic pursuits in which they can be employed to
the greatest advantage. For the beginning, however, we might be wise
to set our sights lower, to get a larger share of the abilities that are
currently listed and scholastically measured over the barriers of class,
wealth, and power. Even today, in spite of these barriers, there is
probably more talent in graduate education than in an average sam-
ple of the population. Graduate institutions should try to educate
their members to the acceptance of ability as responsibility, not
primarily as a negotiable asset in the market. This in itself should not
be at all easy.

The responsibility is to identify the crucial junctions of social
change and to work at them, analyzing situations, investigating
trends, listing alternatives with their implications, finding solutions,
inventing instrumentalities. The overcoming of scarcity, the consequences of the new technology, the structure of a nonstratified society
are not a matter of routine. Without in any way seeing institutions of
graduate education turning into a general staff of social action, the
pool of clear and imaginative thinking they represent cannot and
should not be left out of these processes, where informed and pre-
meditated design is so much rarer, though often much more useful,
than rash and emotional action.

Professions are changing and people are changing professions.
The division of labor is getting too differentiated for the differentiation of professions to follow all the way. A specialist in medicine, law,
philosophy, or mathematics is by far no longer a specialist. Usually he
is supposed to cover a broad band of areas—for example, a specialist
in psychiatry considered competent for everything from depth psychology to victimology, or a specialist in international law expected to
give counsel on anything between international organizations and col-
lision norms regulating currency transactions, of which he has only
superficial knowledge and, owing to his training and experience, possibly a headstart over others to the sources of pertinent information.
The consequence is that initial university education, including
graduate education, is discouraged from the ambition to impart to
future professionals all the information they are likely to need. The
educational effort is thus naturally led toward intellectual fundamentals, toward the general structure of a field, toward many-purposed
methods, toward training for versatility rather than security in an
acquired speciality. Thus prepared, graduates are more ready than
they used to be to move from one area to another or even to switch
between professions. To see people go from the bar to public adminis-

tration, to environmental protection, to social policy; or from chemistry, to biology, to urban planning; or from philosophy to computer engineering, to politics is a more frequent sight presently than earlier, when it was either the sign of a strong though unruly spirit or the mark of a weak and shifty character.

This movement has important consequences for graduate education. On the one side, it helps to approach the ideal of interdisciplinarity, or rather nondisciplinarity, of free play among the mind's basic puzzles, by pushing university education as a whole in somewhat the same direction. On the other, it requires graduate education to open a wide fan of narrowly specialized courses to be taken during one's working life, and even after retirement, as need may be or interest prompt. The two are not necessarily contradictory, and they may complement each other, action-oriented, task-fitted instruction providing the necessary discipline and wide-ranging intellectual search preventing staleness.

The relationship of graduate education to practice is hereby defined as both closer and more distant than we are wont to think of it. At graduate levels education is practice: the research that accompanies it, the two-way flow of information as people come from practice and return to it, the concern with relevance acting as the critical conscience of the educational establishment, all these contribute to a blending of thought and life. Essentially, at the same time, graduate education is not oriented toward immediate short-run results of any practical activity. It is resisting ill-advised though not infrequent attempts to treat it as a university for hire. Actually, these attempts are so manifestly self-defeating, producing neither knowledge nor the results sought after, that the more intelligent among the potential "customers" begin to understand that the best policy in this case is to let them do their damnedest and take whatever seems useful.

Finally, there are the goals and values of future societies and the possible contribution of graduate education to their creation and transmission. The topic is a delicate one. One of the few things that might be safely said about future goals and values is that they will be different from the present articles. Also that graduate education is not going to produce philosopher-kings to ensure the everlasting happiness of humanity. If it were, the most urgent task would be to scrap the whole undertaking while there is still time. It might, though, fulfill a critical function in this respect. Projects for the future tend to suffer, congenitally, from an optimistic bias. If they do not, they are not projects but black utopias, saying in fact, whatever you do, you are doomed. Projectors, however, should be made aware of the unavoidable dark side of the improvements they promise and plan, the drawbacks, the side effects, the opened problems, incidental in the change they advocate. At the highest levels that the systematic education of humans can reach it should at least be possible to inject some rationality into our Great Debates, to direct the sharpest eyes, the clearest heads, the strongest hearts toward a dispassionate examination of our utopias. Certainly not in order to laugh them all out of court or to drown them in a facile skepticism, because some among today's utopias are fated to become the realities of our tomorrows anyway, but in order to see what questions their emergence is likely to pose, to moderate our expectations and so mitigate later disappointments, show us how to lower the costs of transition. Tomorrow's values we ignore. But let us abide, in graduate education as elsewhere, by today's values of rationality and critical thinking in order to have a tomorrow to discover. [See Comments on Pusic and Veysey by Dorothy Harrison.]

Questions and Answers

Q1: I understand that East Germany limits the number of Ph.D.'s by government decree. Is this true of Yugoslavia? Do you recommend such a policy?

A: To the first question, I do not know the situation in East Germany. I would consider this probable and plausible. As in most Eastern European countries, there is personnel planning as a component part of overall planning. You know what number of engineers, physicists, mathematicians, etc., are going to be needed in the next five-year plan. Therefore it is logical that they limit the number of people who are allowed to take the various degrees and enroll in the various disciplines in order to accord broadly with the plan targets.

To the second question, if this is true in Yugoslavia—no, it is not. To a certain extent I would say it is a pity, which is also my answer to the third question. You see this is again a kind of contradiction. It is everybody's right, and should be everybody's right, to choose his field of interest and his field of study. But as it is, at the same time, the field of his productive work, it means considerable responsibility, to let people without adequate guidance make their choices on maybe completely irrelevant criteria. What can be done short of strict planning, saying that so many people can go into architecture, and not one more, or, on the other hand, allowing people to be completely free to choose the profession of medical doctor because it is particularly well paying, leads to high income, and then discover that you cannot get a post as a doctor because there are not enough people and not enough places to pay doctors. Both should be avoided. How this problem can really be solved, well, maybe the most candid answer is, I don't know.

Q2: Could you please comment further on something you said? What do you mean by expanding the span of interest in human possibilities?

A: What I mean is this. The present criterion of passing tests and examinations which is leading to success in the academic world as a student, is a very one-sided criterion. You all agree that it is a very great risk to employ somebody as an assistant professor simply on the strength that he was a good student. At least in our system the risk is very great that his excellence as a student depended on the one-sided ability of an attentive memory. Maybe the student also had ability to express in writing whatever he had memorized. Very often this ability is completely divorced from any creativeness. Such people are often unable to produce any new idea. Our universities are clogged with people who have been recruited from first-class honors students, who went on, and by persisting, made it to full professor after thirty years, to the greatest damage to the discipline. But I do not mean only that. Human abilities are very diverse, there is a great variety of things people can do. And each society has a certain ability criterion which is socially defined and then generalized in order to select people through the whole educational network. This seems to me mistaken. It would be desirable to improve the educational institutional arrangements in a direction in which you have a much wider possible combination of abilities, which lead to some kind of possible academic pursuit. A benefit which might be irrelevant to the present main criterion of success, be it killing enemies or earning dollars. The goal should be simply to expand our system from being selective to being allocative. Allocate people, according to their abilities, to different pursuits. I am aware of a cartoon somewhere in a paper where a man comes along from an ability test, and the tester gets back to him, has a sheet of paper, and says: "Sir, I'm sorry to report that you are not fit for anything." This might and does happen, but I think it should and would happen much less often, if we worked at spreading the span of relevant abilities which we acknowledge in our academic setting.

II. The Prospects of
Graduate Education

Graduate Education as Ritual and Substance

Kenneth E. Boulding

Graduate education is a small but significant subculture within the larger world society. In its most formal sense, it is almost wholly confined to universities and institutions of higher learning; in a more informal sense, it includes all learning that goes on after an undergraduate degree or its equivalent. Formal graduate education indeed is a relatively small part of this postgraduate human learning which is done by very large numbers of people as they acquire skills, take up hobbies, read books, go to meetings, acquire life experiences, and think. I suspect—although I do not have accurate data on this—that even when it comes to formal classes and tests, more graduate education goes on in corporations, government, and other places outside the universities than goes on within the universities themselves. As it is impossible to teach without learning, a great deal of graduate learning goes on among teachers, both inside and outside the universities.

Nevertheless, formal graduate education culminating in a degree is a highly dominant subset of this larger process, simply because it is the prime instrument of certification and of those rites of passage which are the real significance of a degree, whether the student attends a graduation ceremony or not.

There is a difference, however, between the rites of passage into society at large and rites which reflect a selective process symbolizing that the individual has entered a group within the larger society characterized by some standards of achievement or special status. This is the difference between rituals of confirmation like the Bar Mitzvah or the confirmation ceremonies of the Catholic and Lutheran churches, and rituals of ordination which confer special status, like the laying on of hands of a priest, the dubbing of a knight, the coronation of a monarch, or even the beatification of a saint. In our own society the high school diploma has become almost a rite of confirmation, as signified by the opprobrious connotation of the term "dropout." The bachelor's degree has become increasingly a rite of confirmation, even though less than half of the appropriate age group attain it. Only the master's and the doctor's degrees retain the flavor

143

of a rite of ordination, and only in the doctor's degree does this confer a change in title or address. In American society the doctor's degree has become the democratic equivalent of knighthood, "Doctor Doe" being almost a perfect linguistic equivalent of "Sir John." Higher orders of intellectual nobility are conferred by the mutual admiration societies, like the American Philosophical Society, the American Academy of Arts and Sciences, and of course the National Academy of Sciences, which confers the status, though by no means the emoluments, of a dukedom, though only the aristocratic Russians have the nerve to call themselves "academician so-and-so."

Different societies of course take their rites of confirmation and ordination in different ways. In England the symbol of academic ordination was a "first" at Oxford or Cambridge; that is, first-class honors in the undergraduate degree. In my generation at least this was regarded as the passport to university teaching. Few people who got their "first" ever went on to take a higher degree. It was only those unfortunates who just missed it and got a "second" who had to rectify their certificate of inferior status by going on to get a doctorate. If I may be excused a little personal reminiscence on this point: I came to the United States in 1932 with a Commonwealth Fellowship to the University of Chicago. Glowing with the arrogance of youth and the self-confidence inspired by my first at Oxford, I went to see my advisor, Professor Jacob Viner at the University of Chicago, who advised me to take a Ph.D. So I said, "What do I have to do?" When he explained the rigors of this ordeal, I said, "If I do all that, I shall be a broken man," much I think to Viner's disgust. I spent my two years at Chicago very agreeably doing exactly what I wanted to do, writing two or three papers which were eventually published, secure in the expectation that I was going back to England and that I already had my ordination into the academic community. By a set of happy accidents, I came back to the United States and have had a remarkably good life in the American academic community, but still never took a Ph.D., in spite of some deans' eyebrows being raised. In this regard I always thought of myself as the last relic of George III in the United States, and I was probably the last generation that could get away with it.

In spite of my personal experience in getting away without it, I have come to have increasing respect for the Ph.D. and for the subculture which it creates; at the same time I have some lingering doubts and always wonder if there is not a better way of doing it that nobody has yet thought of. My respect for the institution arises mainly because I have seen graduate students do things under the pressures of the disciplines of a Ph.D. program which they would never have done had they been left to themselves or had they pursued a more casual course of studies. I have seen students come to me with vague ideas and formless notions and I have gradually watched these crystallize and transform themselves into a clear, logical, well-argued, well-documented, and well-tested thesis, which would never have taken place without the rather artificial stimulus of the graduate school culture. This happens, of course, all too rarely. We are all familiar with the pedestrian student who just gets away with a pedestrian thesis. When the miracle does happen, and under the pressures of artificial requirements a first-rate, disciplined, yet still creative individual emerges, the reward is so great that it justifies all the donkey work—the hack teaching, the hack teachers, and hack students who occupy the bottom end of the scale. In almost any human activity the bottom 25 percent is what we have to put up with, in spite of the costs of uncertainty that we must pay, for fear that one little pearl should be lost. For the middle 50 percent, the benefits probably exceed the costs. No matter how exhalted the ordination, there will always be a middle ground, and it is these people indeed who keep things going, who do the donkey work, who are the soil out of which the flowers come. The flowers, however, justify the whole, as it is the peak experiences of life and society which ultimately justify the inevitable costs. Only the ecstasy justifies the agony, and it is part of the agony that produces the ecstasy, though which part it is both important and agonizingly difficult to know.

Another aspect of graduate education which inspires me to at least modest cheerfulness is the extent to which it operates as a system of apprenticeship. We are beginning to realize in general that our abandonment of apprenticeship in favor of formal education may have been premature, and that in many fields a combination of formal education and apprenticeship may be what we are looking for. In graduate education, of course, to some extent this is what we have. The graduate student mainly learns to teach by apprenticeship, and it is a rare graduate program where the prospective university teacher gets any formal instruction on how to teach. In research, also, there is a strong element of apprenticeship in many Ph.D. programs, especially perhaps in the natural sciences but also in the social sciences, where the candidate is in effect a glorified research assistant to the professor and his Ph.D. emerges out of a combination of the candidate's and the professor's research. There are dangers in this as well as advantages. Certainly there have been cases where Ph.D. candidates have been exploited by their professors, but the valuable aspect of this is that the professor and the student come to know each other in a way that is almost impossible in undergraduate programs. This is one reason indeed why graduate teaching is so expensive and requires such a small number of students per teacher. In part this is due to the fact that there will only be a small number of students in highly specialized courses and seminars, but it is significant because the personal knowledge which the professor has of the student can easily be the student's greatest asset. The most important part of the student's rites of passage into the profession is not the degree itself so much as the letters of recommendation from his professors. This is the real laying on of hands which confers the ordination. To be effective, however, this does require that a professor know the student well, and this is expensive.

The great problem is to find the optimum degree of discipline and critique. I have come to the conclusion that quality, in the language of evolution, is much more a matter of selection than of mutation. Mutation is a dime a dozen. Change is the commonest thing in the universe. The creativity of the universe, however, the evolutional complexity, comes by selection. The same is true in social life: the capacity to produce novelty is very large. As most mutations in the biosphere, however, are adverse, so are most novelties in social systems. Creativity is not the art of producing novelty, but the art of selecting among the enormous number of novelties that the human mind and the structures of society are constantly producing. We see this in art, where it is what the artist does not do, more than what the artist does do, that makes the difference between creative art and the commonplace. We see this in individual life and in society, where it is taboo, the things that we do not do that we could do, that creates the quality of life. We see it most of all in science, the success of which is almost wholly due to the fact that it developed a subculture within which the testing of the images of the world was overwhelmingly more important than formulating them. We see it in the development of skill of all kinds, which consists essentially in eliminating those things that we might do which are not productive, and so confining our activity to those things which are productive, whether this is in tennis, or writing poetry, or surgery, or teaching, or in the great art of life itself.

Without discipline there is no creativity, and discipline is the right kind of selection operating on a sufficiently rich field of mutation. Those who seek creativity by being undisciplined are tragically on the wrong road. Knowledge is gained by the orderly loss of information through selective processes; perception likewise, as the modern theories of perception stress. Beauty, interest, excitement, or whatever it is that the artist is trying to generate, likewise is gained by creating the improbable; that is, by selecting out of the infinite universe of aesthetic noise those structures which are improbable and which have low aesthetic entropy. The training of a professional involves mainly selecting out of the vast field of the possible those things which are useful.

It is indeed one of the great virtues of the academic disciplines that they do have at least a modicum of discipline. A discipline indeed is a community of critique, in which the exposure of other people's errors is a sure road to promotion if the exposure is generally accepted. I suspect the discipline when it functions well advances knowledge much more securely than the more exciting and more profitable arena of popularizing and the public platform, where the plausible rather than the tested is the key to survival and success.

The graduate school culture is often criticized on the grounds that it is too narrow, disciplinary, niggling, petty, critical, and detailed. There is some truth in these criticisms, as we all know. Every institution and every subculture has its pathologies. Graduate school subculture is certainly no exception to this rule. One recalls the famous definition of originality in a graduate student as "the capacity to present his professor's ideas back to him in a way that he had never thought of before." The graduate student who is so original that he is conceived as a threat to his professors tends to be busted out, and most of us have known such cases. If one could always be sure that it is those who do not need the rituals of ordination who fail to get them, one could have a much more easy conscience.

With every subculture, there is some optimum degree of toleration of nonconformity and of dissent from its dominant ethos. The academic community is no exception to this rule. A department of astronomy would have a hard time accommodating to an ardent supporter of Velikovsky, or even of the Ptolemaic system. A faculty of chemistry would have a hard time with a confirmed believer in phlogiston. Biology departments may have some difficulty in dealing with violently pro- or antisociobiologists. Economics departments have had a very spotty record in dealing with heretics of various kinds, ranging from monetary cranks, through institutionalists, to orthodox Marxists. Heresy has an even rougher time in the Soviet Union, where the penalities for it are much more severe, as we saw in the whole Lysenko episode. If a culture is too conformist, it will suppress changes which might be beneficial to it and will drive out members who might revitalize it. If it is too tolerant, it may disintegrate from lack of internal unity, or it may simply be taken over by an alternative culture against which it has no defense. We see this in the very occasional department that becomes dominated by a particular school of thought and then drives out all those who do not conform to it, because the department has tolerated this school in the first place.

We get the paradoxical dilemma, therefore, that toleration sometimes leads into intolerance, and that the most creative degree of heterogeneity may be unstable; for heterogeneity easily degenerates into factionalism, which can be very destructive in terms of the amount of time it absorbs, even to the point where one faction is driven out and homogeneity is achieved by exclusion.

This illustrates a fundamental principle, that what matters more than anything in graduate education is the subculture of the department, and this may differ widely even within the same institution. The larger culture of the institution has some impact on the departmental subcultures, but I think not very much, except in regard to a general atmosphere of supportiveness or constraint. Universities without exception have some departments which are much better than others, and while this does create certain tensions at the upper levels of administration, so that there are some pressures to improve bad departments—even at the expense of good ones—the truth seems to be that it is very difficult for a university administration to intervene very effectively in the long processes of cultural drift which determine the qualities of particular departments. The random factors here are of great importance. There is luck in the choice of a chairman. Sometimes by accident three or four people may get together and stimulate and complement each other and create as it were a suborganization of great creativity within which each performs much more successfully than might be the case in another setting. The fact that recruitment in departments, and even their defenses against people leaving the department, are to such a large extent within the policymaking power of the department itself, subject to the larger external constraints imposed by the university's financial position, means that departmental cultures perpetuate themselves glacially subject to the occasional eruption of random factors.

Furthermore, the fact of tenure, and the custom of appointing fairly young people who are likely to stay with the department for a long time, means that aging processes, which are highly unpredictable and may themselves have a certain random element in them, play an important role in the cultural drift and in determining the history of the department. Some people age slowly, both physiologically and intellectually, and remain active and innovative in later life; some people who seem to show great promise at the moment of achieving tenure, age rapidly and become rigid, fixated on the ideas of their younger days, becoming an increasing burden which the department has to carry. Unfortunately, our understanding of the aging process is so small that there seems to be no way of dealing with this problem, either at the moment of appointment to tenure or later. Indeed, I would put research on aging as one of the major unrecognized and unsatisfied priorities in our society. The present attack on the rigidities of retirement and the mandatory retirement age represents at least recognition of the problem and of the wholly inadequate solution to it in mandatory retirement. Nevertheless, it leaves the question of the right solution completely open and merely emphasizes our appalling ignorance in the face of a universal human phenomenon. I must confess that as one who perceives himself as a slow ager, I have been vigorously fighting off retirement, with some success, although I recognize that this is a mere scratch on the surface of a much larger problem, to which we do not know the answer.

A crucial element in the subculture of a graduate department is the amount of communication that takes place both among the students, among the faculty, and between the students and the faculty. The formal organization of classes and seminars is designed to achieve at least a small amount of communication between the faculty and the students, and a much smaller amount among the students. The only institution which formally promotes any kind of communication among the faculty themselves, however, is the Ph.D. committee. Invaluable as this is in educating the faculty, one could raise a very serious question as to whether it is enough. There should be a principle of university administration that if you take care of the education of the faculty, the education of the students will take care of itself. Unfortunately, there are very few administrations that give a high priority to this principle, and the education of the faculty is left almost entirely to its own initiative. The institution of the sabbatical of course is a nod in this direction, and this has a certain value in the self-education of the individual faculty member, though it is not always very effective, and it does little to promote the education of the faculty by each other. The two or three hours of a Ph.D. exam, valuable as it is, especially if the student has the wit to get the faculty arguing among themselves, surely should not be the only institutional excuse for interfaculty communication.

I have argued that one of the best ways of spending money on faculty education is the encouragement of some kind of team teaching, even if this only involves having two faculty members jointly teaching a single class. I cannot help feeling that if funds were allocated specifically in budgets for this purpose, the results would be highly productive.

Another device for the education of the faculty, which is too much neglected, is the departmental seminar. Here again, this almost always depends on the chance initiative of one or two members of the department who keep it going. It rarely appears in any budget, it does not figure much in any reward structure, but it can have a very important effect on the cultural drift of the department. Part of the problem here is that of extreme specialization even within the department, which introduces difficulties of communication, which are frequently embarrassing enough so that the communication is abandoned. A department member who cannot understand his own colleagues is apt to keep quiet about this fact. Within the structure of the universities we have never developed the role of a translator of jargon; this is something it might be fun to try. It could even be that this role might in part be fulfilled by students themselves, who are often the only ones who really know what goes on in a department, simply because they are the only ones who experience a variety of the teachers.

If communication within departments is difficult, communication between departments is much more so, and the problem of interdisciplinary education, particularly at the graduate level, which is almost inevitably departmental and specialized, is one that everybody struggles with, feels a bad conscience about, but nobody seems to be able to solve. There is general agreement that specialization is necessary, but that somehow specialists should also be generalists and should be able to integrate their special discipline into a larger framework of knowledge and ideas. Somewhere in all this is the idea, perhaps a leftover from the more elitist nineteenth century, that a scholar should also be a gentleman capable of good dinner table conversation. At its worst, this led to a total taboo on talking shop and a virtual guarantee that all intercourse among different specialists had to be trivial. But still we have a feeling even in this day and age that there is something in it, and that the ideals of Cardinal Newman, that the university is a place of high cultural discourse, are still not obsolete. The very name university suggests that the business of the university is to study the universe, not to be an aggregation of hireling specialists. Somewhere between knowing everything about nothing and nothing about everything there must be an optimum, and we have an uneasy feeling today that we are on the specialist rather than the generalist side of this. Nevertheless, there remains a deep ambivalence. The very term Renaissance man is almost a half insult. There is a slight suggestion of a jack-of-all trades and a master of none. I have been in the interdisciplinary business now for more than thirty years, but a remark which my wife once made, "If you are going to be the great integrator, you ought to know something," still has a not-undeserved sting. Part of the difficulty is that at the level of the student, and especially at the level of the graduate student, all the payoffs are for specialization. A student, and even an assistant professor, who gets too much interested in the wider world, may flunk his prelims or fail to get promoted. The disciplinary structure dominates graduate study even more than it does undergraduate study, and a university, as every administrator knows, is a loose federation of departments with a very weak federal government.

The trouble is that there is even something to be said for this sad state of affairs. As I said somewhere before, the danger with the interdisciplinary is that it tends to slip into the undisciplined. When one's field is the universe, it is hard to get specialized criticism and nobody will get promoted in one department for pointing out that somebody in another department has made a serious error. Philosophy, whose field should surely be the universe, under the chilly doctrines of logical positivism and linguistic philosophy, crawled into a narrow cave and shut the door on the rest of the world and became a specialty of specialties. Somehow the liberal arts became less liberal and more arty, and the university became a multiversity.

It may well be that the only answer to this problem is redundancy, inefficiency, extravagance, and waste. One could argue indeed that the main reason for getting rich, that is, economic development, is that it permits the human race to indulge in these last four delights. Something I have learned from the biologists is the tremendous importance of redundancy and even inefficiency in the survival of species. A really efficient species expands to the utmost limits of its niche and loses adaptability. When the niche begins to close, as it always eventually will, the species that has no redundancy in its behavior cannot have adaptability and will soon become extinct. Extravagance and waste are one of the great pleasures of life and the main argument against poverty is precisely that it demands a grueling and miserable efficiency. It was no accident that science itself emerged as a major social force in the period of the baroque and the rococo. Science itself is an extravagence moved by idle curiosity rather than by practical efficiency. Even further back in time, it was the wasteful extravagance of sexual reproduction, with its spectacular squandering of sperms and eggs, by contrast with the puritan efficiency of cell division and the amoeba, which led to the whole baroque extravaganza of this planet, culminating in Adam and Eve and all that came out of them. Here again, of course, there are optimum points and Aristotelian means. There can be too much redundancy, inefficiency, waste, and extravagance, just as there can be too little. The totally destructive idea is that there should be none.

An increasing problem in universities, and in graduate schools in particular, is the rising demand for accountability, particularly in regard to the expenditure of public funds. There is nothing unreasonable about this in itself, and the question as to whether the taxpayers are getting their money's worth is always a good question to ask. Nevertheless, it is a question to which it is easy to find a plausible but wrong answer. The worst answer is that the measure of money's worth is some simple number, like students per faculty member, and then given this efficiency measure all we have to do is to make it bigger. These procedures can be enormously destructive to institutions which involve risk capital, where the product is hard to measure, so that all the things we can find numbers for will be extremely inaccurate measures of what we really want to know. Creativity requires a degree of trust and even tolerance of error. This is another case where the optimum is very hard to find. A strict holding to imperfect measures of efficiency, however, can be quite catastrophic and can destroy the whole productivity and meaning of the institution.

The demand for greater accountability it seems to me must be met in two ways. On the one hand, universities must not simply shrug it off as meaningless. They should devote resources to improving the feedback from the processes in which they engage. The university should conceive of itself as an experiment in teaching, learning, and the expansion of knowledge. Its information collection apparatus should be designed with useful feedback in view. This is by no means easy. It should be regarded as a challenge worthy of the best intellectual resources of the institution. The problem should not be pushed off onto administrative offices or even the specialized research institute, though there is much to be said for this. And the more both students and faculty and administrators can see themselves as participating in a continuing process of improvement, the more likely is improvement to take place.

Along with this, however, there must also be a constant campaign of explanation directed toward the public at large and to its representatives as to the necessity for freedom, leeway, redundancy, space to move, opportunities for experiment, and so on. Without this, the drive for efficiency can be disastrous.

We are all aware that a chill economic wind is blowing on higher education, several degrees chillier than that which is blowing on our whole society. We all know that in the 1980s the number in the age group of usual college age will decline very sharply and will perhaps be only 75 or 80 percent of what it is in the 1970s. This will have a "divider effect" on graduate education, for the number of new teachers required will shrink much more rapidly than the total number of undergraduate students, and unless therefore there is a sharp decline in the enrollment in graduate schools, they will be producing a large number of Ph.D.'s for whom there will be no employment in the traditional fields. We are feeling this pinch right now indeed, and even in the 1970s we have been educating a lot of graduate students essentially under false pretenses, for their expectations are most unlikely to be realized.

The management of decline, as I have argued elsewhere,[1] is a very painful and a difficult business, much more difficult than the management of growth, or even of stability. The key to it, as far as I can see, is to emphasize an increase in quality as at least a partial offset to the decline in quantity. This is particularly a challenge in graduate education, where the decline in quantity is likely to be quite large in the next ten or twenty years, especially in those fields where the major outlet for the holder of a doctorate is in the teaching profession itself, especially in university teaching. In the extreme case, the object of graduate education is to enable a professor to replace himself, in which case one graduate student per lifetime would be enough. There are not many fields as extreme as this, though there are some in which there are not even opportunities in undergraduate teaching. The decline in graduate enrollment in response to the decline in university teaching opportunities may be offset in part at least by expansion in graduate preparation for other occupations. As the academic community is at present constituted, this would suggest an expansion of master's programs of many kinds rather than doctoral programs. There are many areas of life in which the university has no comparative advantage in the teaching-learning process beyond the master's level.

A possible development here would be a program beyond the master's level which would combine practical experience in business and government with occasional return to the university for a program which would tie in with this practical experience along useful but more academic lines. So far we seem to have given very little thought to this possibility. One could visualize a program worked out in close cooperation with business and government organizations that would keep a person employed in his organization but provide for correspondence courses, sabbaticals, and an integrated program, which perhaps would end up with a degree in ten or even twenty years. This might require a rather new type of professor, who also would take sabbaticals in other organizations.

The economics of higher education, and especially of graduate education, involve an uncertain mixture of exchange and grants. Both of these may be subject to pathologies. The fact that higher education is an investment with a very long-time horizon and at least moderate uncertainties, means that if it is left wholly to the market it will provide examples of what economists call market failures; that is, activities which would be good investments both for individuals and for society, but which will not take place in the absence of opportunities for exchange over time, either through ignorance or through avoidable uncertainty. This is one reason why the grants economy, as I have called it, has been so important in higher education, both in private grants and public grants. There have been many suggestions for moving the finance of higher education more into the market economy, as for instance, the creation of federal educational banks, which might fund a student's education with loans to be repaid as a surcharge on his income tax. These suggestions so far have not found much favor, but we constantly need to keep proposals of this kind on the agenda.

Finally, we need to be reminded that adversity is not always a bad thing, and that sometimes, as Toynbee has suggested, there is a right amount of challenge that produces a creative response. There is no doubt that we are in for challenge. Let us hope that it is just the right amount and that we will indeed have a Toynbeean response.

NOTE

1. Kenneth E. Boulding, "The Management of Decline," paper presented at the Regents Convocation of the University of the State of New York, Albany, September 1974; condensation published in *Change* 7, no. 5 (June 1975):8–9, 64.

Comments by Angus Campbell

I can't begin to respond to all the interesting things Boulding has said but I would like to expand on what he refers to as a fundamental principle that "what matters more than anything in graduate education is the subculture of the department." He points out that the departments exist within the context of the university and the college but he questions how much influence this larger context has.

I think Boulding is profoundly correct in suggesting that the departments have increasingly become the centers of power on the campus. Perhaps this was not always true. When universities were smaller and leadership styles were more authoritarian than they are now, it may have been that the departments were docile colonies within the colleges. But in the large universities at least this is no longer the situation. Whether because these univerisites have become too large to be managed from a central office or because of a general trend toward decentralization, the departments have clearly taken on a life of their own.

Within the limits of the budget they receive from their college, the departments are to a large degree free to determine their own fate. Each department defines the discipline it represents; it sets the boundaries, it decides what is inside and what is beyond the pale. It controls what Boulding calls the rites of ordination in its discipline; by controlling the title of professor of this or that it decides who may present himself as a member of that disciplinary fraternity on campus.

Generally speaking, most of us are probably attracted by the concept of self-determination and the delegation of authority to the local level. Ideally we would like to see a department choose a distinguished chairman and help him or her build a distinguished department. Unfortunately the ideal is not always attained in practice and we not uncommonly see an undistinguished chairman intently building a second-rate department. Then self-determination comes in conflict with some larger sense of standards held by the dean or the higher officers of the university and an intervention becomes necessary which is painful to everyone concerned. Delegation has its hazards in every large organization and not the least within the university.

As departments have become more autonomous they have become very sensitive to their public image. I am not referring specifically to the reputational ratings which emerge occasionally, although they are very much aware of them. They wish to be seen as having certain characteristics and not others. Within the total range of interests and activities they might be concerned with, they value some areas and not others. Referring now to the social science departments with which I am most familiar, the major dimension of concern has to do with the relative importance of the basic-theoretical and the practical-applied. In psychology departments around the country, for instance, there has been a continuing dispute as to whether the training of clinical psychologists is a proper activity for a self-respecting department of psychology. Some have decided it is not. Some sociology departments do not want to be seen as too much concerned with problems of marriage and family life for fear they appear to be involved in some form of social uplift.

Generally speaking those departments with pretensions want to be seen as devoted to pure science. All the social sciences are a little touchy on the question of whether or not they are really sciences; perhaps that is why some social scientists are so anxious to be seen as engaged in basic research heavily wrapped in theory. Glazer observes in his paper that "much of what passes for high theory in the social sciences does not add up to much." That could be argued of course; there is no doubt, however, that many people in the social science disciplines take this "high theory" very seriously. Their graduate students quickly learn what the prestige words are and how one talks theory. My own feeling is that one of the reasons for the general opaqueness of social science writing is the author's attempt to create the appearance of heavy theory. In the words of Professor Higgins in *Pygmalion,* it doesn't matter so much what you say as how you say it.

I am particularly interested in the effect the emerging power of the department will have on the way research is handled in the university. We are all familiar with the fact that research has become a growth industry on American campuses since World War II. This new development was superimposed on a prewar pattern of an individual professor working with a graduate student and that one-on-one format still persists. In the social sciences we have three general levels of research analysis. Macroanalysis depends on the use of aggregative data which in most cases cannot be disaggregated. Economic research is very heavily macroanalytic, so also to some degree is research in sociology, political science, and history. The prewar model of one-on-one is still practical for this kind of research, provided there is a computer backup to handle the often massive computation.

Microanalysis involves the generation of new data, usually from individual sources. This is exemplified by the anthropological field worker or the experimental psychologist. The scope of such research is restricted to the observations a single individual can make and these restrictions are usually severe. Microanalysis at this level also fits the one-on-one format but the product is subject to the painful weaknesses of reliability and validity with which you are familiar and which I will not discuss.

The third type of social science research is almost entirely a postwar development, microanalysis based on large populations. The development of new methodologies, largely during the wartime period, made it possible for social science to "come out of the closet." Our ability to obtain unbiased data concerning large dispersed populations through the techniques of probability sampling opened vast possibilities to social scientists which had earlier been quite unthinkable.

The unfortunate fact is that the social science departments are very badly adapted to the conduct of this large-scale microanalytic research. They do not have, for example, the range of skills that is necessary for this research—sampling, interviewing, content analysis, computing. They cannot add experts in these techniques to their staffs because they would not fit their disciplinary image. The departments also do not have the supporting staff that is required—sampling clerks, assistants in research, interviewers, coders—and it would be very inefficient for them to hire such people for a short-term project. The basic fact is that this kind of research does not fit the one-on-one model; it almost certainly will involve cooperation between several people and more than likely from different disciplines.

Most of the leading universities are aware of these problems and they have taken various steps to cope with them. The most common response has been to set up research centers within departments; on this campus every one of the social science departments has at least one research center within its walls. Less commonly they have created interdisciplinary research institutes outside the individual departments. The University of Michigan took this route in 1946 when it established the Institute for Social Research. Yale University and Columbia University have recently taken similar action and there are no doubt other examples.

To a large extent, however, the universities are not answering this challenge at all. As a result we have watched the growth of universitylike research institutes develop outside the academic grove, for example, the Brookings Institution and the National Bureau for Economic Research. We are also witnessing the growth of a great number of profit and nonprofit organizations supported by government-financed research contracts. Much of the research they undertake would not be appropriate to the campus but some of it undoubtedly would be. In social science research the boundary between what is appropriately academic and what is not is not always obvious. I fear many academics assume that whatever is appropriate to the campus will naturally come to the campus. I believe this is becoming less and less true as time passes.

Boulding has commented on the difficulty the universities have in accommodating to interdisciplinary activities. "The problem of interdisciplinary education . . . is one that everybody struggles with, feels a bad consciousness about, but nobody seems to be able to solve." The problems of interdisciplinary research are even more severe. There are no doubt many reasons for this, but one of them is certainly that the departments have become the basic organizational unit of the college. As I have said, the departments are the defenders of the faith and they have a strong sense of the boundaries of their discipline. The payoffs in the college are in the departments and within the departments they are in the mainstream. There are a few extraordinary people like Boulding who prosper in interdisciplinary space but even they must first establish their legitimacy by some solid achievement well within the approved disciplinary limits. For the ordinary person life on the margin is hazardous. This is especially true for young scholars beginning their careers, and they perceive it to be true. A young scholar who raises doubts in his department as to whether he is a "real" economist or a "real" sociologist is taking his academic life in his hands. Within the social sciences at least the departmental structure is in my view clearly counterproductive to interdisciplinary research.

You may think this an overly pessimistic view or perhaps a view which may have been appropriate at one time but is so no longer. On the contrary I believe that the economic pressures which we are now subject to are increasing the tendencies toward separation of the disciplines. The economic threat is causing the departments to draw their wagons into a circle to repulse the Indians. In the process of conserving, they are becoming more conservative. I expect to see them become more defensive, more parochial as time passes, and, of course, less interested in any commitments of an interdisciplinary character.

Question and Answer

Q: I would like you to elaborate on your closing sentence or two, which told us that austerity represented an opportunity for improvement in quality. Most of us grew up in an era when the problem was how to manage abundance. What I would like to know in navigating the stormy seas of austerity is what you would use as stars and benchmarks.

A: Just to go back to Toynbee again: a challenge sometimes produces a response, but by no means always. Austerity sometimes produces imaginative responses. I am terribly puzzled by the circumstances under which it produces imaginative responses. I suspect that a strong random element is in this. On the other hand, we may have to think in terms of new types of institutions. One of the functions of this conference is to think about something we haven't thought about for a long time; we didn't have to think about graduate education for the last thirty years. I certainly hope this is only the beginning of it. And if I could add something to Campbell's excellent remarks, which I entirely agreed with—one thing that isn't in my paper, is the role of the research institute in the university and in graduate work. It is potentially of very great importance, not only as a source of outside support, but also as a way of loosening the stranglehold of the department. One of the functions of an institute is to legitimate inequality in the faculty. Departments are very egalitarian, so they tend to be highly suspicious of excellence, for the most part. It is easy for departments to become like Adam Smith's Oxford, in which as he says, everybody spent most of their time condoning the sins of their fellows in which they also wanted to indulge. Almost any isolated and rather secure group will tend to do this, and the institutes do provide an opportunity for some variety to offset the sins of departments.

The Disciplinary and the Professional in Graduate School Education in the Social Sciences

Nathan Glazer

It seems inevitable, when we deal with relatively new topics—and, as the prospectus for our conference points out, the literature on the philosophy of graduate education is very thin—that many of us will be tempted to resort to autobiographical experience.[1] This sets for each of us what is problematic in graduate education today. We see it in contrast to some past: pre-World War II, still marked by the Depression; the war with its peculiar demands; the early postwar and somewhat halcyon period, before the flood of expansion induced by increasing numbers of undergraduates and increasing funds for graduate student support and for research from government and foundations; the period of high optimism and expected endless expansion—shall we date it from Sputnik to the Columbia University revolt?; and finally our current period, in which expansion has ceased in many fields, to be replaced by decline, and in which an incessant demand for justification in a more rationalized and organized world imposes new and unexpected demands on graduate education and those who argue for and defend its budgets and resources.

But within this larger history, there are individual trajectories, representative of general but less global changes, which mark each individual perspective. If one senses and believes that one's experience is not completely idiosyncratic, one will be tempted to draw general lessons from it.

After this elaborate justification, let me make the personal report that my experience in graduate education has been one in which I have moved from what we consider in the social sciences "theoretical" knowledge, pursued very much for its own sake, to more "practical" knowledge, knowledge for use. My first exposure to graduate education was in the fields of linguistics and anthropology at the University of Pennsylvania, during the war. Strangely enough, that most exotic and pure branch of learning, linguistics, and in particular the descriptive linguistics developed by Edward Sapir and Leonard Bloomfield

160

and their student Zellig Harris, had been found of use in World War II by the armed forces. At least during my involvement in it, this practical aspect of linguistics was considered by leading scholars only a means to support research in abstract and theoretical issues, linked not only to the study of language as such, but also to the study of basic human behavior.

The corridor on which the professors of linguistics of the University of Pennsylvania had their offices symbolize to me a pure and uncorrupted phase in the history of graduate education, as remote from anything ordinary or ordinarily useful as one can imagine. At one end of the corridor was the office of the professor of Sanskrit; at the other could be found the offices of the professors of Semitics and Chinese, and in between one found the professors of Indo-Aryan languages, more versed in the early descendants of Sanskrit and ancient Persian than in Hindi or modern Iranian. That even this remote seat of linguistic study could be reached by war and found useful for it tells us something of the all-embracing character of World War II.

Let me contrast this first location for my graduate studies with my current one. I now teach in a graduate school of education. Theory is not banned from it. Professors of psychology, political science, sociology, and economics would recognize the theory taught as their own, for our professors come from those disciplines. We study human development, sociolinguistics, government policy, the costs and benefits of different approaches to education, and in all of this we are deeply engaged in the world of practice.

Now, having presented this much autobiography, let me point out that however unique my personal career may be, it does represent general trends which I believe characterize all the social sciences in graduate education. They have moved from a stance toward the world that emphasizes detached observation and analysis, inevitably an analysis somewhat remote from the daily practice of governments, business, schools, cities, prisons, and hospitals, to a stance in which observation is increasingly mixed with participation, analysis with judgment and advice. The social scientist today relates to institutions less as an uninvolved scholar seeking for general truth, than as a participant whose concerns are close to the concerns of the practitioner, either because the social scientist shares these concerns, or because both share the same concerns in their general role of citizen.

This development characterizes each department of graduate education in the social sciences. Of course people in these departments in the past have always to some extent been involved in the world; and even today, the greater part of the scholars within these fields pursue, at least part of the time, theoretical studies, however defined in their respective fields. Yet I am convinced that it is not only the shift in my own interests and location that leads me to see a surprising degree of involvement in the world in graduate education, where, if any place, one would expect the theoretical foundations of a discipline to be pursued.

Let me give an example: The sociology of health and medicine is one of those specialized branches of sociology that developed in the postwar world. Sociologists and anthropologists studied the ward or the hospital by means of extended participation, interview, etc. In this early work researchers saw themselves as contributing to their disciplines. They were not primarily, or even secondarily, interested in improving the effectiveness and efficiency of the ward or hospital they studied. They were interested in contributing to the development of role theory, or of the theory of the social structure of occupational groups, or of labeling theory, or what not. But now sociologists of health are interested in the central issues of medical practice, and have moved away from interest in or concern with sociological theory at the level at which they once pursued it. They still have theoretical interests, which is to say, an interest in generalizing, in rising above the issues immediately presented by one's empirical research. But now theory in the sociology of health will more typically arise directly from issues in the field of health, rather than being imported from a purer and more remote discipline where the theory was forged. One will move from roles, or labeling, or marginality—all of which did serve to bring some useful perspectives to the field of health care— to reasons why group practice succeeds or fails, problems in deinstitutionalizing the mentally ill, factors affecting the performance of doctors. The sociologist, at least as I see it, moves closer to the field of health and the issues it raises, rather than coming to it with the preformed issues his discipline has raised. He has a more practical orientation.

One type of theory that is increasingly popular everywhere in the social sciences is Marxism, a hopelessly vague term, which also has its own form of presumed practicality, dubbed "praxis" to show its distance from vulgar "practice." This orientation, whatever its problems, also leads to a closer engagement with practice and practitioners in many fields. Thus, the Marxist emphasis in sociology and history has led to much work on the history and nature of the professions. The Marxist as well as the non-Marxist social scientists have moved from a stance of detached observation and analysis to one in which observation and analysis is mixed with participation, judgment, and advice.

There are still of course substantial differences; the Marxists hope to give their judgment and advice to clients and subjects, rather than administrators and professionals, and they hope their advice leads to that fundamental change in social and power relations that they believe it is possible to introduce throughout society, whereas the non-Marxists hope only to improve the functioning of existing institutions. And to my eyes, even as they involve themselves in practice, Marxists, because of the origins of their outlook, tend to be distant from the realities of current practice. But Marxist theory, whatever its weaknesses, just as non-Marxist theory, has found the subjects and sites of research increasingly of greater interest in their own right, and theory has been in greater degree either allowed to rise from the subjects and sites of research, or brought up closer to them. So, in the sociology of health the hospital was in the beginning seen as a site for sociology; it is now of interest and concern in its own right. We can say the same for the sociology of education, of crime, and for other subfields, and I believe we can see the same development in other social sciences. The social scientist working in a subfield of practice has greater commitment to improving or revolutionizing practice, less to general theory.

One reason for this development, of course, is that as the subfield develops, jobs in the field of practice develop too. We now find sociologists of medicine and health care in almost every medical and nursing school. We find them on major research projects, not only as technicians of their distinctive methodology, but as participants in research formulations and research analysis. But I would argue that the shift from a more theoretical, remote, and isolated position—isolated, that is, from central issues of practice—to a more involved position has occurred not only because job opportunities in teaching and research and planning and administration have become available, but because the intellectual orientations of the disciplines have changed, too. Theory may still be the area of greatest payoff for the career of the scholar, but it too is increasingly less theoretical. It is more closely based than it was on practice, practice observed, practice engaged in, practice analyzed. The perspective of the professionals in a given field of practice has increasingly prevailed over the perspective of the theoretical discipline. What this means is that we see greater attention to effect, to consequence in the real world of action, in the teaching and research of the graduate departments of social science, less attention to theory and the perfecting of the discipline.

I am uneasy in making this generalization because this has been so much my own course, and I am afraid of imposing my own autobiography on large trends in graduate education, but as I concentrate more closely on specific areas, I believe this generalization can find substantial support. Thus, if we take the area of poverty and equality, we will see a movement from early work which was ethnographic and descriptive, what is it like to be poor, and theoretical, what is the function of class difference, to work which increasingly deals with governmental policy, not only with its effects but also with the questions of what specific policies should be formulated, and what might we expect their effects to be. One reason for the decline of a disciplinary approach is that where one engages with a problem, one must consider the problem on its own terms, independent of the discipline's capacities and interests. As soon as one begins to consider what is good policy, one already breaks out of the shell of a discipline, which looks at one abstracted side of any issue, because policy must include everything relevant to something working: not only the function of poverty in a society, but how one reduces it. There economics and political science are as relevant, or more so, than sociology. This is an example of what I mean when I say that in general a professional perspective, the perspective concerned with practice and effects, gains over a disciplinary perspective, the perspective in which the dominant issue is the advancement of science, which must always have something of a general or abstract character.

One can see the same development in the study of crime and juvenile delinquency: We have moved from an emphasis on causes, functions, or how crime fits into a society, to what one does about it. If one is interested in what one does about it, it is no longer possible to be a pure sociologist or pure political scientist; one must also be something of an economist, a politician, an administrator, an evaluator of how incentives and disincentives affect different kinds of behavior. Of course there are those who stick to pure disciplinary approaches. It is they who often frustrate policymakers when they are consulted on topics on which they are purportedly experts, and who are themselves frustrated when they consider the whole range of considerations, far from their discipline, that must become relevant when one considers real action, real effects.

I have called this concern for the problem, as against a site for research and theoretical elaboration, a professional one, in that it is linked to the kind of work that goes on in professional schools, and have argued this perspective gains within the disciplines themselves. It is interesting, for example, to contrast texts in urban sociology and race relations ten or twenty years ago with the same texts today. The earlier ones could limit themselves to strictly sociological considerations in which the concepts of sociology—class, race, role, function, social change—could be manipulated to cover the field. The newer ones must deal with governmental action, political organizations, economic factors, and economic policies. They become more policy oriented. This creates quite a problem when we consider what is suitable education in the scholarly disciplines. To me the issue is not that the purity of the disciplines has been muddied by the intrusion of the real world and its opportunities. Undoubtedly the disciplines change in part because research funds become available, and because jobs in these areas are opened to graduate students trained in a social science discipline. But it would be to radically underestimate the inner sources of intellectual and disciplinary change, indeed to engage in a kind of vulgar Marxism, to leave the matter at that. The world has changed too, not only in its opportunities, but in its structure and character.

From the vantage point of sociology, but also of the other social science disciplines, I would emphasize three changes. One is the enormous expansion of government in many spheres. For sociology, this means that processes that had been seen as having a "natural" character, reflecting the crescive movements of people and groups, became seen as increasingly affected by organized human intervention, principally government. Thus urban sociology changed sharply from analyzing a kind of social drift to analyzing governmental or corporate policies influencing or causing urban change. The same occurred with the fields we call deviance, social problems, criminology, marriage and the family.

Second, institutions such as hospitals, prisons, schools, and social work agencies also changed radically. Just as government underwent much more rapid growth and change in recent decades, so did these institutions. From being seen as stable backwaters in which people engaged in routine activities, they became fields of rapid and confusing change, and for this reason alone the theoretical disciplines increased their interest in them.

Finally, growth and change both in government and these institutions became seen as increasingly problematic, something to be questioned, challenged, defended. This development within sociology occurred both among what are now considered conservative sociologists (they call themselves liberal) and radical and Marxist sociologists. Social change, seen in the past as consisting of such processes as technological change, cultural lag, social movements, revolution, now increasingly become seen as owing to change in the behavior and scale of government and in the service institutions which had become so large a part of governmental activities.

I emphasize a change in sociology. One can see parallel changes in economics: increasing concern with governmental policies, and particular branches of social policy—health, education, crime, etc.; in anthropology: a shift to modern societies, to governmental roles affecting the poor, to governmental influences on backward societies; and in political science: a rising emphasis on governmental impact in given realms of social policy, supplementing the concentration on governmental institutions as such.

And so today, schools, prisons, hospitals, housing, public administration, once seen as involving purely practical skills, are now considered linked deeply to and implicated in the structure of society, reflecting and shaping its values, creating the world we all live in. If this seems obvious, let me remind you how boring these institutions appeared to the teacher of the social sciences, or the graduate student in them, twenty or thirty years ago. Obviously something has happened when books on these institutions are seen as among the most challenging in the social sciences. The study of these matters is no longer left to the narrower and more practical professional school.

The matters studied as well as the styles of work of the graduate departments in the social sciences and certain professional schools have come closer together. I have in mind not the professional schools of the major or learned professions, medicine, law, and divinity, but the newer professional schools dealing with the newer and more ambiguous professions that are engaged in social and public service: education, social work, criminology, lesser health professions (nursing, health administration), public policy, city and regional planning.[2] The word "professional," attached to an occupation or a school, raises many difficulties, and has been analyzed at great length, and in the present context I cannot avoid the ambiguity created by the fact that academic social scientists, working in graduate departments of social science in universities, are also "professionals," engaged in educating and shaping successor "professionals," yet I contrast them with the teachers in graduate professional schools. The first are professional in some senses. They are not amateurs at being sociologists, economists, political scientists, etc., and the organized discipline in which they are involved also has the characteristics of a profession. But the teachers in professional schools carry on a rather different tradition, and are professional in another sense. In the model of the classic professions of law and medicine, they have clients to whom they provide a professional service, based on some expertise.

Even though the academic social scientist can legitimately call himself a professional, I consider him as carrying on a disciplinary perspective, one whose traditions emphasize learning and research for their own sake, the advancement of theory and understanding independently of their usefulness for practice. I contrast this with the traditions of professional schools, which have taken as primary the preparation of students for practice in some field. It has always been a wonder why these two were so far apart—sociologists and social workers inhabiting different worlds, for example. It was not always so. But disciplinary and professional styles of education have been sharply differentiated in the American university.

The developments I have described have inevitably caused them to draw closer together. The graduate departments of the social sciences have moved closer to the professional schools dealing with social services in selecting subjects for research; the professional schools have moved closer to the graduate departments in their style of teaching and research. In the typical school of education some years ago, and perhaps in some today, theory was often a crude and distant hand-me-down from partially understood and half-forgotten work in the theoretical social-science disciplines, and the main course of study often dealt in picayune detail with minutiae that one could pick up on the job in a fraction of the time devoted to them in the professional school. But as the institutions they deal with have become more interesting and problematic, as the practice for which they train their students has come under criticism and been questioned, the better professional schools have reached out to the graduate departments for teachers in the theoretically oriented social science disciplines.

Simultaneously, the theoretically oriented disciplines themselves were independently changing as practice in all the professional fields grew, as government expanded in its involvement with them, and as accepted practices and procedures in the professional fields, and in education for them, were increasingly seen as problematic. The local government agency, the federal bureau, the hospital and mental hospital, the prison and police department, the welfare department and the city planning office, under the impact of these developments, no longer served only as sites for research to advance disciplines whose practitioners were indifferent to the actual and presumed objectives of the enterprises they studied in their search for generalized theory. Social scientists now are concerned with whether the welfare office really overcomes dependency, the prisons really rehabilitate convicts, the police department really reduces crime, the school really teaches, and the hospital really cures, and what causes the successes, and more commonly, the failures of these varied institutions. This has brought them to larger questions of governmental capacity, professional effectiveness, and the impact of social intervention on the lives of individuals, families, and larger nongovernmental and nonprofessional associations.

The role of high theory thus has been reduced and increasingly joined by theory based on concrete and grubby practice. The position of research and analysis devoted to social institutions and their effectiveness, justice, and ends, was enhanced, and its prestige rose. While one can connect this kind of work to high theory, it requires an initial task which becomes ever more demanding and absorbing in its own right, that is, understanding these institutions. My own conversion from the larger and more abstract issues to what I quite candidly present as smaller and more concrete ones has been more radical than for some of my colleagues, but the change has marked generally the social scientists of my generation. And the fact that books on the family, prisons, schools, and social work may be among the most challenging of any season, as against the rather dull texts for practitioners in professional schools they once were, is one indication of the scale of the change.

As I have suggested, this change in what the social science disciplines did and were interested in has also changed the character of professional education. In many schools teachers are now increasingly scholars trained in one of the disciplines, rather than practitioners or graduates of the professional school itself. In schools of education, city planning, criminology, or social work, one increasingly finds economists, sociologists, political scientists, anthropologists making up the faculty, in addition to teachers and "educationists," city planners, criminologists, and social workers.

But it is what this involvement in the world of practice has meant for the traditional social science disciplines that here concerns me most, and it has received surprisingly little attention.

Let me first emphasize what may not be necessary: I am not a critic of these developments. Much of what passed for high theory in the social sciences, certainly in sociology, does not add up to much. It consisted mostly of a rehashing of the contributions of the masters, and it was no great loss if graduate students got involved in the study of institutions for their own sake, as well as for the sake of high theory. Nevertheless, this development does create some problems. How does one teach for practice, or the understanding of practice, when theory remote from practice has been the mainstay of teaching in graduate social science?

There are conflicts between study and research for its own sake and study and research for use, and they are particularly sharp in the social sciences. In the physical and biological sciences, there are close and organic links between theory and practice, "basic" research and "applied" research. Understanding the structure of the atom permits us to build weapons or produce energy, understanding the structure of genes permits us to cure genetic defects. For those more deeply involved in these fields there are undoubtedly serious issues in drawing lines between theory and practice, basic and applied, but to the social scientist the connections seem enviably simply, justifying strong claims for support all along the chain from the most abstract to the most practical, and permitting work anywhere in this broad spectrum to legitimately claim a home in a graduate department. The situation of the humanities does not, to my mind, even raise the question of the theoretical and the applied in any sharp form. What after all is application in the humanities? There is no large and clearly demarcated field of practice or application set off from a field called theory in the humanities. There is of course the teaching of the humanities, to undergraduates, to graduate students, in professional schools (e.g., courses in the ethics of the profession), to lay people, but this is not practice or application in the sense in which we can use it in the social sciences and the sciences. For these, practice or application takes place outside of teaching situations, in other institutions such as businesses, research institutes, hospitals, jails, schools.

It is for social scientists in the graduate schools that the connection between teaching and research for its own sake and teaching and research for practice raises the most difficult issues. One reason is that what one learns, teaches, and researches changes sharply as one approaches the frontier of practical work, the kind of work that professionals in fields of social policy do.

Education within a discipline is very different from education within a profession, and as one moves from one to the other, the strain shows. There is a very different flavor to each. One significant element of training within a discipline in the social sciences is that the writings of masters is crucial. This is what theory is all about. The way one studies the discipline is by studying texts, developing their implications. This is no longer true in economics, an indication of how closely economics has moved toward the sciences, but is certainly true of sociology, political science, and anthropology. One analyzes Marx, Toqueville, Freud, Max Weber, Leo Strauss (and whoever Leo Strauss analyzed), Malinowski, Radcliffe-Brown, Talcott Parsons, Claude Levi-Strauss, Robert Dahl, etc. One's status in the discipline depends on the degree to which one has contributed a text worthy of such analysis, one which is itself an analysis of the texts of earlier fathers of the discipline. One does see some of this in professional schools, but in contrast with the academic disciplines, one examines practice, through courses (which are unfortunately not able to gain the discipline of organization about major texts), through field experience, through doing, through analysis of governmental regulation and professional standards.

One may say, to put the matter in an extreme way, that as one moves from the disciplinary to the professional stance, the relevant texts move from the writings of the masters, ancient and modern, to the regulations propounded by professional associations and government and its various manifestations, legislature, executive, judiciary. The office of the professor of a discipline is filled with books and journals. The office of the professor in a professional school is filled with reproduced reports, decisions, regulations, and comments on regulations. In his teaching, he may increasingly use cases in business school style, dense masses of fact, statistics, and regulation. The professor in a discipline will continue to look for elegant, abstract, theoretical textbooks. I suppose that on the whole there is a decline in quality of writing, of coherence, profundity, significance, generality, as one moves from one setting to the other. Yet not in every case. The lucubrations of a minor theorist in the social sciences may lose considerably in contrast to a well-written and argued court decision.

But the contrast is indeed striking. I teach a course in higher education. Most of the students are from the graduate school of education; there may be a few from sociology. The topics they select for research are very different. The sociologist will be interested, for example, in applying some generalization from a theorist of modern social trends — Daniel Bell or Talcott Parsons or Alain Touraine — to data drawn from higher education. His concern is basically in theory, and he will engage in what can only be considered an intellectual tightrope walk, trying to get from the large generalization to the somewhat mute data which may or may not demonstrate that the theorist is right or wrong. He moves from the text to the data. The graduate student in education is doing the same thing. But his text is something like a Department of Health, Education and Welfare regulation requiring states to set up planning bodies for higher education in their state. A very different exercise in comparing a text with a reality. In one case one sharpens the wits in comparing words and concepts, in engaging in a chain of complex reasoning; in the other one expands the capacity to see certain kinds of practical complexity.

But as I pointed out earlier, the two are coming closer together. If we look into the professors' offices, again, we will find that both may be filled with printouts, and while the research of the professor in the discipline may be more sophisticated than that of the professor in the professional school, this is probably only marginally true. The theoretical texts of the discipline migrate into the profession, the laws and regulations and rulings and standards of the profession increasingly migrate into the discipline, not only as subjects of study, but as necessary parameters if one is interested in effect, impact, action, policy.

Is the profession being corrupted by disciplinary theory, moving away from its true objectives? Is the discipline being corrupted by practice? I would argue neither of these things. I think a necessary adaptation of the social science disciplines to a changing world is taking place—a world increasingly created by law, regulation, judgment, large organization, as against the atomic action of individuals and small organizations. On the whole this is a healthy development. There is to my mind an aridity to the endless examination of the writings of the masters when they deal with a world that is gone and are applied to a radically different world that is undergoing change. Undoubtedly certain things in the social world are relatively unchanging and in that sense the insights of the masters are crucial. But there is a necessary balance in how far one carries them, and the enormous effort of young social scientists to "save" and "apply" Marx or some other master, in sociology, political science, economics, has something unreal and even farcical about it. This is something from which the professions are more likely to be saved—it is not their style. But then one can make the opposite criticism: The concentration on the world as it is and how to act in it is also narrowing and deadening. The larger perspectives generally provided by the disciplines bring in air and light. To emphasize an education based on rules and regulations is undoubtedly narrowing, and I believe there is less of this in the professional schools than there used to be particularly since laws, regulations, and codes change so rapidly. But at the same time, the professional perspective relieves the social sciences of their own kind of aridity, their own kind of airlessness, one in which concepts dance, and the life of society goes on far away, as if under glass.

Of course, as we all know, there are now strong practical reasons why the disciplines and the professional schools are being brought closer together. There may be more job opportunities for the graduates of a social science discipline in a professional school than in a college or university. The latter decline, while the former still, in many fields, expand. Under these circumstances it is an advantage for a graduate student to have done his research in a field linked to professional practice, rather than on a more theoretical issue closer to the heart of the discipline. Research opportunities are more likely to be available from a grant-giving agency in a field of practice than from one which is willing to advance the discipline as such.

But I would argue that there are more than practical reasons for the professional perspective to infuse disciplinary study. There are good reasons from the point of view of the development of the disciplines. The disciplines, after all, in some respect model the real world, and must be compared with it. And this world is increasingly shaped by professional practice. When the internal development of a discipline is too fully based on those issues most centrally identified with it, it remains at too far a distance from its ultimate objects of study, man and society, as these actually exist. Most important to my mind, the objects of study have themselves changed with the growth of government and with the growth of intervention in social development at every stage, and in every sphere. These provide new questions for the discipline, new areas in which what the disciplines have to contribute to practice should be displayed. It is thus not only jobs and research money that bring the disciplines closer in styles of research and in styles of teaching to the professional schools. And it thereby became a major issue in graduate education to compare the styles, to see how they may interact productively, and how both professional education and disciplinary education may avoid the specific defects they tend to develop when the two styles stay at a far distance from each other.

NOTES

1. I have benefited in preparing this article from comments by David Riesman and an unpublished manuscript by Nathan Keyfitz.

2. On these schools see Nathan Glazer, "The Schools of the Minor Professions," *Minerva* 12 (July 1974): 3, 346–64.

Comments by Angus Campbell

I find Glazer's argument not unrelated to what I said in discussing Boulding's paper. Glazer believes that the social sciences are moving from a single-minded concern with theoretical knowledge to an interest in what he calls practical knowledge, knowledge for use, from theory to social problems. He feels this is happening not only or primarily because money is available to study social problems or because work on social problems promises job opportunities for our young Ph.D.'s. He argues that we are less and less a traditional society and increasingly a managed society. Govermental intervention with massive social programs creates new objects of study—Affirmative Action, Head Start, Model Cities, Job Training and the like. These programs attract social research.

Glazer believes that this growing concern with problems and practice thrives most actively in the professional schools. He sees the departments remaining the citadels of the discipline and of basic theory but even they are being influenced by the perspective which characterizes the professional schools. Overall he detects a decline in attention to theory and the perfecting of the disciplines with greater attention to the real world of action. He is clearly not disturbed by this change in emphasis.

I must confess that I find Glazer's argument a little overstated but it raises some very interesting questions to which I would like to respond. If there is an increasing concern with social problems among social scientists (and I agree that there is) why is it primarily located in the professional schools? There are several plausible reasons. Many professional schools are established specifically because of an interest in practice—medicine, law, education, for example. Professional schools find it easier to build an interdisciplinary staff and therefore to be concerned with interdisciplinary problems. The professional schools do not have to conform to the specific set of values, methodologies, and theoretical dogma of any particular discipline. Career success in the professional schools depends less on one's ability to impress important gatekeepers with facility in the manipulation of disciplinary theory.

The professional schools, or at least some of them, undoubtedly offer a congenial environment for research on social problems. But this is only half the story. The social science departments, or at least many of them, are actively uncongenial to such research. They see this as applied research and there is surely no more damning word in the lexicon of the true disciplinarian than applied. Problem-oriented research is going into the professional schools and research institutes in part because the departments feel their scientific image would be compromised if they showed an interest in such activities.

Glazer teaches in a graduate school of education where he says the faculty come from the disciplines of psychology, political science, sociology, and economics, the whole range of the traditional social science departments. He states that in schools of education, city planning, criminology, and social work one increasingly finds social scientists making up the staff. I do not quarrel with this observation but it may be useful to point out that there are other professional schools where the invasion of the social scientists is hardly visible. The schools of law, for example, whose subject matter overlaps that of the social scientists at many points, have made hardly more than token efforts to bring social scientists onto their faculties. If I were to risk a generality I would suggest that those professional schools with a relatively short history of scholarly achievement will be the most likely to recruit faculty from outside disciplines rather than from their own graduates. They are likely to be less rigid in their definition of a proper faculty member and, like Avis, they may be trying harder.

Glazer believes that the departments and the professional schools are moving closer together in their interest in research on the real world. In the long term that may be happening but in the here and now one has to be impressed by the chasm which exists on some campuses between the social science departments on one side and the professional schools on the other. To take Glazer's discipline for example, I do not think it would be an exaggeration to say that the typical sociology department regards the sociologists in the education, public health, or social work faculties on their campus as well below departmental standards. They do not offer them joint appointments and they do not want to be associated in the pubic eye with them. Some of this is simple snobbishness, no doubt, but basically it comes from a traditional conviction that theoretical sociology is the true sociology and problem-oriented sociology is somehow inferior.

I believe, however, that Glazer's argument has time on its side. It seems to me very likely that the research programs of the professional schools and research institutes will continue to develop. This will depend on an increasing number of social scientists going through the conversion which Glazer says he has experienced, from primary concern with theoretical knowledge to a major interest in practical knowledge. And it depends also on the ability of Glazer and others like him to attract the best of the young social scientists into these extra-departmental appointments. I agree with Glazer that the tide is flowing in this direction.

It is not so clear to me where or how fast the departments will move. It may be that we will see a time when the most exciting research and scholarship will be going on in the professional schools and interdisciplinary research institutes. This will surely happen if the departments draw back into the historical confines of their disciplines, invoking the names of the old masters, reading from the old scrolls, while, in Glazer's felicitous phrase, "the life of society goes on far away, as if under glass."

Reply to Campbell

Campbell has suggested some cautions and qualifications in connection with my thesis on the influence of what I called the professional perspective in graduate education in the social sciences over the more narrowly disciplinary perspective. I agree with much of what he says: The theoretical has more prestige than the applied; the disciplinary has more prestige than the professional; the members of a discipline within a department named for that discipline have higher prestige than and generally look down upon the members of a discipline who work in a professional school. And the gap as well as the relative prestige is indicated by the fact that a department representing a discipline almost never has a member someone whose basic training has been in a professional field, while a professional school often, and I believe increasingly, has faculty members who have been trained in a discipline. Perhaps the gap is wider than I suggested, and the rate at which professional perspectives influence disciplinary perspectives is slower than I suggested. And yet despite the cautions and qualifications, Campbell agrees he sees something like the trend I have described. I still find compelling the fact that the kind of topics discussed in the past almost entirely in professional schools, now provide exciting subjects for disciplinary research and theory.

But I have to add some qualifications too. First, we must separate the schools of the newer professions—education, social work, city planning, public policy, business—from the great professional schools, in particular, law and medicine. Whereas the newer professions raise their prestige as they take faculty who have been trained in a discipline, rather than in a professional school or in the profession itself, this is not true of law and medicine. Thus the merging of disciplinary and professional perspectives in the great professional schools, we would expect, proceeds at a slower rate, if it proceeds at all. Second, matters differ from university to university. In some, a professional school may have as much prestige as the departments to which it is closely related. This I believe is true of the schools of public policy at the University of California at Berkeley and at Harvard, for example.

But my larger argument was that what is taken up in the professional schools is increasingly taken up as leading subjects of research and study in the disciplines, and from this point of view there is no difference between the older professional schools of high prestige and newer professional schools. Both of them provide to the social science disciplines topics for research more interesting and provocative than the internal development of the discipline itself provides. Inevitably this focusing on common issues, or some common issues, whether the organization of medical care, the role of law on social policy, the effects of education, brings the disciplines closer to the subject matter and approaches of the professional schools, even if they would not dream of adding faculty from professional backgrounds.

Graduate Education in an Age of Stasis

Laurence Veysey

It is now nearly an entire decade since the boom climate in American universities abruptly vanished.[1] The period of drastically lowered expectations has accumulated its own history. It is as if we were now able to look back on the events of 1929 and 1930 from the vantage point of 1938. However, that is a less than perfect historical analogy, since for us there is every prospect of deepening decline in the long run—what we are still far too tempted to think of as a depression, an unnatural interruption in the normal thrust of growth, is instead the likely new order of things, bound to continue for our lifetimes.

It has grown increasingly clear that all the one-time adversaries of the 1960s were wrong about the future. The radicals were, of course, enormously wrong about the readiness of American society to endure a social revolution. Liberals failed to foresee the declining impetus of their own philosophy, based upon faith in the federal government as the active promoter of social justice. And spokesmen for the imperial dream of the universities as "knowledge factories" were wrong both in their projections of an unlimited expansion of institutions and in their faith that the executive branch would increasingly rely upon their expert counsels. To be sure, that last argument retains some validity at its core, at least in such fields as weaponry and public health, but we have learned that higher education is still considered eminently suitable for long-term retrenchment despite its own desire to make itself useful.

To predict the future is far from easy, as these recent examples show. Can one be any better at it in 1978 than in 1968? Historians, diagraming the past, remain aware of the intervention of the unexpected. Mindful of such caveats, which come to me straight from the wisdom of my own academic discipline, I shall nonetheless argue that it is indeed possible to see the future more clearly from 1978 than it was in 1968. If I am wrong, like all those earlier diverse prophets of the 1960s, then I shall be happy.

The kind of future I see stretching forward even beyond the year 2000 is bright neither in terms of quantitative projections nor in the more elusive realm of public recognition of what we do. It requires, to

177

anticipate briefly, that our morale and sense of mission come not so much from the externals of size and popular applause, as from our unswerving belief in the intrinsic value of the intellectual life, whether in the raw, materialistic America of 1840, the seemingly more receptive America of 1960, or the hedonistic, tax-conscious, postindustrial America of 1980 or 2000.

Future historians will increasingly come to view the period roughly from 1958 to 1970 as a highly unusual mini-epoch, an aberration. Once again, this has to do not only with the spectacular outburst of radicalism it contained, but equally with the imperial mood of aggressive academic expansion. Further, I believe the two phenomena—seemingly so antagonistic at the time—were in fact deeply connected. The history of radicalism is peculiarly intertwined with the history of elite groups in the society, if only because radicals so often are members of the elites. Though of course without the Vietnam War radicalism might never have become so widespread, much of its temporary optimism paralleled, and may well have sprung from, the perception of the society's willingness in those years to grant a larger place to intellectual pursuits in general, wherein the mushrooming of universities played the most visible part. To drop out of society was an expansive act, born of that optimism, at a time when fears over one's ability to gain access to reasonably rewarding careers had not yet arisen. Meanwhile, the academic boom of that period appears to have had two major causes—fear of the Russians, and economic prosperity in an atmosphere that had not yet become qualified by a sense of future limits. It was thought possible to have guns, butter, and knowledge all at once, and at least the social sciences as well as the physical could promise to make an urgently needed contribution to national survival in the cold war. Even the humanities got dragged along, booming equally in graduate enrollments, though not of course in research funding. Like all booms, this one fed itself, the measure of it being that between 1960 and 1970 the share of Americans of working age boasting professional status rose from 8 to 13 percent.[2]

It is hard to take stock successfully in a period of aberration. I think the signposts, in terms of long-range trends, are much clearer now. In some respects, since 1969 or 1970, we have returned to normal, as deepseated tendencies in American culture have reasserted themselves. In other ways, the entire society has entered a genuinely new period, distinct from anything in its past. It would be inaccurate to term it a "no-growth" period, at least as yet, but the rate of growth is slowing drastically, and growth increasingly takes new forms, forms relatively uncongenial to our role as scholars and teachers, especially in the arts and basic sciences.

A major respect in which the post-1970 period constitutes a return to the classic pattern of American culture involves the nebulous but not inconsiderable area of values often called anti-intellectualism. The distrust of expertise, of fanciness of language, and of abstraction for its own sake, which was to a degree suspended in the post-Sputnik climate, surged up again in the neopopulistic mood that elected President Carter. It simply was not true, as technocratic spokesmen had tried to imply in the 1960s, that the American people had broadly been converted to a docile posture toward the role of experts of all kinds as they impinged upon their lives. Instead academics were forcibly reminded of a wide current of popular suspicion, no doubt much stronger in some parts of the country than in others, directed against them. Perhaps worse, they had to contend with a growing indifference. To the chagrin of most scientists, astrology and fundamentalism boomed. More respectable forms of irrationalism edged into the academic curriculum, often in interdisciplinary programs. And yet we must see all this in longer perspective. New challenges here mingle with very old ones. Basic scientific research has not usually been popular, or its rationale adequately comprehended, on a mass level in America. Even within the educated elite, humanistic countermovements of many sorts have consistently been present.

Recent questionings of the value of technology as distinct from science appear to strike a more genuinely novel note. Questions of land-usage have attained truly wide impact within American communities. Yet it remains to be seen whether Americans will sacrifice profit or living standard to a degree that cuts deeply into their established patterns of life, short of national emergency. Moreover, unlike the return to a greater indifference toward basic science, the hesitation over technology mounts no potential threat to the core of graduate education. It promises, to the extent that it is sustained, to shift students away from destructive fields of expertise toward others concerned with ecological values—or, perhaps in larger measure, to bring about a demand for internal redefinition of such fields as chemistry, earth sciences, civil engineering, and city planning. Attitudes may shift more greatly than numbers of experts.[3]

In the larger sense of suspicion toward science itself, popular anti-intellectualism is not among our newer worries. Since the mid-1960s we have merely returned to a condition rather more like that of 1926, when Sinclair Lewis' novel *Arrowsmith* dramatized the lack of resonance of the research ideal in America and when fundamentalism and mystical cults were also flourishing, than it is to the climate of the 1950s and early 1960s. If other factors were different, particularly the economic, than graduate schools could successfully swim against those currents as they did for most of the period since their origin. (Popular anti-intellectualism went through one previous period of rather mysterious abatement, from about 1880 to 1900, the very time when our first major graduate schools were being founded; partly a result of the new respect for Darwinian science, it was also a season when imitators of European high-cultural norms and institutions gained surprisingly uncontested influence in America, though mainly on the basis of private philanthropy rather than public appropriations.[4]) Academics, particularly those in administration, have long discovered means for enabling basic scholarship and research to continue—at private universities, by appealing to their intrinsic value, in conjunction with the social prestige conferred by the allied undergraduate operation, at many publicly supported ones, by sending up a smokescreen in which all—even the Byzantinist at the University of Wisconsin—appears to be safely utilitarian. These strategies would go on dependably working to produce expansion if money were in loose supply in a nation where everything else was also rapidly growing. Even in our present climate of tighter money and retrenchment, we can hope to count on such appeals for our basic survival.

In the future, it is only to be expected that the mood of anti-intellectualism will have its further peaks and valleys. We would be ill-advised to project the immediate atmosphere surrounding Ronald Reagan, Jimmy Carter, and Jerry Brown steadily to the year 2000. But, despite such periodic shifts in the cultural climate, I would be tempted to guess on the basis of the entire American record so far, that seasons of pronounced admiration for highly trained experts in the imaginations of ordinary voters will continue to be exceptional. So, to reiterate, when we separate anti-intellectualism from all other factors, it would appear that since 1970 we have in the main merely returned to the more usual state of affairs in our relationship to the surrounding culture, though it may seem rather different in a time of newly intensified competition for economic resources.

Quite another variable relevant to the future of graduate education needs to be brought out into the open, though it rarely is, by reversing our perspective and asking why the suspension of popular distrust of experts occurred in the 1950s and early 1960s. It would seem unquestionably true that the fortunes of the American university, and of graduate education in particular, depended at that time to a large extent on the fear of war. The urgency of the cold war produced the only major relaxation of popular anti-intellectualism since the turn of the century.[5] From this one might conclude that not war itself, but the feeling that one should rationally prepare for war, is good for universities. Periods such as the present one, when prolonged peace again becomes the general expectation, conversely might be linked with the relative inattention given to advanced training, especially no doubt in the sciences with appropriate technical applications. But I believe that this argument, when applied to the present and future, is too simple. One measure of the recently declining influence of universities may be that they are no longer so closely linked in the popular and governmental mind with national survival. Weapons research now proceeds more often outside them. A shrewder, more narrowly calculative spirit among governmental planners links preparedness with a less far-flung range of activities, more fully under the control of the government itself. The post-Sputnik mood, pouring resources into universities with abandon in the name of a defense emergency, may then after all not reveal any intrinsic connection between the universities and the threat of war, but only the more naive expansiveness of a people not yet so disillusioned about the fruits of government expenditure.

The truly central factors affecting the scope of American graduate education in the future are those having to do with the economy, the birthrate, and the degree of ability to recruit students from nontraditional sources. The first two of these are primary; the third, I shall argue, has severe limits, given the continuity of certain other long-held American values.

The economy and the birthrate are both areas in which, unlike anti-intellectualism, I believe that the period since 1970, and extending into the very long-range future, will be utterly distinct from the American experience at most earlier times.[6] Models in these key respects which in any way take off from the longer past become hopelessly obsolete. As an historian I am certainly aware of the very real danger of projecting too much of the immediate present onto the long-term span ahead, just as happened so often in the 1960s. And if the predictions I now make are proved foolish in another ten year's time, the part of me that has no real faith in such prediction will eagerly join in the headshaking that follows. But there are considerations, I believe, both with regard to the economy and the birthrate, that make it rational to say the United States is entering a genuinely different era than ever before.

This may become clearer if I digress to offer you a chronology of recent American history that is slightly unorthodox but which has come to seem persuasive to me in teaching and reflecting upon the subject, and which I think throws light upon the kind of turning point that may exist around the year 1970.

The distinction between industrial and postindustrial society, made by Daniel Bell and others, is now widely accepted.[7] While I think that Bell seriously misreads the future in terms of his optimism about the role in it to be played by experts and the institutions they foster, the underlying point remains—an important shift occurs in the history of a nation such as the United States when we move from the production-oriented stage of initial heavy industrialization to the consumption-oriented stage, marked by greater leisure and mass spending power, that we label postindustrial.

It appears to me that key criteria for the existence of a postindustrial society are the highly developed mass market, the shorter work week creating leisure, and such specific inventions as the everpresent automobile and the mass media—radio, films, and later television. If so, then I would argue, somewhat against the common wisdom, that its existence in America really begins with the 1920s. For, though the prosperity of that decade was somewhat thin, and the depression afterward temporarily gave it a major check, these several basic indicators all point to a fundamental continuity in the fabric of our lives from the 1920s forward. Most important of all, the length of the work week (in manufacturing industries) had already declined to about forty-four hours at the beginning of the 1920s and was down to its present forty hours by the early 1930s, where it has remained ever since. The short work week crucially sets the stage for a consumption orientation at all levels of the society. Again, there were 21,000,000 automobiles in America in 1929 to serve 122,000,000 Americans grouped largely into families. I see the 1920s as the first years of our own time.

I belabor this earlier history in order to argue that in many ways we have already had over half a century of experience as to what it is like to live inside a postindustrial society.[8] Past experience in a society with large amounts of time and money to spend can offer us more guidance than we often think in projecting trends for American values in the future. Further, it is likely that this far longer period can better inform our sense of the choices that postmodern Americans make than can the unusual decade following Sputnik.

What overriding lessons can we learn, then, from the behavior of Americans in the nearly sixty years during which, according to my reckoning, they have been living in a postindustrial society? The strikingly continuous theme, surely, has been the growth of hedonism—a pleasure-oriented attitude toward life. We may debate how deeply the work ethic has collapsed, or how unimaginatively Americans continue to define their private pleasures.[9] But we surely will not contest that the shift has been toward the legitimization of pleasure as its own end, at least during the major fraction of each week and year when one no longer has to be employed.

The ways in which Americans pursue pleasure become highly relevant to the prospects for graduate education. Property-oriented individualism has remained strong, based in families in the 1950s, but increasingly centered in the single male or female individual in our own day, to the point that observers such as Christopher Lasch refer to an advancing tide of narcissism in our society.[10] This individualism affects graduate education in two distinct ways. First, it suggests a deepseated unwillingness to extend tax support to esoteric pursuits during a period of worry over declining living standards. Second, on the mass level its style focuses on consumption patterns that by and large do not any longer require major new technological break-throughs. In the main, Americans enjoy—and want to go on enjoying—pleasures of a relatively homely, simple character, in which such items as alcohol, the automobile, the boat, the color television, and possibly sex loom extremely large.

For the minority who want to experience a more deliberate pattern of self-growth, psychological advice is often necessary, and the advisors require some degree of advanced training, so that clinical psychology in fact temporarily became one of the few boom areas in graduate study during the early 1970s (it leveled off after 1975).[11] And, to a lesser extent, the impulse toward self-development can lead to a desire to take courses in a wide variety of academic or semi-academic disciplines, but far more often at the undergraduate level, or in the extension programs that have already bloomed so abundantly, than in serious graduate study.[12]

Despite these exceptions, the more basic point remains, most Americans consume pleasure in forms that require neither advanced education nor further technological innovation at this point in time which would stimulate whole new areas of research. In many respects, Daniel Bell's conception of postindustrial society neglects these sustained indications of mass taste pursued upon privatistic and purely hedonistic lines, to fasten instead upon a conception of culture in the lives of an elite enmeshed in technocratic organizations.[13] It will at the very least be interesting to discover, after the 1980 census is published, whether the professional and managerial sectors of the work force have been able to sustain any further growth at the expense of lower-level occupational categories, after their enormous bloating during the 1960s. More likely, in my view, is a static or declining role for high-level functionaries, a peaking of their relative impact brought about all the sooner by their recent overproduction. An adequate definition of postindustrial society needs to take account of the great bulk of the population and its behavior over the whole of the long time span which is now available for us to study.[14]

Yet, graduate education of the most serious kind experienced its great upsurge in this same postindustrial half century, until about 1970. The turning point that seems to have been reached in 1970 involves the climate of growth, both economic and demographic. In an era when men still believed that limitless expansion lay ahead, so that even the Great Depression was considered abnormal, the growth of universities could be supported in a rather heedless spirit. Postindustrial society and its characteristic pursuits continue, but its priorities become more sharply defined when there is competition for what is now perceived to be a limited pie. Values do not change so much as they intensify. An insecure lower middle-class increasingly sets the tone of debates. It wishes at all costs to hang on to material advantages precariously gained. Arcane knowledge, once tolerated for its eventual usefulness, comes to seem like a mere luxury, especially as the pace of inventions slackens. In this altered atmosphere, even the elite loses some of its venturesomeness. It may seek solace in the irrational, like Daniel Bell in some forms of vaguely-comprehended religion.[15]

If, as I believe, postindustrial values are relatively stable, though revealing an altogether less pleasant side when the prospect of growth is suddenly removed, what then of the bedrock factors of the economy and the birthrate as we try to peer into the future? It would be falsely dramatic to call the years stretching ahead toward 2000 an era of "no-growth." Instead, what seems inescapable is a prolonged slowing of the rate of growth in America. This induces alarm in terms of previous expectations fostered in the boom years of the 1960s.

Let us begin with the basic demographic picture. Though in broad outline it may now be very familiar, it requires reiteration in any assessment such as this one. Given the present birthrate, it will take over half a century for the population of the United States literally to stand still. Moreover, the continuing immigration here of poor people from countries such as Mexico, who are not yet accustomed to birth control, adds a slight note of greater growth potential to prospects for the future.

Against this is the fact that the birthrate is still falling, if at a less rapid rate since 1973.[16] We have no idea when the decline will stop. There is no reason to believe, from the recent statistics, that today's rate is anything more than a way station along a downward path that will continue into the indefinite future. Contraceptive practice still has some distance to go in penetrating the entire social spectrum and the entire age span of possible fertility—as shown by the fact that so many poor women and teenage girls still seek abortions.[17] Hints are leaked of new technological advances in this one area that promise to make contraception still easier than at present.

However, with contraception already so widely in vogue, the voluntary decisions of couples as to their desired family size become still more relevant. The baby boom of the period after World War II was basically produced by such a rush toward large families. The present low birthrate is the result of contrary attitudes. It is notoriously difficult to predict in this area. The baby boom was not foreseen. Third world countries present a variety of results, at least in degree, which are probably not too relevant to the United States. What makes me expect that, for the next long period of time, the birthrate will continue to fall even lower, rather than flattening out or rising again, is the current trend, especially powerful in the college-going middle class, toward emphasizing the individual human being, not any longer the stable family unit, as the focal point for one's aspirations in life. Thus marriage rates have declined in recent years as well as birthrates, while divorces rise. As more women want careers of their own, they often decide to postpone, and perhaps ultimately abandon, childbearing. For both men and women, children come to be seen as at least partial encumbrances, though not always abstractly rejected or disliked. From all this, I see still fewer children being born in the future than now, especially at upper-income levels of the society, which, of course, furnish the major market for graduate school attendance. Moreover, if economic anxiety is added to the mix, further incentives toward a still lower birthrate will be present, in this case of the same kind as greatly lowered it during the 1930s.

The state of the economy may well prove to be rather more volatile in the future than the birthrate. Changes in taste in the existing population, even within the overall context of hedonistic continuities, may be sufficient to spark new booms in some areas, even as other industries long thought to be economic mainstays (steel, to our recent shock) decline in the short-term. The economy is not of a single piece, and it may have some very bright spots in it for a very long time to come.

But we must face the fact that the United States is now an old industrial power, without the benefit of having had its plant destroyed during the Second World War. It faces increasing competition from countries like Japan, where much lower wage levels are accepted. And, as we all know, the energy situation threatens to cut ever deeper into our living standard as time passes. The automobile, deeply entrenched in that notion of an adequate way of life, is the evil temptress of our age. As more and more money is spent on scarcer supplies of petroleum and natural gas, while real income levels no longer advance in general, it is hard to envision a regaining of the economic expansiveness of the 1960s which produced the almost careless willingness to spend large amounts on higher education.

Of course at some point in the growing scarcity of energy will come a sudden willingness to seek alternative technologies on a truly massive scale, and some of these may swell advanced-level study once again in certain highly specific areas. But the general effect of all this is more reasonably to be seen as a deepening impulse toward cost saving in most areas of education, including most sectors of the graduate school. If the automobile is defined as basic to American life, the study of history, English, or even psychology at an advanced level is going to be regarded by most persons as a relative frill if there is no longer believed to be sufficient money for everything. This does not mean that graduate education literally disappears, any more than it does now in New York City, only that it can be expected to endure prolonged hard times until, if ever, the atmosphere of crisis dissipates.

Recently there has been an effort to find relief from the limitations imposed by the birthrate and the economy—and to present a more broadly democratic appearance at the same time—by seeking to recruit graduate students from wider sectors of the population than in the past, in terms of age, sex, social class, and ethnicity. Presumably we all favor such forms of outreach, while possibly disagreeing over the appropriateness of particular means to obtain it. My only concern here is with the question of how greatly such efforts are likely to modify the bleak enrollment picture presented by the economy and the birthrate. Wider demand would certainly enable universities to make a far more effective case in seeking sustenance.[18] In brief, I believe that such a deliberate broadening of recruitment will have only minor effects on the overall aggregate. Blacks equaled 5.99 percent of the national graduate enrollment in 1976; women rose from 35.5 percent in 1970 to 40.8 percent in 1976.[19] If blacks and women were represented in graduate enrollments in proportion to their share in the national population, the number of blacks would double and the number of women would rise less than 10 percent.[20] This would not cause the total number of graduate students in this country to mushroom enormously. Moreover, the effort to improve school systems so that disadvantaged persons can realistically conceive of attending college and graduate school appears to have slackened in recent years, as cost consciousness and tacit indifference to social injustice have prevailed.[21] A renewal of the brief zeal of the 1960s in these respects seems hard to prophesy, especially if the economy remains riddled with anxieties. In the absence of an enormous campaign, deep-seated obstacles very much present in American culture and in the existing peer-group youth cultures of specific ethnic groups and classbound sectors of the population—these last having to do with certain kinds of ambition in life—are strongly apt to go on prevailing. In sum, the great bulk of graduate students will probably continue to come from advantaged groups in the population. And, though figures seem lacking, it is hard to believe that the influx of markedly older students will assume gigantic proportions in the basic disciplines. They are, at any rate, a source that can be used only once.

Finally, attendance at graduate school is limited by the pool of college graduates. Interest in or ability to attend college has been declining in proportion to the population in recent years. The share of eighteen- and nineteen-year-olds who have completed a year of college fell from 13.6 percent in 1970 to 10.9 percent in 1977, despite a countervailing rise of .3 percent among women.[22] Perhaps those youth not now choosing to go to college are not the sort who would in any event have gone to graduate school. But the fact remains that, if this trend continues, fewer people relative to the population will be available as a source for recruitment, and this may cancel out other kinds of efforts at wider outreach.

Graduate education, because it deals with a relatively young age group, has felt the effects of the new post-1970 phase within postindustrialism more rapidly than the commercial sectors of the economy.[23] In the fall of 1976 graduate enrollments in America, including all fields, both applied and basic, for the first time entered the period of literal "no-growth."[24] Yet, in deference to the many imponderables of the economy as a whole, I have avoided that phrase in titling these remarks and have chosen instead, with some care, the word stasis to describe the period we are now living in and which may be expected to continue. The most relevant dictionary definition for stasis is "a slackening of the blood current, as in passive congestion." The current flows on. The slackening is relative to what had gone on before. The congestion is due to the effort to maintain institutional structures at something like the artificial boom level of the 1960s, despite an already greatly reduced demand for degreeholders in most areas of study.

In very brief compass, I have tried to examine the major cultural and material factors which might affect the size and resources of graduate education in America over the next substantial period of time. I have projected a model of American society which differs from the past in the crucial respects of degree of economic growth and population rise, but one which posits continuities in the attitude of indifference or suspicion toward advanced abstract learning and, to a crucial degree, sadly, in the willingness to go to extraordinary lengths to open up realistic opportunity to the great share of the population now seldom inclined toward graduate school.[25] An increasingly anxious and unhappy majority may well, in this new and far more static phase of American history, fall back on traditional values that are among the least lovely aspects of the national inheritance. Hedonism, the desire to protect one's living standard, seems likely to outstrip every other consideration. At least this is the quite gloomy view of one historian who has been asked to look at the future.

A further important trend has already revealed itself within graduate education during the 1970s. This is the relative decline of the arts and sciences within the total mix of fields, and the ever-growing share of enrollments in applied programs of various kinds, even if many applied fields have now also peaked numerically.[26] Every indication is that fields identified with basic scholarship and research will go on declining, and do so, moreover, at a rate faster than the applied fields.[27] Morale may suffer unduly in such a situation, which makes it appear that not just the larger culture, but the educational institutions themselves, give increasingly less attention to basic research.

And yet a rational response to recent enrollment figures in the arts and sciences must be that they have not declined nearly enough. Between 1970 and 1976, the annual numbers of graduate students in these areas dropped only 10 to 14 percent. In other words, we are still today producing graduate students, year by year, at 85 to 90 percent of the level at the peak of the artificial boom period, and at a time when there is close to zero demand for Ph.D.'s in some of the humanistic disciplines. After most of a decade in which to comprehend our true situation, we have scarcely begun to adjust to reality, in terms of the magnitude of overproduction.

I wish to make it plain that I am not advocating a reduction in enrollments tailored to estimates of the job market. To do this would crassly eliminate the individual's sense of choice as to aspiration in life; besides, it would just about destroy the disciplines. A reasonable goal, as one scans the figures given in table 1, might be to reduce enrollments to something like their 1960 level in each field. This would mean lopping off well over half of all our present arts and sciences graduate students. Let us face the fact that we could perform this surgery without by any means killing the patient. Instead, we would be converting to a leaner type of operation geared to far higher expectations of quality.

Against the force of all the trends that have been discussed, there is only one real recourse. That is to continue to take an intrinsic satisfaction in what we do. Having stared coolly at our prospects, we should turn around and count our many blessings. We do not face extinction. Even if, slowly or more rapidly, we returned to the numerical scale of 1960, we would be enjoying one of the most favorable settings in world history for the pursuit of science and humane scholarship. If we allow ourselves to be demoralized by this sort of change in climate, we will be part and parcel of the atmosphere of clinging to recently won pleasures which I reluctantly believe will dominate the larger population in America.

What I suggest is that, despite everything, we should simply reaffirm the worth and the excitement of what we do. The psychologist Nevitt Sanford, recently reminiscing about changes in graduate education since the 1930s, pointed to an unwholesome tone of careerism, without larger intellectual perspectives, during the boom years. Then he speculated:

> It may be possible to take advantage of the present phase of retrenchment in moving toward some needed reconstruction. Since it is now clear that ... advanced degrees are no guarantee of bigger jobs, it may be possible to revive interest in more fundamental goals of education. ... It ought to be possible, at a time when the problem of numbers of students is not so great, to conceive and plan for a career in graduate school that is broadening and humanizing, and in the course of which students learn a variety of skills and values needed for intellectual leadership.[28]

A similar call for a cleansing operation, as a response to retrenchment, was made several years ago by the historian Lawrence Stone.[29] In the metaphor of stasis, such an operation may help to unblock the flow of our genuine lifeblood. We should return to our primary concern for intrinsic quality. This means not succumbing to

TABLE 1. Enrollment for Master's and Doctor's Degrees, by Field of Study, United States and Outlying Areas, Fall 1960 to Fall 1976

Field of Study	1960	1965	1970	1972	1974	1975	1976
All fields	314,349	535,332	816,207	858,580	965,000	1,053,769	1,030,007
Agriculture and natural resources	5,493	8,039	10,432	11,322	12,601	14,674	15,206
Architecture and environmental design	585	1,085	5,433	7,240	9,208	10,231	10,128
Area studies	669	1,412	2,262	4,016	4,198	4,165	4,091
Biological sciences	14,775	27,165	36,499	38,914	42,518	44,157	43,957
Business and management	25,342	50,920	87,487	98,762	123,387	144,953	149,976
Communications	868	1,190	2,503	6,153	8,108	9,315	8,791
Computer and information sciences	(a)	816	7,937	8,826	10,379	10,856	11,852
Education	94,993	150,300	257,605	275,053	327,113	349,087	324,475
Engineering	36,636	57,516	64,788	56,006	56,037	59,402	57,330
Fine and applied arts	6,287	12,539	19,858	24,890	28,016	30,708	30,222
Foreign languages	5,903	13,001	18,567	16,796	14,618	13,891	12,808

190

Health professions	5,842	8,909	14,242	23,692	30,378	35,463	38,101
Home economics	1,580	2,358	4,611	5,336	6,693	7,664	8,085
Law	1,651	2,465	2,533	2,870	3,493	3,604	3,586
Letters	18,228	35,214	51,167	49,382	48,132	46,464	43,982
Library science	1,360	8,567	12,416	13,554	14,395	14,731	13,307
Mathematics	11,770	20,198	22,672	19,238	16,739	16,168	14,926
Physical sciences	25,707	36,506	40,113	36,047	34,936	35,497	36,147
Psychology	10,677	15,551	25,342	29,157	32,794	35,318	35,363
Public affairs and services	8,235	13,465	19,671	28,272	40,588	47,711	53,032
Social sciences	28,373	53,284	76,805	73,207	72,505	71,213	67,128
Theology	5,314	7,028	7,194	10,334	12,558	15,222	16,791
Interdisciplinary studies	4,061	7,804	26,070	19,513	15,606	33,275	30,723

Source: United States, Department of Health, Education and Welfare, National Center for Education Statistics, reports on *Students Enrolled for Advanced Degrees.*
Note: Data for 1960 exclude students enrolled for first-professional degrees, including some master's degrees in such fields as business and commerce, education, library science, and social work. Data for subsequent years include all students enrolled for master's and doctor's degrees.
  a. data not available

the temptation, in a buyer's market, of tailoring the education to fit the prescientific or preaesthetic world views of more casually motivated students. It means preferring to reduce numbers rather than to welcome all stray comers in order to maintain them. In this connection, we should be indifferent to the collapse of entire graduate programs at universities of low or middling caliber.[31] We should in some respects actually welcome the decline in numbers and resources, though humanely aware of the personal costs to faculty who find themselves caught in the reductions. We should expect that we shall become an increasingly smaller part of the American scene, as it continues along its pleasure-dominated course but moves into a less expansive phase.

But the absolute base, gained during the quiet years of the 1950s and the turbulent ones of the 1960s, remains in existence, especially at our high-quality institutions, both private and public. If we provide an example of maintaining or improving quality in apparent decline, our memory ought to prove an inspiration to at least some of the very long-term survivors of events, such as those in international relations, which it is still less easy to predict.

NOTES

1. For very helpful readings of this essay, I thank Alan Richards and David Riesman. This essay was written in early 1978, and I now (1980) believe that it is too optimistic, especially its last pages. I was not aware then of the extent to which high-quality students are declining to continue on to the Ph.D. in liberal arts fields at major institutions. Low numbers of good students, rather than the high numbers of graduate students carried forward on the books, now seem to me to be the real problem.

2. This is my own calculation from the United States censuses of 1960 and 1970, counting only Americans of both sexes between the ages of twenty-five and sixty-four, and using the census' definition of professional occupations. By comparison, figured similarly, the share of this age group in the professions advanced only from 4.4 percent to 8 percent in the entire forty-year span from 1920 to 1960. Thus, even by the general standards of growth in the professions assumed by the model of a postindustrial society, the decade of the 1960s reveals an unnaturally bloated character, which demographic and economic trends since 1970 bring into still sharper relief.

3. Enrollment figures by fields through the fall of 1976 show a doubling of graduate students in architecture and environmental design between 1970 and 1975, then no change from 1975 to 1976, suggesting the numerical boom there may already be over, while the number of engineering students (of all kinds) decreased 14 percent from 1970 to 1972, then remained just about

constant through 1976. See United States Department of Health, Education and Welfare, National Center for Education Statistics, *Digest of Education Statistics, 1979* (Washington, D.C.: Government Printing Office, 1979), p. 96, table 90.

4. See Laurence Veysey, *The Emergence of the American University* (Chicago: University of Chicago Press, 1965), pp. 14–18, 263–68; Laurence Veysey, "The Plural Organized Worlds of the Humanities," in *The Organization of Knowledge in American Society, 1860–1920*, edited by Alexandra M. Oleson and John Voss (Baltimore: Johns Hopkins University Press, 1979).

5. The brief flurry of attention given to "brain trust" experts at the start of the New Deal produced little institutional impact within the academic community, and it brought forth a rapid counterreaction against planning-oriented experts, highly visible and in many respects successful by 1935–38. David Riesman informs me of the considerable tolerance for basic research within such organizations as the United States Navy during the early cold war.

6. The birthrate fell sharply in the 1930s, but it has been dropping steadily beneath those earlier historic lows ever since 1965. After a brief very temporary halt around the year 1970, the decline plunged at a much quickened rate in the years 1970 to 1973, into depths never before seen. The rate of decline slackened from 1973 to 1976, and the decline fluctuated in 1977 and 1978, but the current rate is nearly the lowest in history. See United States, Department of Commerce, Bureau of the Census, *Current Population Reports: Population Characteristics: Population Profile of the United States, 1978*, series P-20, no. 336 (Washington, D.C.: Government Printing Office, April 1979), table 3. Still more recent reports in 1980 show a halt in the decline.

7. Daniel Bell, *The Coming of Post-Industrial Society* (New York: Basic Books, 1973), and *The Cultural Contradictions of Capitalism* (New York: Basic Books, 1975). The idea was already apparent in Walt W. Rostow, *The Stages of Economic Growth* (Cambridge: Cambridge University Press, 1960) and in David Riesman et al., *The Lonely Crowd* (New Haven: Yale University Press, 1950).

8. Even the 1930s, seemingly so opposite, showed surprisingly little change in terms of these indicators of a postindustrial society. Gasoline consumption declined only very briefly around 1932–33 before it started rising again. The media (radio and the movies) were growth industries during the otherwise bleak 1930s. The work week did not lengthen. And, interestingly, the Lynds reported in their study of Muncie, Indiana, in 1935 that there was no decline in hedonistic values or sexual freedom there as a result of the depression, no return to puritanism. See Robert S. and Helen Merrill Lynd, *Middletown in Transition* (New York: Harcourt, Brace and Co., 1935), pp. 170, 267. Daniel Bell identifies these kinds of long-term changes with the 1920s, yet elsewhere says that "a post-industrial society . . . is only now beginning to emerge"; see *The Cultural Contradictions of Capitalism*, pp. 74–75, 198. David Riesman, in commenting on a draft of this paper, affirms: "We are still an industrial society which has become in its attitudes and values post-industrial before we can afford it in a world economy."

9. See Tibor Scitovsky, *The Joyless Economy* (New York: Oxford University Press, 1976).

10. Christopher Lasch, *The Culture of Narcissism* (New York: Norton, 1979); Henry Malcolm, *Generation of Narcissus* (Boston: Little, Brown, 1971).

11. Graduate enrollment in the field of psychology grew by 29 percent in the period 1970–75 (most of the growth taking place in the clinical side of the discipline, not the side devoted to basic research). It then remained almost exactly unchanged from 1975 to 1976. See note 3.

12. For vivid indications of contemporary popular taste in adult extension-type courses, see the *New York Times*, January 26, 1978. The graduate school is seldom a suitable place for their exercise.

13. E.g., see Daniel Bell, "Toward the Great Instauration: Reflections on Culture and Religion in a Postindustrial Age," *Social Research*, 42 (1975): 385–86. In *The Cultural Contradictions of Capitalism*, Bell worries enormously over hedonism but exaggerates its imaginativeness on the mainstream level and the links between it and the artistic avant-garde; his extreme denunciations have the odd effect of lending it more glamor than it has really very often possessed.

14. A book far more relevant to the gaining of such understanding, to my mind, as it involves ordinary taxpayers, is Lillian B. Rubin, *Worlds of Pain* (New York: Basic Books, 1976). The work of the sociologist Herbert Gans is also highly relevant.

15. Bell, op. cit., pp. 412–13.

16. See note 6.

17. Though the birthrate for blacks has fallen as sharply in recent years as that for whites, it remains above the white birthrate at present. We should expect it to drop even more sharply until it merges into the white rate. For recent statistics on the rise of teenage pregnancies, see the *New York Times*, January 31, 1978.

18. Entirely different issues are raised regarding admissions to a few highly sought-after fields, such as law, or to a wider range of fields in high-quality institutions, where there is still intense competition for places. Those issues have to do with the balancing of concerns for intellectual merit and social justice. The present discussion, looking macrocosmically at the longer future, assumes what is likely to be far commoner—a shortage of qualified students, at least relative to established expectations.

19. United States, Department of Health, Education and Welfare, National Center for Education Statistics, *Fall Enrollment in Higher Education, 1976: Final Report* (Washington, D.C.: Government Printing Office, 1978), table 11, p. 55; table 29, p. 181.

20. Indeed, probably less, as women have in all likelihood continued to advance in their proportion of enrollment since these figures.

21. According to some figures, the proportion of blacks attending college has very recently declined again, at least in integrated institutions.

22. *New York Times*, December 15, 1977.

23. In addition, most economic activity depends upon the repeated con-

sumption of items by individuals. But a Ph.D. degree is usually received by a given person only once.

24. *Digest of Education Statistics, 1979,* p. 96, table 90; see also table 1 in this article. From 1970 to 1975, the arts and sciences had already begun to decline, but growth in the applied fields more than balanced them. Now the applied fields themselves have become highly spotty in this respect—education declining while business still grows slightly—producing for the first time a slight overall decline.

25. A very low birthrate in the established middle class, along with continuing inflow of population from cultures whose members cannot mainly envision an advanced education (such as Mexico's), may, in the absence of any special effort to bring members of disadvantaged groups into the better sectors of higher education, result over time in an actual narrowing of the effective base within the national population from which graduate students are recruited.

26. Another kind of shift that had been feared, away from high-quality institutions toward those of lower quality, did not occur at least by 1973, according to a careful national study. David W. Breneman, *Graduate School Adjustments to the "New Depression" in Higher Education* (Washington, D.C.: National Board on Graduate Education, 1975), pp. 13, 23–24, 35, 41, 76.

27. The biological sciences constitute a distinct exception, growing in enrollment 17 percent between 1970 and 1976. Concerning the apparent exception of psychology, see note 11.

28. Nevitt Sanford, "Graduate Education Then and Now," *American Psychologist* 31 (1976): 762.

29. Lawrence Stone, "The AHA and the Job Market for Graduate Students," *AHA Newsletter,* March 1972, pp. 26–27.

30. Interdisciplinary programs are no great intrinsic panacea since they vary so much in quality. The overwhelming bulk of the intellectual vitality present in American graduate schools lies within the established disciplines. Yet there are genuine cases (for instance, in fields like social philosophy or the history of ideas) where recognized student interests on a high level are not adequately served by existing departments at most institutions.

31. I have acted on this premise in consistently working for the abandonment of the Ph.D. program in history at my own institution, and we have now done so. I must acknowledge that my position on graduate school enrollments is inevitably affected by my location, uniquely among the American authors of these papers, at an institution which has no large existing stake in the maintenance of high numbers of graduate students.

Comments on Pusic and Veysey by Dorothy Harrison

Before opening the discussion on Pusic's and Veysey's papers, let me pursue a bit further the implications which some of the social and economic factors we've mentioned will have on the future of graduate education.

Over the long run, say the next fifty years, the United States population will probably stabilize, in sharp contrast to the steady growth which has characterized our history. We have seen a change begin; its effect is now being felt in the high schools. The number of high school graduates reached its peak in 1976. In 1990 it will decline to about the number of 1960.

A decline in the rate of growth of the American economy is also likely over the next half-century and it is a major factor in long-range planning. The rate of growth of productivity is likely to decline, because those segments of our economy which have increased productivity the most in the past are becoming increasingly less important.

Manufacturing, which has made up about 30 percent of the American economy, has generally remained stable, even with the introduction of automation. In contrast, agriculture increased its productivity spectacularly over the past seventy-five years. At the end of the nineteenth century, one-half of the population of the United States engaged in agriculture. Today, only about 4 percent of the population is able to produce enough to feed us all. Even if agricultural productivity were to double in the next generation, it would release no more than 2 percent of the work force. Thus, the spectacular productivity increases in agriculture have reduced it to an insignificant element in the economy.

The probability of slowdown in the American economy, then, with the declining importance of capital-intensive segments and the increasing importance of labor-intensive segments like the service industries seems pretty high over the next half century. There simply is not much opportunity for increases in productivity in these fields.

Over the past twenty-five years, we have reduced poverty in this country by about 50 percent. That is, the percentage of families with incomes below $3,000, below $5,000, and below $7,000, in constant 1972 dollars, was cut in half between 1947 and 1972. The percentage of families with incomes over $15,000 was quadrupled during the same period. However, we accomplished this by increases in productivity, not by any relative redistribution of wealth. The relative distribution of income today is almost exactly what it was twenty-five years ago. Declining productivity will make it impossible to advance further in this way.

You can see what all this means for tax revenues at all levels of government. In combination with a steadily aging population, which will seek a higher proportion of available resources committed to services for the elderly, the prospects for commitment of resources to education and other areas traditionally seen as serving youth are bleak.

While our graduate institutions can produce skilled manpower, they cannot create the demand for it. The Catch 22 situation which former President Gerald Ford described in his 1974 Ohio State address—you keep going back for more degrees to be competitive in the job market and when you have the doctorate you're told you're over qualified—is one we're all quite familiar with. What then are we to do?

Professor Veysey would have us confront this problem by eliminating all but first-rate programs and thereby the number of over-qualified people.

In a national study of graduate education in the humanities that I've been working on with Ernest May and Lew Solmon, we conclude that it is simply out of the question that numbers of Ph.D.'s will diminish to match the number of college teaching jobs or jobs which are designed to encourage independent research in a scholarly field.

The reasons are many. Some of them are crass. Universities have developed undergraduate programs that assume and depend upon a constant influx of cheap labor in the form of graduate teaching assistants. Some are idealistic. Were the graduate student population to be cut back to numbers matching the numbers of respective academic jobs, training would simply cease in some specialties. And in many fields, whatever the job market, students will continue to come.

Thus, for the long and short run, the best universities in the country will be producing more Ph.D.'s than traditional markets can absorb. We estimate that all jobs in English, including those in all community colleges, during the 1980s could be filled by the Ph.D.'s that will issue from fifteen institutions. All jobs in philosophy could be filled by the products of ten institutions; all jobs in history by the products of six institutions: Columbia, Wisconsin, Harvard, Berkeley, Chicago, and Yale, leaving no jobs for Ph.D.'s from Michigan, Stanford, Penn, Princeton, Cornell, Duke, Johns Hopkins, etc. We estimate, in fact, that from elite institutions such as those just named, five out of six Ph.D.'s in the humanities will not find academic employment. From less prestigious and less well-connected universities, nine out of ten Ph.D.'s will not find academic jobs.

If we're right about these numbers, and I believe they err on the high side, then we haven't the choice of simply contracting and continuing as before; we may have to explore, as Pusic suggests, new ways of increasing impact and connecting graduate education with the transmission-creation of the goals and values of future societies.

Questions and Answers

Q1: A brand-new unpublished study, done at the University of Michigan, projects a much more optimistic picture than yours concerning undergraduate enrollments in the 1980s. The argument runs that we should not simply count the numbers produced by the birth rate in raw terms, but take into account the following three factors: (1) more parents with college educations will be present in the mix, making youth more prone to attend college than in the past; (2) more youth will come from small families, which will give their parents greater financial resources to send them to college; (3) there will be more older students than in the past. Taken together, these factors are projected to cancel out the 25 percent decline expected in the raw age cohort. How would you respond to that?

A: Let's take these arguments in turn. The first one, the greater number of parents with college educations in the future, seems formidable. But if so, why shouldn't this factor already be noticeable in the recent past? The enormous boom in college enrollments occurred in the period of the G.I. Bill after World War II, and the children of these parents were attending college from 1965 onward. Yet, as I pointed out, the proportion of the population going to college declined noticeably between 1970 and 1977. It may be that more and more children are making these decisions independent of their parents. The second argument about smaller families seems far-fetched, especially in a period of economic anxiety and rising complaint about the cost of college education. The third argument about older students is really analogous to a change in a tax collection date designed to produce the impression of new income. You can only use this device once. Moreover, in literal terms, it seems doubtful that an enormous flood of older students will descend upon the university, above and beyond their numbers in recent years.

But let's suppose that these arguments are valid, and that college enrollments will not decline in the 1980s. At most, the authors of this study project a static enrollment situation over that decade, not a rise. And static enrollments will not create more demand for Ph.D.'s in the arts and sciences.

To sum up, it seems that there has been considerable playing with figures to produce the more optimistic picture in the new study that has been cited. Howard Bowen's more optimistic paper, elsewhere in this volume, likewise admits that its projections are very "iffy." Meanwhile, Dorothy Harrison's statistics are more devastatingly negative than my own. I would of course like to be proved wrong.

Q2(Pusic): Your analysis of American culture relies heavily on the concept of hedonism, which is, of course, extremely broad, perhaps indeed so vague as to be nearly meaningless for analytical purposes. Could you comment on this?

A: Philosophers such as Jeremy Bentham who promoted the idea of hedonism of course did so in such a sweeping way that the pursuit of pleasure became synonymous with all behavior. I mean to employ the term in a more popular, everyday sense, as the pursuit of immediate pleasure, at the expense of deferred gratification. Attendance at college, and especially at graduate school, is one of the most striking cases of the prolonged deferment of gratification. It means willingness to sacrifice for years and years. Now, of course the popularity of medical schools shows that, for the promise of a very high reward later on, many people will still make such a sacrifice. So, in a lesser way, does the continued high level of college enrollment. I do not deny all this. I simply question whether the broadest trend in our society is toward increasing sacrifice of this and other kinds, or whether it runs in the opposite direction. And I do believe that, although the concept of hedonism is indeed vague when it is pressed to the point of an ultimate or universal psychological principle, it is meaningful in contrast to an ethic of work and sacrifice.

Q3: Historically, have there been any successful attempts by universities to take the offensive and influence the values of the society to get themselves out of the bind imposed by such social pressures as anti-intellectualism?

A: I'm convinced that in a few important cases, at least, universities have indeed directly influenced the values of the larger society. One such case is the anthropological message on the scientific worth of racist theories and beliefs.

But take another instance which lies closer to our present concerns, namely, the role of universities in influencing Americans to trust in the benign power of the federal bureaucracy to tackle and solve a host of social problems, such as those besetting our cities. For decades the social science departments within universities have been spreading a liberal message of this kind. Yet the last ten years have seen a great turning away from this faith in the role of the federal government as an active agent promoting social justice. Instead there is rising tax-consciousness and mounting cynicism about our ability to win wars on poverty and other evils. The universities appear to have lost this crucial battle in the attempt to influence public opinion.

With this mixed record, I certainly wouldn't advocate defeatism. A soberly realistic evaluation of our box score should spur us to greater efforts. We must continue to try to convert people to a more positive view of well-grounded expertise and, more basically, we must work for a return to the belief that it is worthwhile to expend effort in programs that help people. It may be that we are only experiencing a brief conservative season at present, and that after 1980 there will be a resurgence of the liberal faith. Much depends on the state of the economy.

Institutional Policy Setting:
A Dynamic View

William F. Miller

When I first came into my present office, I had, sitting on my desk, a self-composed aphorism which said: "The substance of the University is contained within the processes by which we do our business." I left it out for awhile, but before long put it away because it was too cryptic to explain itself and my visitors thought I was more interested in process than in substance. I am interested in decision making in both the processes and the criteria. I shall go a step further: I believe that it is absolutely essential that we think of the processes for decision making together with the criteria, for one without the other will leave us organizationally sterile or impotent—sterile if the criteria fail us, impotent if the processes fail us.

There are two primary reasons why attention to the processes as well as the criteria of academic decision making is very important. First, in a very complex world, the ability to get an issue decided and the credibility with which one gets the issue decided may become as important as the decision itself. Second, we are in a very dynamic, rapidly changing world. Even if the present rate of change of institutional and social needs slows down, I still foresee a world in which the periods of change are short, compared with the professional lifetimes of our university graduates. In order to accommodate to this rate of change, in the words of Eric Ashby,[1] "Universities therefore have to strike a balance between an adaptation which is too pliable and an adherence to tradition which is too inflexible. To achieve this balance, universities need to initiate and control their adaptation to society, not to allow it to be imposed on them from outside." The processes of decision making are of paramount importance in maintaining this balance between adaptation and adherence to tradition.

The university enterprise is a derivative of societal needs and higher education itself constitutes one of those societal needs. Eric Ashby, in discussing the forces that shape a university, identifies four:

1. Interlogic, by which he means faculty interests and the needs and forces of academic disciplines;

2. Student needs and student interests;
3. Manpower needs of society; and
4. Patron interests, be they public or private.

These forces have always been present to some extent. However, today they are more obvious, for two reasons: the increased prominence of higher education, and the greater emphasis on accountability of all our institutions. Higher education has always been an adaptive system responding to society, but in today's world it has become so important to the economic life of the country that societal forces are keenly felt. I believe that it is perfectly clear to all of us that universities today cannot be driven entirely by their own interlogics. On the other hand, the reason that most of us are gathered here today is that we believe that we should not be simply buffeted around by societal needs and interests. Therefore, I conclude that institutional policy needs to be shaped by processes and criteria which bring together the interforces within a university as well as societal forces acting upon the university.

In dealing with change, in response to society, there are two issues. First, how does one prepare students (and here we speak principally of graduate students) for a changing world at any given time? And second, how do institutions change over time to accommodate new interests and new needs while at the same time preserving the important and best from the old programs?

There are three kinds of changes for which our students must be prepared. The first are those changes within their own disciplines—that is, the introduction of new methodologies, new paradigms, or new frontier problems. Our traditional practices of sabbatical and other leaves of absence, faculty seminars, combined with the pressures and challenges within a discipline, deal with this issue in a reasonably adequate way. The disciplines have been developing for centuries by these more or less traditional practices, and although change is much more rapid today in many disciplines, compared with the lifetime of a researcher, what simply may be called for is a more frequent utilization of the leave opportunity than in the past.

There are two other areas of career change for which our traditional practices do not prepare us. There often arise associated new problems within a discipline where the new problems themselves do not have their origins in that particular discipline. For example, engineers and physical scientists now have to deal with issues of environmental protection in order to practice their professions, and medical research scientists now have to deal with issues of public

health and human subjects in order to carry out many of their research activities. In order for scientists to deal adequately with these
problems, they must develop the understandings of the social scientists, including lawyers; conversely, social scientists and lawyers, working on these broader social issues, must develop considerable understanding of the scientific and technical implications of various
projects.

There is a third, more dramatic, change involved when individuals make whole new career changes. This might occur when new
career opportunities become available if the individual feels prepared
to make that change. New needs in government or industry might
provide such opportunities or, on the other hand, a subject area may
be playing itself out, becoming less interesting to an individual so that
there is a motivation to seek new career opportunities. Such changes
require rather new skills and understandings, as well as confidence in
one's ability to exercise those skills and capitalize on those understandings. This is a more dramatic change than the second category
simply because in that area one can often call upon colleagues for help
but a new career requires the personal exercise of new skills and
understandings which is more demanding.

The most important opportunity for preparing graduate students for a changing world comes during their undergraduate education. I firmly believe that a liberal education is a very practical education, and that a liberal education during the undergraduate years
does more to prepare an individual for facing new issues, new demands, new environments, than anything we can do during the
graduate years. By liberal education I mean an education which prepares the mind for unfettered inquiry into new ideas, based on the
solid understanding of old ideas.

I see the tight link and the essential character of undergraduate
education as preparation for graduate education and beyond. Professional school faculties are more accepting of this notion than the
faculties of the traditional academic disciplines. The professional
school faculties have not yet taken much serious action on this issue,
but there is discussion across the country on the prerequisites for
professional school admission, especially in the medical schools.

I am not suggesting here that the undergraduate should not have
the opportunity to major in some disciplinary area, but a four-year
curriculum provides sufficient opportunity for a student to acquire a
solid liberal education, as well as sufficient preprofessional training or
preparation in an academic discipline as a major. A change in the
prerequisites for admission to professional and graduate schools

could stem the trend toward more and deeper preprofessional and discipline training and could turn attention back toward interest and understanding of the ideas and culture of our society.

A signal from the professional and graduate schools that this was an important prerequisite for admission would not only indicate to students that they should devote more time to those parts of the curriculum that contribute to a liberal education, but also that they should engage in those studies with seriousness of purpose and thought—and not view them as unfortunate university breadth requirements that are imposed upon every undergraduate.

Beyond the undergraduate program, there are some opportunities within the professional graduate schools to contribute to better preparation for a changing world. At Stanford University, there is no universal language requirement at the institutional level. Some departments and schools require one foreign language, but many have no foreign language prerequisite for the awarding of the Ph.D. I suggest that in earlier days requirements outside the discipline were considered normal and important. This would suggest that one might adopt a program which is probably still common in some institutions, that in addition to the major subject area of Ph.D. research, the student must include some minor area of study. Additionally, one might include courses in public policy. For instance, it may make sense to have all engineering students take a course in environmental law. I am sure that there are many cases where academic departments are at least encouraging such broader studies, if not actually requiring them. This is not a very radical idea. In fact, it is simply an adaptation of the earlier notion that there were tools and understandings beyond one's own discipline that were important for the development of a research scholar.

Beyond the provision for broader understanding while in graduate school, we need to provide specialized opportunities for renewal and change in the postgraduate years. There seems to be a plethora of opportunity for short courses, long seminars, and for continuing postgraduate education, but whether or not these opportunities are adequately serving the purpose of preparing our professionals and scholars for change I'm not prepared to say. There seem to be opportunities and a rather public acceptance of capitalizing on those opportunities may be sufficient to deal with that issue.

Some of the processes and criteria employed in our decision making at Stanford University, develop the social functions derived from both the interlogic and interinstitutional needs of disciplines in faculty as well as from those external forces in society working on the institution. Many institutions follow very similar processes and have very similar criteria to Stanford's, but perhaps these processes have been refined to a point uncommon at other institutions. Even more to the point, we have a program for articulation to the various constituencies on the basis of decision making—that is, the criteria and the processes, in such a way that we have developed confidence and credibility of our various constituencies—students, faculty, staff, trustees, and patrons of the institution. Decision making is surely an imperfect art and mistakes are made; furthermore, not everyone agrees with our conclusions. However, within the University and the faculties and the alumni and patron constituencies that there is a substantial understanding that we have reached our decision by rational thought and that our decisions are based on informed judgments, even though any given individual may have come to a different conclusion.

The processes and criteria for decision making have to serve two purposes; first, the administration and implementation of academic policy, and second, to derive from internal and external considerations the institutional educational policy.

Stanford has four principal academic processes which, taken together, constitute the mechanisms for academic administration, implementation of academic policy, and the derivation of academic policy. These four processes are: (1) academic planning and budgeting; (2) the development of the faculty manpower plan and the appointments and promotions process; (3) facility planning and capital budgeting; and (4) the development of academic priorities and plans for fundraising.

The latter activity is rather unique to a private university, but there are a number of parallels in the way in which we relate ourselves to external constituencies.

Each of these four processes yields explicit results, with varying degrees of flexibility and concreteness. The academic planning and budgeting process yields, first, a long-range financial forecast, second, operating budget guidelines for a given year, and eventually, the operating budgets of the various academic units. The faculty planning process yields a faculty manpower table, including plans into the future, and the appointments/promotions process yields recommended candidates which fill the positions in the faculty manpower table. The facility planning and capital budgeting process yields a document which is a plan for future academic facilities and the related capital budgets. It includes estimates of cost, details of sources of funds, as well as a description of the program requirements for these facilities. The process of developing academic priorities for fundraising is an important administrative process in which great care must be exercised to develop a list of approved fundraising targets that are consistent with the academic planning and the academic manpower considerations.

Many people fear too much attention to processes. The complaint most commonly heard will be that too much attention to processes develops inertia, that the processes take on a life of their own, and that they diminish the opportunity for judgmental considerations. Others would argue that planning is difficult at the very best and impossible under rapidly changing conditions; therefore institutions are better served if they simply muddle through their decision making with opportunistic decisions. Indeed, there are dangers in well-defined processes. One of the greatest dangers is that they do take on a life of their own and tend not to serve the institution. Whether or not that happens depends on the attitude of the administration and faculty of the institution. Good processes provide for checks and balances, and evaluations from various faculty peer groups, as well as opportunity for exceptions.

If the processes work well, one develops guideline documents which become baselines for the directions of the institution, baselines from which one may depart with reasoned judgment.

Academic planning and budgeting principally draws from within the institution on the interlogic, as Eric Ashby calls it, the faculty interests, the discipline drives and directions, the academic philosophy at various levels, student interests, and so forth, whereas the fundraising activity interacts these needs with societal interests.

In academic planning and budgeting there are criteria for the associated decisions in that process. Academic leadership is often called upon to make clear its academic priorities. In a complex institution dealing with very complex subject matter, this is extremely difficult. Furthermore, emphasis on priorities is a bit misplaced in the sense that a priority suggests an ordered preference scheme. Rather than priorities, we have some fundamental criteria which become the basis for decision making.

There are four general criteria as fundamental for the judgment of programs, be they ongoing programs or new programs which are under consideration for start-up, or old programs under critical examination for possible elimination.

They are: (1) Is the program academically important? (2) Is there now and will there continue to be a student interest? (3) Can we, as an institution, be outstanding at this program? and (4) Can the program be securely funded? What is immediately obvious without even further explanation of these criteria is that no one of these is sufficient in and of itself but each is a necessary criterion. That is to say, one must have an affirmative answer for each of the questions aimed at each of these criteria, but an affirmative answer for any one or even all may not be sufficient.

Let me extend a bit the discussion of each of the four criteria.

1. Is the program academically important? This requires the judgment of some peer review groups, principally faculty, but it may include some students. If a particular program is considered sufficiently important by the institution, this consideration might outweigh all the others to the point that one would mandate student interest and plan to secure appropriate faculty to be outstanding and also mandate the funding of the program. For example Stanford is in the process of reexamining the need for a western culture requirement for undergraduate education. There once was such a requirement, but it was abolished in 1969, following the study of education at Stanford. Since then there has been a substantial return of emphasis to undergraduate teaching and the undergraduate curriculum. It has not yet been settled as to what form the western culture course sequences will take or what form this will be required of the undergraduate student body. It is clear, however, from the discussions in the task force working on this program, that there is substantial feeling that this is of such high importance that it outweighs the other academic considerations. In graduate education, there are fewer cases where any single program is of sufficient importance to outweigh all the other considerations.

2. Is there now and will there continue to be a student interest? In the graduate education area in particular, student interest is an important consideration and especially the opportunity for the graduates (which feeds back to student interest). One has to assume that the marketplace is operating to a certain extent. It may well be that students will still undertake graduate programs in areas where job opportunity is not great, but they should do that knowingly, and if certain areas hold sufficient attractiveness to students to work in those areas in spite of few job opportunities, that consideration should weigh in on a decision about a program. Future student interest may

have to be estimated from enrollment trends or other indications of new interests (such as attendance in seminars or single courses). In the end, one needs, again, a judgment as to what these data tell us.

3. Will we be outstanding at this program? This judgment requires both peer evaluation and administrative evaluation. One can always take the attitude that if we allocate enough resources to a program, we can be outstanding, but as a practical matter, that is sometimes a very difficult course to pursue. In an effort to build up a particular program, one might carry a lot of baggage that would make it difficult, but not impossible. Professor Frederick Terman, when he was provost at Stanford, always emphasized building on what he called "steeples of excellence." In a certain way, that's the principal I'm suggesting here. Given the choice between two programs, similar resources to allocate, etc., one should be making better use of the overall resources of the institution and providing better opportunity to the students if one supports those programs in which we can be outstanding.

4. Can the program be securely funded? Are there obvious and secure ongoing sources of financial support for salaries, equipment, library support, student support, and so forth? Again, one will often hear the argument that any program can really be supported because there are controllable sources of financial support, so it is simply a matter of deciding the priorities and allocating accordingly. To a certain extent that's true, but by and large that is a rather misleading concept.

Setting aside those few programs that are so central that they would qualify at all cost, one is then led to ask, if it is not easy to develop a priori priorities concerning academic programs, how does one finally arrive at the yes/no decision concerning the allocation of resources. In the final analysis, it is on the informed judgment of academic administrators that the decision rests. Thus, it is clear why process and style are so important. The processes must guarantee and be perceived to guarantee that the judgments are informed, and the style must communicate the issues, the criteria, and the basis of deriving those judgments in order to give credibility to the decisions.

One might ask why the emphasis on credibility for the decision. Actually, there are different reasons for each of the various constituencies with which a university administration has to deal: faculty, students, staff, trustees, and external supporters such as alumni, donors, and other volunteers.

The faculty has a special responsibility in a university, both intellectually and operationally. It is often said that the faculty is the university, although that does not tell us how to organize the faculty to develop decision making. In particular, either by explicit delegation in the bylaws of the institution or by established custom, the faculty is responsible for the awarding of degrees and the evaluation of the achievements of students. From that responsibility stems an ongoing responsibility for the quality of the overall curriculum. In order to conscientiously discharge their responsibility for the awarding of degrees, the faculty collectively must have confidence in the processes which lead to the development of academic programs.

Additionally, it is clear that both faculty and staff carry out their duties with greater enthusiasm and sense of challenge if they are confident of the administrative processes. Higher performance is reason enough to adopt a style that provides for critical review decisions and develops credibility for the outcome of those decisions.

The student body needs to have a sense of confidence in the decision making of the university. Although only a few students are actively concerned with management decisions of the university, there are obvious reasons why tuition-paying students and their parents or other supporters should be confident that the university is well managed and that the student is getting a proper return for his or her tuition.

I would like to digress here for just a moment to point out that all the emphasis that is given at Stanford to explaining our budgetary processes, the decisions, the criteria, and drawing in the participation of faculty and students, has had a very clear impact on the academic programs in the following way. As soon as it became clear to faculty and students alike that the operating budget depended very centrally upon tuition from the students, one began to hear from various faculty groups that we must pay a great deal of attention to the education we provide these students in order to ensure that it is worth the tuition that they pay. I can easily trace through the discussions of various committees that report to the faculty senate a growth of interest in improving the quality of teaching, concern for the content of the curriculum, and concern for advising students, all of which was motivated by the realization that the education students received had to be worth the tuition.

In most universities, private universities in particular, trustees are persons who are not active in internal management of the university. Nevertheless, trustees have a fiduciary responsibility that goes beyond merely making certain that the institution is in sound financial shape. One of the principal ways in which a board of trustees discharges its broader responsibilities is to continue to examine the processes and the criteria associated with them through which the university conducts its business. Clear processes that lead to guidelines, even though they may be only base guidelines, make it possible to reveal to the trustees the ongoing directions of the institution and permit them to discharge their responsibility with greater confidence.

The last constituency to be dealt with is one called the volunteers—donors, alumni, friends of the university—all of whom work for and contribute to various programs. Their continued support is essential to the successful operation of the private university, and there are parallels to the public universities. Special attention must be given to communications with this constituency. They are not in continuous contact with the university and thus seldom have the full context for decisions which affect their particular interests. This group must remain confident that the trustees are carrying out their responsibilities of proper overview of the management of the university; they must have confidence that the administrators and faculty are meeting and discharging their particular responsibilities.

The academic planning and budgeting process is a year-round process, and is a two-way process. That is to say, considerations, constraints, and issues are communicated from the central administration to the schools and departments, and program considerations, needs, and judgments are communicated from the departments and program officers to the central administration. The schedule of the processes at Stanford is as follows.

At the March meeting of our board of trustees, the operating budget guidelines for the following academic year, which begins September 1, are discussed, evaluated, and approved. Subsequently, during the next month or so, budget guidelines are implemented and, at the same time, some of the studies of the previous year are evaluated and the analytical work that must be carried out during the summer is planned.

During the summer, the planned research and analyses of programs, enrollments, faculty needs, financial aid issues, with a special focus on the institutional-level planning issues are carried out. Long-range financial forecast and economic context document are then developed. In the economic context document, we discuss the various national and regional trends that impact the university economically and then present a long-range financial forecast on the various budget parameters of our operating budget—that is, the projections of different components of income and expenses under a variety of assumptions about enrollment levels, tuition rates of increase, financial aid requirements, gift support, return on endowment, etc.

The long-range financial forecast is reviewed by the faculty senate and the board of trustees in October or November. It provides a certain context for the discussion throughout the remainder of the year in the development of the operating budget.

Early in the academic year, in September or October, a set of documents called budget protocols are developed and distributed. These are sent to the schools and administrative offices and support offices (such as the library). The budget protocol documents and the responses to them constitute a transfer function between the institutional-level planning and the program planning that goes on at the departmental and school levels. The budget protocol documents do two things. First, they set forth the constraints and criteria that have been developed independently through other processes, and second, they solicit data and judgments about program needs and academic directions.

The budget protocols set into motion a process of discussion between the central administration and the deans of schools, and between the deans and the chairpersons of their departments, and between various faculty oversight committees. At each of the various stages of consultation and decision making, the general criteria that I outlined above are brought to bear on the decisions. Many decisions are small ones and do not require a lot of machinery to examine, but major programmatic considerations have these general criteria brought to bear on them.

All of these back-and-forth discussions eventually lead to responses to the budget protocol documents, which are then evaluated and sorted out. The process has the advantage of bringing together at a single point on the calendar all the major planning and management decisions involving resource allocations.

There are many presentations of the work in progress and the final results to different bodies within the university and to the various committees of the board of trustees. There are generally three major presentations to the faculty senate, the first of which is a presentation and discussion of the long-range financial forecast (usually presented in the early autumn). Early in the winter quarter, there is a preview of next year's budget parameters. This is really an update of the forecast as it would be applied to the following year. Finally, there is a discussion of the operating budget guidelines before presentation to the board of trustees.

There are three similar presentations to the board of trustees: the long-range financial forecast, an intermediate view, and then the guidelines for the following year's budget.

This process has proved invaluable to the university; it permits the institution to develop informed judgments based on various data and studies as well as the judgments of various appropriate peer groups. We have sufficient leeway to prevent the system from becoming inertia-bound and developing a life of its own, and at the same time the process is sufficiently systematic so that people have confidence that the judgments are not whimsical. These processes have permitted us to undertake two rather major budget adjustment programs when the institution foresaw a financial crisis, and at the same time these processes made it possible to reevaluate, shift resources, and develop new programs within the schools and between the schools.

Just one year ago, Stanford completed a very successful major fund-raising campaign in the face of considerable economic distress in this country. It started in a period when there was a relatively low confidence of the general public in higher education. A plan was developed for explaining to patrons the basis of decisions and the reasons behind the adoption of various courses of action by the university. We also listened to their interests and clearly responded to patron interests in some ways, never allowing patron interests to dictate the academic judgment of individuals, but those interests clearly helped shape the general direction of the university. It is a means of having societal impact on the institution. As an example, there was a great need for development of a basic neurobiology program to complement the many different programs in various aspects of the neurosciences. In this particular case, a patron of the university, the Sherman-Fairchild Foundation, has a great interest in such a program. Without doubt, matching their interest with Stanford's need helped considerably to shape the direction of these programs.

An institution has a great deal of control over these directions. A proper articulation of the reasoning for developing programs is not only important, but generally rewarding. The donor public is reasonably susceptible to good argumentation in these directions. I might hasten to add that monies offered have not always been accepted. The bases for not accepting offered contributions might be that the conditions are too controlling or that it would be for programs that we could not sustain or are not sufficiently academically important.

There were four thousand volunteers during the fundraising campaign. We had a very active program of the faculty explaining their work, their general programs, to these volunteers, who, in turn, articulated this to the potential donors. It is very important to devote a great deal of time to explaining one's self to the government, federal and state, and to the private supporters of institutions, and at the same time, to listen to their concerns because they reflect societal concerns which also have to be taken into account in developing the policy and rationale for institutions.

Let me conclude by saying that I believe that there are many forces for change within and from without the university and that institutions have to be sensitive to them. We need to bring together our own inner logic and the interests of society. I would like to repeat my initial thesis that our processes need to be so developed that they derive the ongoing academic policy and practices which bring together these internal and external interests—processes which permit an evolutionary attitude toward institutional policy.

NOTE

1. Eric Ashby, *Adapting Universities to a Technological Society* (London: Jossey-Bass, 1974) p. 1.

Comments on Miller and McMurrin by Ernest Bartell

I would like to make a few comments on the subject of liberal education, which was raised by both McMurrin and Miller, with several converging points in both papers. The discussion of the useful versus the useless as an antinomy raises a question of the current role of liberal education. It suggests that the distinction itself may not be the most operationally useful today. With so many of the fundamental values in our society up for question, not just within academe, but in the press, on television, and everywhere else, it is hard to imagine any form of education that someone cannot find useful in some sense. Increasingly, we find at the Fund that people dealing with some of the new clientele, at all levels of education, are looking for liberal education again, and I find evidence for that in rather strange quarters. This leads me to believe that we do not have to be terribly defensive any longer, that perhaps our role at this particular time is to put our best foot forward. For example, one of the projects the Fund is supporting is basically a storefront school in Black Harlem, intended to pick up adult minorities who have dropped out of the educational stream, who want to get back in it, and who really do have graduate and professional aspirations. Now this particular program, called Malcolm-King, has been extremely successful in sending over 95 percent of those who have completed its two-year program on to graduate and professional education. They have turned out Ph.D.'s, M.D.'s, and lawyers. There is a large waiting list of people trying to get into the institution, even though they are charging tuition. And they have no trouble collecting the tuition. I think it is interesting that the curriculum of the program is a very traditional one. It is also a fairly rigorous and disciplined curriculum, with a degree of discipline that I am not sure that I would be able to enforce in that same setting as well as the people in the local community can enforce it. I'm not sure they have any cut policy at all or that they allow a great deal of choice and election of courses. It is a rather rigid set of distribution requirements, and yet the results are so impressive in terms of later performance of the students that it has received very widespread support in the community. There is simply no question of the distinction between the liberal and vocationally oriented content of higher education in that setting.

I hear the same thing from people in the deep South who are operating storefront type schools, that their clients are looking for not immediate job skills, but basic skills, generic skills, the abilities to respond to opportunities, to express themselves more articulately. It is interesting that the only models that some of these storefront type schools have are those drawn from conventional core curricula in the universities, which they are applying.

I do think that we need not be so defensive about liberal education any longer, but perhaps we have an opportunity to pick up upon a trend. Liberal education is relatively cost effective. I think that one of the reasons we see more models of alternative education at the undergraduate level than at the graduate level is precisely because of cost effectiveness. One can do lower-level liberal education things in a variety of settings; whereas at the graduate level there is so much involved in the research enterprise and the teaching enterprise that I think that contributes to the relative paucity of alternative models to the traditional university settings. Graduate education will continue to be highly university based, though with links and ties into the other sectors of society; while at the other levels of education we see more individual efforts on the part of libraries, museums, community-based agencies of one kind or another, to get into the education business.

The question as to when liberal education takes place has implications for graduate education because, in addition to the traditional pattern of having basic liberal education take place in the first couple of years of undergraduate school, we also hear now, with the whole lifelong learning movement, that perhaps liberal education ought to take place after specialized training. I suppose one can debate this and a variety of cogent arguments can be made. Some of the results of a new study by Dean Whitlat, who is Director of Institutional Research at Harvard, attempting to measure some of the outcomes of the conventional four-year liberal education both in elite, private universities and in state colleges, indicate that perhaps more happens than we are willing to admit during the liberal education phase of a young person's education. He found, for example, that values do change during four years of undergraduate school; moral attitudes do change, generally to a more liberal position, more tolerance for alternative views is developed, a more liberal view is held on social issues, and this may contribute to the discussion of what the importance is of the formal education. What is interesting is that I don't think some of these changes in attitudes could be traced neatly to individual programs or courses within a curriculum. They are in some sense a result of the total experience. I think we have always to keep in mind that students learn from each other in the dormitories, in their social life, and in their discussions in the bars and the libraries, and everywhere else. And all of this comes perhaps at a time in life when the results will be most significant.

At the same time, he found that even the relatively short period of specialization in the typical liberal arts major's experience, a two-year major in some particular discipline, did seem to be highly correlated with the outlook of the student on a whole range of life problems and issues. He and his colleagues have interpreted their results to mean that the major itself does shape the student's thinking; that even a small degree of specialization shapes the individual's world view and outlook. Of course, statistically one might turn it the other way around, and argue that the student chose the particular major because he or she had a particular world view that was consistent with the methodology of the major. But nonetheless, it does raise the possibility that even a relatively modest degree of specialization has wider ripple effects than we might anticipate. I think questions such as these really have to be addressed if we're going to determine when general education versus special education should take place in the entire ladder.

We are faced with the whole question of common core versus individualized learning needs which we have not yet resolved. Both points have been raised in both papers: to some extent we need absolutes and we need standards and that implies sometimes an argument for a common core curriculum; on the other hand we talk about the importance of the individual. Miller's paper ends on that very strong and important note. It is not clear that we have the curricular capacity yet to cope with those two poles; there is much discussion going on now, although focused at the undergraduate level. It is today's graduate students who are going to be the faculty members making those decisions before too long.

As to the question of articulation between levels of education, not just from secondary to undergraduate, but from undergraduate years to graduate and professional schools: several points have been made about the importance of assessing the student's performance and competence at the moment of articulation, at the moment of moving on, and historically we have done that through some mix of standardized tests, transcripts, recommendations, and all sorts of artsy-craftsy systems which are themselves up for scrutiny. In our experience at the Fund in attempting to come up with better measures or assessment procedures for performance, particularly in dealing with one's prior accomplishments in liberal education, we have not been terribly impressed with the results to date, so we continue to criticize the typical standardized tests as not being very good predictors of later performance. I am not sure that we have come up with good alternatives yet; I am not sure that statistically it is even possible to talk about any kind of standardized assessment procedure to evaluate the individual, the single case, particularly when one is dealing with such nonquantitative fields as the arts and humanities. Still, if we don't get into that, the alternatives tend to be very expensive if we want to do a better job than we are doing now. Obviously graduate faculties could spend a good bit of time interviewing applicants themselves and probably would develop, based on their own experience and knowledge of the profession and their previous students, a very good capacity for picking and choosing among students with sufficient time and input. But that is a very expensive use of a very scarce resource. We really have not yet come to grips with that problem.

This brings me to perhaps a second set of questions that are raised, especially in Miller's paper—the cost problems that are associated with so many of the goals involved. Both papers took a very strong stand on the preservation of quality. At the same time there is concern for access, even for traditional students, not to mention the nontraditional students such as the low income people and the minorities coming along. We all know that the preservation of quality is very expensive, and that there are not many labor-saving possibilities in higher education. As the point was made earlier, technology has been talked about as a great savior of higher education for as long as I have been going to school, and I have yet to see it come along and replace the very expensive inputs of people. I think we are faced with an increasingly inflationary problem that is going to be with us endemically, and it is going to affect survival issues for many institutions. Graduate programs in many institutions are the victims of some of this squeeze, not in the best established institutions, but clearly in a large range of middle institutions that serve a large part of our population. I am not sure that we have really come upon any solutions for dealing with the cost factor as it applies to the relatively expensive graduate programs in institutions that are not particularly solvent. We are also faced with the danger that, if indeed some of those middle-level institutions choose to retrench by cutting graduate programs simply because there is no demand at the moment for the graduates of those programs, it may not be many years before we have a shortage of the very scholars and teachers of which we now seem to have a surplus. We are not notoriously flexible in higher education, and the time lag can turn out to be socially embarrassing in the not too distant future. Even *Airline Magazine* carried an article about the increase in the birthrate that all the demographers are predicting for the next decade. If that comes to pass and creates a whole new clientele for education, and in the meantime, we have retrenched because there do not seem to be great opportunities for our graduate students, then just at the time when we need that lost generation they won't be there, and we will be right back where we were in the postwar years. Maybe the Ford Foundation will come to our rescue again and we'll be all right, but I fear that history can repeat itself and the burden of that rests at the graduate level. We face problems in the rigidities of tenure and faculty appointments that raise questions about the internal flexibility of institutions.

Finally, on Miller's paper, I want to comment on a kind of political premise of his whole explication of the processes and criteria for planning in a great university. I am very impressed with the application of both the process and the criteria. At the same time it is very clear that the successful working of those processes and criteria depends upon the establishment of credibility. Credibility building among all of the constituencies depends a great deal on a kind of trust that I hope we can always assume before forces to which he referred really translate very quickly into political constituencies on a campus, as becomes quite noticeable when there is any activism or breakdown in shared consensus as to what the whole enterprise is all about.

Now I think most all of us here lived through a period of that not too many years ago when it was very difficult for administrators to assume the administrative roles that Miller interprets so accurately in terms of administrative responsibility for the direction of decision making with adequate participation from all of the constituencies. That social fabric is a bit fragile and I worry that it could recur at some future time when the administrative and managerial issues demand levels of sophistication. If we had to repeat the late 1960s in the 1980s when financial issues and all may be much more acute than they were in the late 1960s, the extra burden of that might tax the political and social fabric of the institutions a great deal. In the meantime, in many institutions we face the specter of unionism, for example, among the faculty as an expression of social change; the implications of this for quality, especially at the graduate level, are horrendous to consider, but it is nonetheless a specter still on the horizon for a large number of institutions.

Reply to Bartell

This is a response to the very last point on consensus building and the fragile character of the political forces. I'm sure that the forces are fragile; on the other hand, an administration has a great deal of opportunity to get out in front. I am reminded of the advice my track coach gave me when I was entering into a new distance run. I asked him how shall I run this race, he said, "It's pretty simple. You get out in front and steadily improve your position." Actually an administration has many opportunities to assert leadership and get itself out in front and so articulate its positions. I am reminded of advice which we were able to use in the era of disruption—advice which turned out to be very fruitful and had many side effects. We had on our campus a news and publication service which was run by Bob Beyers. I went to Lyle Nelson and Bob Beyers and said that I would like them to hire what I would call an academic reporter. This person would report new academic things going on. They hired a young woman named Nancy Donham. My instructions to her were very simple: get academic issues on the front page of everything you can get them on, in particular our own campus report and the campus journals. She did a very fine job of this; every time a faculty member won an award, rather than just report it, she wrote a story on the work and background. Every time there was a new academic undertaking in some committee a full report on this went out. We were able to report that a lot of good things were going on at the university besides disruption. And faculty began to realize that they got recognition for doing something besides participating in all of these activities. They got recognition for their own academic enterprises. Little things like that can go a long way to keep you out in front.

Future Social Needs and Demands for Highly Educated People

Howard R. Bowen

A prominent feature of higher education in the past several decades has been an unprecedented growth in the number of persons engaged in advanced study. This growth has been judged by many to have been excessive. A major policy issue confronting educators, and also those who supply the resources for education, concerns the future magnitude and scope of advanced study. My remarks are directed primarily to this issue. I am using the term advanced study to cover all formal education beyond the baccalaureate degree whether graduate study in the arts and sciences or professional training. Most of what I have to say applies to both.

Four basic propositions about the nature and uses of advanced study have emerged from the conference discussions and are germane to the question of the future magnitude and scope of advanced study. These propositions are as follows:

1. The basic objective of advanced study is to help interested people to achieve, over their lifetimes, mastery of a field of knowledge.

2. Since any field of knowledge may be used in various ways, only one of which is teaching, persons who undertake advanced study should be helped to acquire reasonable versatility and mobility in their careers and in other lifetime experiences.

3. Advanced study should be conducted in ways that will help individuals to become well-educated and cultivated persons as well as professional experts.

4. Advanced study in the aggregate should bring about certain outcomes for society, for example, manning the institutions of society with competent professionals and leaders, providing a pool of human resources available to meet social exigencies, serving as carriers and

developers of the cultural heritage, promoting sound national economic development, etc.

Drawing upon these four propositions, I conclude that access to advanced study should be very open and strongly encouraged, and that it should be guided primarily by the free choices of individual students rather than by strong social control. I shall begin by commenting on several widely held opinions about American higher education and then proceed to a consideration of needs and demands for highly educated members of the labor force.

One common opinion is that the American people are disenchanted with our colleges and universities, or that they are immersed in a wave of anti-intellectualism. It is true that the euphoria of the 1960s has cooled down. But when one applies the acid test of financial support, it is surprising—in view of the fast-moving inflation—how well higher education has fared. In all previous periods of inflation, dollar amounts available for higher education have not increased and the real income of colleges and universities has declined sharply. In the present inflationary period, funds have about kept pace both with inflation and with growth of enrollment. This is a major triumph. Moreover, the public expresses greater confidence in the leadership of higher education than in virtually all other leadership groups in our society including those in government, business, the church, and independent professions. Also, an overwhelming proportion of the population want and expect their children to attend college. More important, enrollments continue to rise and the interest of adults in further education is rapidly growing. My sense of the situation is one of amazement at how well disposed is the public toward higher education, not how shabbily it is being treated.

A second widespread opinion is that the labor market is, and will be, unable to assimilate all the products of advanced study. However, the admittedly worrisome job situation for holders of advanced degrees must be viewed in the context of a temporarily congested labor market. The nation has been trying to assimilate into the labor force an unprecedented number of workers (see table 1). Women have been flooding into the labor market in large numbers. At the same time, because of the postwar bulge in the birth rate, young people have also been entering in greater numbers than ever before. But ironically, at the very time when hordes of women and young people have been trying to find their way into careers, the economy has turned sluggish. Under these conditions, the labor market has been

TABLE 1.   Trends in the Labor Force, 1960–76 (in percentage)

Year	Adult Women in the Labor Force[1]	Persons of Ages 22 to 24 in the Population[2]	Unemployment in the Civilian Labor Force[3]
1960	34.8	3.6	5.5
1965	36.7	—	4.5
1970	42.6	4.8	4.9
1975	45.9	5.2	8.5
1978	47.1[a]	5.4[a]	7.0[a]
1980	47.9[b]	5.6	—
1985	—	5.4[b]	—
1990	51.4[b]	4.5[b]	—
2000	—	3.7[b]	—

1. United States, Department of Commerce, Bureau of the Census, *Statistical Abstract of the United States, 1976* (Washington, D.C.: Government Printing Office, 1976), pp. 355, 358. Refers to women 16 years of age and over.
2. Ibid., pp. 6–7, 27.
3. Ibid., p. 355.
a. author's estimates
b. official projections

congested and young people of all levels of education have faced exceptional difficulty in finding their chosen careers. Nevertheless, the economy has performed surprisingly well. It now provides over 90.5 million jobs as compared with 78.6 million in 1970, an increase of 12 million jobs. But even this increase has not been adequate to accommodate all the entrants. Nevertheless, the unemployment rate for educated people, even including young people, has been consistently and substantially less than that for less-educated people. The sketchy reports I have received from several major universities about the employment of Ph.D.'s indicates that the vast majority, around 93 to 95 percent, are employed in jobs related to their fields of study. Clearly, the market is not as strong as it was several years ago. In some fields there is great difficulty in placement. Over the next decade, however, as the unusual numbers of new entrants are assimilated and if the economy improves, the situation could be strikingly different from what it is today.

Another factor in appraising the situation is the present and prospective educational level of the American people. There is a widespread belief that the American people are saturated with education. The in phrase is "the overeducated American." In fact, of the adult population twenty-five years of age and over, about 11 percent have baccalaureate degrees only, fewer than 3 percent have master's degrees or equivalent, and about 0.6 percent have doctoral degrees or equivalent.[1] All together, about 14 percent of the population twenty-five years of age and over have attended college four years or more (see table 2).

These percentages of persons with college degrees are of course increasing as shown in table 3 which traces an age cohort through the educational system. For example, in 1965 there were 3,093,000 persons of age 18. Of these, 2,665,000 graduated from high school, and 1,442,000 entered college. Several years later, in 1970, 798,000 received bachelor's degrees and still later in 1975, 384,000 received advanced degrees. It seems that at each stage in the progression through higher education, about half the students drop out. The number of advanced degrees is about one-eighth of the age cohort and the number of doctor's degrees is 34,000 or about 1 percent of the cohort. The flow of young people through the educational system is still not producing vast numbers of persons with degrees. In my opinion, the data do not support the contention that America is becoming an over-educated society.

There are some who argue that higher education, even if it has not grown out of proportion to the relevant labor market or to social need for educated people, is overexpanded in relation to the amount

TABLE 2.   Years of School Completed by Persons Aged Twenty-five Years and Over, 1975 (in percentage)

	Men	Women	Men and Women
Elementary school			
under 5	4.7	3.8	4.2
5–7	7.5	7.2	7.4
8	10.2	10.4	10.3
High school			
1–3	14.5	16.6	15.6
4	32.3	39.7	36.2
College			
1–3	13.2	11.7	12.4
4 or more	17.6	10.6	13.9
	100.0	100.0	100.0

Source: United States, Department of Commerce, Bureau of the Census, *Statistical Abstract of the United States, 1976* (Washington, D.C.: Government Printing Office, 1976), p. 124.

TABLE 3.   Flow of Students through the Higher Educational System,
Cohort Entering College in 1965

	Year	Number (in thousands)	Percentage of Age Cohort
Single-year cohort, age 18	1965	3,093	100.0
High school graduates	1965	2,665	86.2
Entering (first time) degree credit college students	1965	1,442	46.6
Bachelor's degrees awarded	1970	798	25.8
Advanced degrees awarded	1975	384	12.4
Master's		294	9.5
First professional		56	1.8
Doctor's		34	1.1

Source: American Council on Education, A Fact Book on Higher Education 2 (1976): 78–79; 4 (1976): 213.

of qualified talent available. We can all agree that there are students in college or in advanced study who do not belong there by reason of inadequate ability or motivation. As a footnote, I believe that many of these people are inadequate because of environmental disadvantage and not because of inherent incapacities. I also believe that modifications of the higher educational system would enable it to accommodate many students who are not well adapted to the present system. But without going into deep questions of heredity versus environment or of educational reform, one may confidently assert that there are many qualified people who are not in college or in advanced study.

To take up first the question of numbers in college, there are about a million fewer women than men in college.[2] And at the professional and doctoral levels, the relative difference in numbers of women and men is much more pronounced. In 1975, women received 45 percent of the master's degrees, 12 percent of the first professional degrees, and 21 percent of the Ph.D.'s.[3] The number of persons from low-income families are proportionately far less than those from high-income families. Also, the percentage of young people attending college varies widely among the states—in some states the percentage is half what it is in other states. In addition, there are literally millions of adults who would enter higher education if arrangements for student aid, release time from work, and the like were more widely available. There are enough potentially qualified students to double higher educational enrollments over the next generation—if women were to attend at the same rate as men, if the enrollment of poor people were expanded, if laggard states expanded educational opportunities, and if circumstances were made more favorable for adult learners.

On the matter of future enrollments, I have been much impressed by recent studies conducted at the University of Wisconsin and the University of Michigan. These estimates take into account the reduction in family size, the ability of parents to send children to college, the effect of the spread of higher education among parents on college attendance of their children, and the increasing attendance of age groups beyond the usual college age. These studies suggest that college enrollments may remain steady or even grow during the 1980s and 1990s. The authors of these studies point out that a possible error in many recent forecasts has been concentration on the future number of eighteen-year-olds to the exclusion of other significant factors.

My intention is not to make a prediction about future enrollments. It is only to point out that the range of possibilities is very wide. What actually happens will depend on tuition rates, student aid, the convenience of time and place at which education is offered, the kinds of education available, and the state of the job market—not merely on demographic trends for eighteen-year-olds. The state of the job market, in turn, will depend on what the nation will be doing. It will differ if the nation is at war or peace; if it is exploring space, the bottom of the sea, or the interior of the earth; or if it is dealing with environmental pollution, natural resource supplies, urban problems, and other great social problems.

I have dwelt on undergraduate enrollments because persons with baccalaureate degrees are the source of supply of students for advanced study. Of course, not every person with a baccalaureate degree is qualified for advanced study, but a great many of those who are qualified elect not to go on to graduate or professional programs. The limit on numbers is clearly not due to lack of qualified talent.

It is likely that many more students would be attracted to advanced study if additional economic opportunities were opened up. Indeed, as undergraduate education has been expanding, growing numbers of young people have been aspiring to the kinds of professional and administrative work for which advanced study is a preparation. Moreover, increasing numbers have been hoping for life fulfillment and personal development through advanced study. There is a serious moral question as to whether the opportunities for people to develop themselves should be restricted to the number of related jobs the economy provides. To apply such restrictions would be tantamount to saying that people should be kept ignorant and their talents undeveloped because the economy fails to supply enough of the kinds of jobs that would use their abilities. A better moral position would be to hold that the economy should provide the jobs necessary to use the abilities of the available people.

So far I have been considering the supply side of the labor market. Let me now turn to the demand for highly educated people. There are two conflicting theories of the demand for higher education. One is the manpower theory which holds that the number of persons to be prepared for each occupation should be determined by the number of jobs the economy is expected to provide at various dates in the future. This theory is commonly followed in socialist countries which run their economies on the basis of long-term economic plans. In these countries, the higher educational institutions are considered an integral part of the economy and therefore of the planning process. In developed Western societies, the manpower theory does not fit very well for two reasons. One is that forecasts of manpower requirements are notoriously unreliable, and the other is that free individual choice of field of study and of career is regarded as an inalienable personal right.

The one significant application of the manpower theory in the United States has been in medical education. In my judgment, it has been a disaster. All that it has achieved is to create and perpetuate a monopoly, to deny a great many well-qualified people the right to choose their preferred vocations, and to induce others to accept an inferior medical education by studying abroad. It has also resulted in an enormous brain drain of physicians to the United States from other countries which could ill afford to lose them.

The alternative to the manpower principle is the theory that people should have considerable freedom in their choice of fields of study and careers. This theory assumes that educational choices should be influenced by the interests and the career aspirations of people and by their own judgments about future labor market opportunities. It is assumed that individuals will make reasonably prudent decisions taking into account their personal interests and aspirations as well as prospective employment opportunities and earnings. There is evidence that their decisions in the aggregate are reasonably sensible—at least as good as those made by manpower planners—though it is true that student responses to market conditions are somewhat volatile and lead to problems in educational planning.

The underlying weakness of the manpower theory is that it assumes that the economy provides fixed quotas of jobs of various kinds and that the workers must adjust to these quotas. It treats people as means and not ends. In a free society, the number of different kinds of jobs available is not rigidly fixed, and the workers do not have to adjust to preordained quotas. Rather, in the long run, there is an interplay between the jobs the economy provides and the jobs workers are prepared to accept. Of course the workers cannot ignore the economy, but at the same time the economy, that is employers, must adjust to the workers available and must provide the kinds of work they are willing and able to perform. Historically, under the free-choice principle, millions of unpleasant or monotonous jobs have been automated, and workers in many kinds of menial jobs have virtually disappeared—for example, household servants, telephone operators, many kinds of bookkeepers and clerks, many kinds of assembly line and agricultural workers, ditchdiggers, and shoeshiners. Indeed, the continued existence of many menial jobs has been possible only because of the immigration of uneducated and unskilled workers from abroad, and because teenagers have been willing to take such jobs, often on a temporary and part-time basis. Meanwhile, the relative number of white-collar jobs has increased steadily until now these jobs represent well over half of total employment. Yet, despite the enormous expansion of higher education, unemployment among college-educated people, and especially those with advanced study, has been and continues to be much lower than unemployment among less educated people.[4] Over the last fifteen years, for example, the unemployment rate among scientists and engineers has run about one-fifth of the unemployment rate for the total labor force.

Enormous shifts have occurred in the deployment of the American labor force over the course of this century (see tables 4 and 5). For example, there has been a steady shift of the working population from goods-producing to service-producing industries. Technological progress has been concentrated in the goods-producing sector with the result that vast increases in goods production (i.e., in agriculture, mining, manufacturing, and construction) have been achieved with small absolute increases in the work force and with a rapidly declining proportion of the work force. The people not needed in the goods-producing sector have found employment in the service-producing sector (government, finance, wholesale and retail trade, transportation, professional services, and miscellaneous services). The nation has now reached a point at which two-thirds of the workers are engaged in producing services, almost exactly the reverse of the situa-

TABLE 4. United States Employed Labor Force
by Major Industrial Sectors (in thousands)

	Goods-producing Industries			Service-producing Industries[3]			Grand Total All Industries
Year	Mining, Manufacturing, and Construction[1]	Agriculture[2]	Total	Government	Other	Total	
1900	7,252	11,680	18,932	1,094	6,832	7,926	26,858
1910	10,238	11,770	22,008	1,630	9,829	11,459	33,467
1920	12,732	10,790	23,522	2,371	12,331	14,702	38,224
1930	11,943	10,560	22,503	3,148	14,333	17,481	39,984
1940	13,204	9,575	22,779	4,202	14,971	19,173	41,952
1950	18,475	7,870	26,345	6,026	20,721	26,747	53,092
1960	20,393	5,970	26,363	8,353	25,487	33,840	60,203
1970	23,336	3,606	26,942	12,535	34,745	47,280	74,222
1975	22,375	3,168	25,543	14,771	39,668	54,439	79,982

1. United States, Department of Commerce, Bureau of the Census, *Historical Statistics of the United States*, vol. 1 (Washington, D.C.: Government Printing Office, 1975), p. 137. Figure for 1975 estimated on the basis of number of wage and salary workers, *Economic Report of the President*, 1976, p. 202.

2. *Historical Statistics of the United States*, op. cit., p. 139. Data for 1970 and 1975 projected on the basis of employed persons in agriculture, *Statistical Abstract of the United States, 1975* (Washington, D.C.: Government Printing Office, 1975), p. 359.

3. *Historical Statistics of the United States*, op. cit., p. 137. Figure for 1975 projected on the basis of *Economic Report of the President*, 1976, p. 202.

TABLE 5. Percentage Distribution of United States Employed Labor Force
by Major Industrial Sectors

	Goods-producing Industries			Service-producing Industries			Grand Total All Industries
Year	Mining, Manufacturing, and Construction	Agriculture	Total	Government	Other	Total	
1900	27	43	70	4	25	29	100
1910	30	35	65	5	29	34	100
1920	33	28	61	6	32	38	100
1930	30	26	56	8	36	44	100
1940	31	22	53	10	36	46	100
1950	35	15	50	11	39	50	100
1960	34	10	44	14	42	56	100
1970	31	5	36	17	47	64	100
1975	28	4	32	18	50	68	100

Source: Based on data in table 4.

tion in 1900 when two-thirds were employed in goods production. Further shifts of this kind are likely, not only between goods production and service production, but also within the service sector partly because fewer people will want less-desirable jobs. Along the same line, there have been enormous absolute and relative increases in number of professional, technical, and administrative jobs since 1900 (see table 6).

The economy and the labor force have an amazing capacity both to generate social changes and to adjust to these changes. One of these changes has been technological advancement which has made possible the production of goods with ever-decreasing labor per unit of product. Another of these changes has been the great migrations of peoples from rural underemployment to remunerative jobs in urban areas. At the same time, new products and services have been invented, the tastes of the public have been modified, and the goals of our society have been altered. Meanwhile, there have been changes in the interests, career aspirations, and qualifications of workers. Throughout all these changes, the spread of education has played a significant part. There is no reason to suppose that these fundamental

TABLE 6.   United States Labor Force by Major Occupational Groups

	Numbers (in thousands)				Percentage Distribution			
Year	Professional, Technical, and Kindred Workers	Managers, Officials, and Proprietors	All Other	Total	Professional, Technical, and Kindred Workers	Managers, Officials, and Proprietors	All Other	Total
1900	1,234	1,707	26,089	29,030	4	6	90	100
1910	1,758	2,493	33,040	37,291	5	7	88	100
1920	2,283	2,861	37,062	42,206	5	7	88	100
1930	3,311	3,654	41,721	48,686	7	8	85	100
1940	3,879	3,808	44,055	51,742	8	7	85	100
1950	5,000	5,131	49,099	59,230	8	9	83	100
1960	7,090	5,733	55,167	67,990	10	8	82	100
1970	11,018	6,285	63,300	80,603	14	8	78	100
1975	12,639	6,528	66,471	85,638	15	8	77	100

Source: United States, Department of Commerce, Bureau of the Census, *Historical Statistics of the United States*, vol. 1 (Washington, D.C.: Government Printing Office, 1975), pp. 140–41. Figures for 1975 estimated on the basis of data in *Statistical Abstract of the United States, 1975* (Washington, D.C.: Government Printing Office, 1975), p. 359.

social changes will cease, though no one knows the precise direction they will take in the decades ahead.

In appraising the employment prospects for educated workers it is useful to consider the future goals of the nation and the needs for educated people that will flow from these goals. Looking backward, the demand for educated workers was affected by World War II, the cold war, the Vietnam war, the expansion of scientific research following World War II, the growth of education at all levels, the space program, and the electronics revolution. Today we seem to be at a kind of historic turning point in our national purposes. The old programs influencing demand seem more or less played out, and we do not have a firm grip on the future. As a nation we have, however, identified a long list of serious and urgent national problems with which we must sooner or later come to terms. I need only mention them because they are all familiar. These problems include:

Ignorance;	Natural resource depletion
Poverty;	(the energy problem);
Crime;	Simultaneous inflation and
Ill health;	unemployment;
Discrimination and inequality	Third World poverty;
among persons;	War; and
Urban decay;	Personal alienation.
Environmental degradation;	

Progress toward the solution of most of these problems would call for substantial numbers of persons with advanced study. For example, suppose the nation were to attack the problem of ignorance by improving its educational system from the cradle to the grave. This might be done in several ways: (1) by expanding early childhood education and day nurseries; (2) by enriching programs and reducing class size in elementary and secondary schools; (3) by providing compensatory programs for the underprivileged and work-study arrangements for teenagers and young men and women; (4) by coordinating work and study for adults and providing financial aid suited to the special needs of adults. These programs could, of course, be carried out only over a period of years but over time would require at least a million additional teachers and other professional workers.

Suppose the nation were to push scientific research and technological development to deal aggressively with problems such as energy supply; conservation of land, energy, and other natural resources; and abatement of pollution. If these things were done, the need for scientists, engineers, and administrators would increase by hundreds of thousands.

Suppose the nation were to embark on a determined effort to deal with urban problems including land planning, transportation, housing, utility development, crime abatement, legal services for low-income people, public health improvement, etc., a great variety of professional and administrative persons in huge numbers would be needed.

Suppose that under a national system of health insurance, medical, dental, and psychiatric services were made available to everyone to the same extent that they are now available to upper income people, vast increases in the number of health professionals would be needed.

Suppose the nation became more involved in economic and social development abroad and in the education of foreign nationals, an increase in virtually all kinds of professional people would be needed.

Suppose serious efforts were made to promote the arts—including applied arts such as architecture, household decoration, and design of products—hundreds of thousands of humanists and artists would be needed.

To conclude this line of thought, one has no difficulty in conjuring up social needs, or objectives, that almost anyone would admit are desirable or even urgent and that would require literally millions of trained professional and administrative persons.

It is one thing to recite a long list of social needs, and another to translate these needs into social demand backed up by dollars. To convert most of the social needs I have enumerated into actual demand would require governmental decisions involving the expansion of public budgets. But today the people of this country have become generally skeptical toward the solution of problems through big government, bureaucracies, and increased taxes. In the last election, most candidates of both parties found it expedient to campaign against big government and to promise cutbacks, reorganization, and elimination of waste. Many people question whether programs such as those associated with the New Deal, the New Frontier, and the Great Society achieve their purposes. Further, the political acceptability of governmental programs is weakened by the constant threat of inflation and by the conflict between long-run environmental goals and the immediate bread-and-butter objective of jobs. Also, the glamour of programs like the Manhattan project and NASA seems to have worn off. For all these reasons, the short-run political outlook for meeting the social needs I have mentioned and for creating the professional and administrative jobs they would generate is less than promising.

In the longer run, I think the outlook for professional and administrative employment may be more favorable than it now appears. Let me review some of the factors that might affect future trends in the deployment of the labor force. To begin, the needs of our society as I have enumerated them are real and are felt by increasing numbers of people. Incidentally, the sensitivity to these needs is due in no small measure to the spread of education in our society. Whether we like it or not, these problems will inevitably involve government and will call for increasing taxes. This is not to say that government must carry out all the activities involved, but that it must supply much of the leadership, the decision-making processes, and the funds. Much, but not all, of the actual work can be conducted in private enterprises and other nongovernmental organizations—just as is done with production for national defense, research and development work, etc.

On the matter of governmental involvement, despite the widespread belief that governmental efforts to cope with social problems have failed, the true record is far from being an unqualified failure. We are beginning to have second thoughts on the record. For example, Levitan and Taggart in a thorough and objective appraisal of President Johnson's Great Society programs concluded:

> . . . The Great Society did not eliminate poverty, but the number of poor was reduced and their deprivation significantly alleviated. The Great Society did not equalize the status of blacks and other minorities, but substantial gains were made which have not been completely eroded. Significant redistribution of income was not achieved or sought, but the disadvantaged and disenfranchised were helped. The Great Society did not have any magic formula for prosperity but its policies contributed to the longest period of sustained growth in the Nation's history. It did not revamp education, or assure health care for everyone, or feed all the hungry, but as a result of its efforts, the disadvantaged were considerably better educated, fed, and cared for.[5]

These authors might have added that during the Johnson years, the women's movement gained momentum and higher educational opportunity was greatly extended.

Henry Aaron of the Brookings Institution has also written an important book on the role of government in the solution of our national problems under the title, *Politics and the Professors*.[6] Aaron points out the need for governmental action and observes that "despite intense skepticism and disillusionment about government efficiency and honesty, surveys repeatedly indicate that the public wants the federal government to take an active role in solving social and economic problems and has faith that it can do so."

Two former chairmen of the Council of Economic Advisers and the present chairman have all recently commented on these matters.[7] Paul McCracken, the first chairman in the Nixon administration, recently noted in arguing for increasing public works that "The volume of public construction is now, in real terms, about 25% lower than a decade ago—in an economy that, in real terms, is 30% larger. Public construction is now so low, in fact that the real value of public capital is probably not being maintained."[8] Charles Schultze, the present chairman, pointed out shortly before he took office that federal expenditures over the past twenty years have fallen, relative to GNP, from 18.2 percent to 15.8 percent of GNP (after adjustment for inflation as it had affected different parts of the economy).[9] Walter Heller, the chairman in the Kennedy and Johnson administrations, recently expressed his view "that expenditure restraint has been carried too far" and indicated his support of "more adequate spending for social programs." He then commented, "Perhaps the greatest enemy of adequate federal funding of social programs is the widespread impression that they have been costly, cumbersome, and inefficient in administration." Heller suggested that this impression is overdrawn, but that nevertheless expansion of social programs must occur with "deliberate speed" if they are to be successful.[10]

Future attention to the many social problems will also be encouraged by newly recognized limitations on the production of physical goods and by the resulting difficulty of employing our population in conventional production. The production of physical goods is limited by the supply of natural resources and by the capacity of the environment to absorb pollution. These limitations when combined with continuing technological progress, mean that employment in goods production will probably not increase very much in the years ahead and may even decline. Under these circumstances, the obvious way to employ people usefully is to tackle the big social problems. An example of the possibilities is the recent bill signed by President Carter on February 27, 1978, calling for annual expenditures of over $6 billions for research and development relating to energy. This bill is already having an effect on the employment of scientists and engineers. Incidentally, enormous investments in physical capital will be needed to improve the environment, to conserve natural resources, to rehabilitate the cities, and to deal with the many other problems. Since capital investment tends to be custom work rather than mass production, the demand for scientists, engineers, economists, architects, planners, and other professional persons would increase.

Another factor which will undoubtedly affect the deployment of the labor force is changes in the supply of labor. As I have indicated, the availability of different kinds of labor is one of the variables to which the economy must adjust. It is a great mistake to assume that the demand for different kinds of labor is fixed and that workers must adjust to the economy as it now is. The adjustment is mutual and interactive. Moreover, political decisions about the direction of economic activity are affected by the interests of the labor force. As the number of educated people increases, the weight of their political influence will be directed toward projects and programs that will use their talents and skills.

My final comment relates to the employment of persons with advanced study in business and governmental careers. One of the greatest blind spots in our present graduate programs is the concentration on teacher training. The prevailing attitude is that any person with an M.A. or Ph.D. is a failure or an anomaly if he or she finds a career in an occupation other than teaching. In my view, our society would be greatly benefited if these people could fan out into all parts of our economy. For example, the preparation of teachers is by no means a narrow training, and people with that background should be, and usually are, easily adaptable to a wide range of jobs—especially those in which an understanding of people is needed. Similarly, I would count it a blessing if many Ph.D.'s in psychology, political science, anthropology, or history found their way into executive positions in government or business, the foreign service, journalism, and other areas. I would say the same of Ph.D.'s in the humanities and sciences. I believe these people could bring new dimensions to practical affairs and that many of them would find practical affairs as challenging as teaching. To bring an infusion of a new kind of brains and a new kind of outlook into practical affairs would, however, require a change of attitude on the part of both university faculties and employers. It might also help if there could be modest changes in the way Ph.D.'s are educated, changes that would in no way impair their ability to teach if fate should after all lead them into academic life. Universities should help to facilitate the flow of persons with advanced degrees into business and government partly by helping them to see new opportunities and partly by helping to introduce employers to a new and largely untapped source of talent. I am pleased to note that important beginnings in this process are being made.

As I see American society, it suffers from two major incongruities:

> *a)* Between the nature of the urgent problems we face and the political attitudes toward governmental solutions—which are the only solutions available; and
>
> *b)* Between the potential talent, skill, and learning of the population and the jobs available in the economy.

In dealing with these incongruities, one possible alternative would be to ignore the social problems, expand goods-production, and cut back on education and on technological progress so as to avoid creating a surplus of persons qualified for professional and administrative work. The more desirable alternative would be to attack the social problems, slow up the growth of goods production, and maintain or even expand advanced study.

It would seem that the nation must face both of the incongruities I have mentioned. On the one hand, it must go forward to meet the great problems, and it must keep opportunity open for human development. Having said all this, however, I want to make it clear that I am not predicting a vast increase in the demand for highly educated people. Rather, I am suggesting that the existential situation will persuade or compel us in the long run to bring about a substantial expansion of the opportunities for persons with advanced study. Meanwhile, it would seem prudent from both a practical and moral standpoint for the universities to do their best to open up new channels to educational opportunity, and not merely capitulate to the conventional view that higher education is overextended.

The United States has pushed formal education further than it has ever before been extended. The nation is exploring new territory. The effects will not be known for several generations. Clearly, the spread of education has not yet brought the milennium, though it has produced great benefits as I have tried to show elsewhere.[11] It has given us new capabilities and new values. In my opinion, if we are able to push ahead, and to continue to raise the educational level of the whole population, we have a chance of achieving a great and humane civilization in which for the first time in history the vast majority of the people will be mainstream participants.

NOTES

1. Estimated on the basis of historic data on degrees awarded. See United States, Department of Commerce, Bureau of the Census, *Historical Statistics of the United States*, vol. 1 (Washington, D.C.: Government Printing Office, 1975), pp. 385–86.

2. United States, Department of Health, Education and Welfare, National Center for Education Statistics, *Projections of Education Statistics to 1985–86*, (Washington, D.C.: Government Printing Office, 1977), p. 17.

3. American Council on Education, *A Fact Book on Higher Education* 4 (1976): 220.

4. Howard R. Bowen, *Investment in Learning*, (San Francisco: Jossey-Bass, 1977), pp. 454–55.

5. Sar Levitan and R. Taggert, *The Promise of Greatness*. (Cambridge: Harvard University Press, 1976).

6. Washington, D.C.: The Brookings Institution, 1978.

7. Walter Heller, Statement before the Joint Economic Committee, United States Congress, February 7, 1977.

8. Quoted by Walter Heller in testimony before the Joint Economic Committee, United States Congress, February 7, 1977.

9. Henry Owen and Charles L. Schultze, *Setting National Priorities: The Next Ten Years* (Washington: The Brookings Institution, 1976) p. 331.

10. Heller, op. cit.

11. *Investment in Learning*, op. cit.

Comments by Harold Shapiro

Bowen makes a number of interesting and provocative points in his paper. Before attempting to deal directly with some of the issues he raises, however, let me say a brief word or two about my own basic perspective on universities through which I attempt to analyze issues such as those raised by Bowen and others at this conference. The perspective I speak of relates to what Pusic and Mandelbaum call the social context of education.

In the current social context, the university community's base of authority in society stems from both its expertise and knowledge and its peculiar position in society that allows it to engage in thoughtful, independent social criticism. This privileged position is also the source of our fundamental obligation to develop and preserve knowledge and to generate throughtful criticism of society and its developing institutions. In reference to our role in training teachers, for example, Passmore says it well in telling us that we must ensure that our future teachers "understand critically the subject he is going to teach . . . its place in human culture."

In terms of the issues raised in Bowen's paper, our obligation is not simply to assess whether over the next two decades, or longer, the American society, economy, or personality could require increasing amounts of what Bowen calls advanced study. Clearly, such a scenario is possible and Bowen makes a rather plausible case for such a development. Our obligation, however, is a deeper and more complicated one. At least two critical questions must be addressed in this connection.

First, should American society increase, decrease, or stabilize its commitment of resources to advanced study in the decades ahead? As Pusic has noted, we are still in an age of scarcity in the sense that our list of articulated needs exceeds our capacity to satisfy them. Public policy, therefore, must still be concerned with the allocation of scarce resources to alternative uses. Second, whatever the level of resource commitment, should such advance study take place in the nation's universities? Let me address each of these points separately.

It seems to me that the age of the amateur is over. In this I agree with the inference drawn by Bowen that the problems most likely to be faced by our society require advanced expertise. Thus, we are nowhere near the satiation point in terms of a level of human capital needed by society to assist it in confronting the problems that seem certainly to lie ahead. I further agree with Bowen that we certainly have not exhausted our potential in this respect. Thus, an increased commitment to advanced study, in its broadest sense, may not only be advisable but quite likely.

The second of the issues raised above, the role of the university particularly in graduate education and advanced training, is a good deal more difficult to decide, at least in my own mind. Boulding has already pointed out that a great deal of advanced study has always been located outside the university. Quinton has made the same point and urges us to consider further moves in this direction. Passmore notes that we pay little attention in our graduate programs to students headed for employment in industry and government and that, in any case, industry may be a more fertile environment for training in interdisciplinary problem solving. Unfortunately, Vlastos rather completes the circle by reminding us that we are not training teachers either. Should the university, therefore, be entrusted with the task of providing the necessary advanced training in these areas? Historically, as Quinton notes, universities have not always undertaken this role. We do not, of course, have to resort to history to find alternative roles. Such alternatives exist in other societies today. In America, however, universities have clearly exercised an increasing monopoly in this area over the last century. The key question we must ask ourselves is whether the broader role occupied by university training in our society has been a productive development with respect to our fundamental responsibilities to scholarship and to society.

Thus, society has really two fundamental problems to decide in this respect, and it is our obligation as members of the university community to develop appropriate alternatives. First of all, it will have to decide if it wishes to take on the type of social problems enumerated by Bowen. Will society move to strengthen the programs and commitments of the New Deal and Great Society or will it rather revert to the "New Narcissism?" Further, even should it move in the former direction, will the government be the chief instrumentality through which such programs will be mounted and developed? Clearly, the government will play an important role, but it may do so by providing the appropriate incentives for the private sector, rather than undertake the programs directly. This decision will have important implications regarding the location of certain types of advanced training. Society must decide which institutions will provide the expertise undoubtedly necessary to develop solutions in these areas. We in the university community tend to take this issue rather as an article of faith. That is, if advanced study is going to be necessary, the university must certainly be the obvious location for it. I believe, however, that we must rationalize this faith and demonstrate in some convincing way our suitability for this role. The university community has undoubtedly played a major role in the tremendous scientific and technological developments in the United States during the last century, but the nature of this role is not completely clear and, in any case, it does not seem to me to provide a sure guide to the future place of the university in society's development.

Now let me address a few narrower points in Bowen's paper.

1. It may be that we have overemphasized in our graduate programs preparation for a teaching/research career. If this is so, however, and if increasing numbers of our Ph.D.'s will be heading into different types of careers, this shift has major impact not only on curriculum design and on the feasible set of research possibilities in the university, but as noted above, on the institutional location of advanced study.

2. We must develop a strong case for increasing the resources devoted to advanced study and not simply say with more opportunities (i.e., resources) more students would present themselves at the university's door.

3. Some final points on some economic issues:

    a) Undoubtedly the large shift from agriculture to industry enabled us to release an enormous amount of productive potential for our society. It is much less clear that the current shift in industry from goods production to service production can release the same potential. It is also worth noting in passing that, if inflation continues to be a problem for society, this will set up forces which tend to work against the trend of moving from goods production to service production.

    b) In a labor-intensive industry such as higher education, if productivity gains continue to lag below the national average, one of two things is bound to happen. Either the relative price of higher education will rise or salaries in higher education will fall relative to national averages. This has important implications for both access to higher education and its capacity to attract the best talent.

    c) I certainly want to agree with Bowen that the high unemployment rates we have been experiencing in recent years are, at least in an important way, heavily influenced by marked changes in labor force behavior which can be expected to work in the opposite direction in the years ahead. Thus, we want to be careful before overreacting to what has undoubtedly been a difficult labor market in the last few years.

Finally, I believe that the combined impact of future economic growth and demographic changes on higher education have not been well thought out. We have concentrated on what I would call "first-round effects" (e.g., falling birth rates, decreased rate of growth and labor productivity). In most areas, economists and other social scientists have adopted a general systems approach which recognizes the complex dynamic interdependencies in a society's evolution of its ideas and its institutions. We seem to have forgotten this lesson in our prognostications on the future of higher education. Compared to other societies, America has had a love affair with education despite, as Veysey has noted, the often-quoted sentiments of distrust of the ivory tower. My own view is that if we are up to the challenges ahead, we shall be given ample opportunities by society.

Reply to Shapiro

I shall comment on two aspects of Shapiro's remarks: first, on the role of the university in our society and second, on the place of government in the solution of the many social problems I referred to as the agenda of the future.

There are many ways of organizing education and research and different societies choose different ways. In the United States we have chosen to operate several kinds of higher educational institutions, and to assign to the higher educational system an important place in basic research. The major universities are the most influential centers of basic research in our society, but other types of institutions also play a part. It is widely recognized that American universities and colleges have discharged their research responsibilities well; indeed, there is some opinion that the considerable achievements of America in basic research are in part due to the decentralization of basic research among the universities and colleges. I believe that higher education should continue to have an important place in research.

Shapiro raised the question of whether government is the proper agency to take the lead and to carry the major responsibility for attacking the social problems I enumerated. I agree with him that much of the actual work involved can be carried on by private enterprise. For example, the activities associated with developing new energy sources, improving quality of air and water, urban improvement, etc., can be done by private enterprise. But I believe that much of the initiative and financing will have to be the responsibility of government. Many of these activities are inherently nonprofit making or involve risk or distant returns beyond the capacity of private enterprise. The analogy is that of defense production for which government provides the initiative and funds but private enterprise produces the goods. In some cases, however, government might operate through positive incentives to private persons or organizations rather than through direct intervention. For example, the government might use tax incentives or positive rewards to encourage individuals and industry to avoid air-polluting behavior, instead of funding large programs for air quality improvement or passing laws outlawing certain types of behavior that contribute to pollution. It is surely not necessary for everything to be done by and through government, but a large role for government is indispensable in serious attacks on most of the social problems I alluded to.

Questions and Answers

Q1 (Veysey): I would embrace the kind of future you've portrayed for us—solving social problems intelligently and resourcefully with highly trained manpower in all the areas that you laid forth. However, I suppose I would share, to some extent, hesitation about the growth of governmental bureaucracy. But the question in my mind is not primarily the desirability of the rather liberal utopian future that you laid before us, but whether it is feasible. I am concerned with the question of projection: how do we tell what's really going to happen? We both agree on the difficulty of predicting the future. I tried to make clear in my presentation that historians tend to be skeptics about prediction, and it was in the context of that skepticism that I tried to predict at all, and I limited myself largely to demographic predictions. You have introduced new factors relating to intentions to attend college in the future. The point about families with higher education in their own backgrounds seems to be becoming an important factor. The other point about smaller family size leading to more college attendance seems, on the face of it, a bit more dubious. It seems to me that values and attitudes regardless of family size might play a much larger role in the decisions of parents than mere family size.

A: In my judgment, family size is third in importance of the three factors I mentioned affecting college attendance. It should have some influence, but I don't know how much. On the question of predicting the future, I am not opposed to prediction, but I feel that it is more significant to form judgments about good policy for the future, than it is to guess what may happen. The range of possibilities are very great. It is conceivable that in the years ahead higher education may experience anything from deep depression to great prosperity. One could trace out scenarios that would lead to either extreme or to many possible intermediate conditions. Prediction is based on an assumption of predestination about the future—predestination that tends to be self-fulfilling. For example, if it is believed that enrollments will drop because of expected demographic changes, then this is likely to happen. People will not inquire into the range of possibilities based on nondemographic factors. The study of policy, on the other hand, tends to open up the variety of options and to set the stage for trying to make the future a desirable one rather than a predestined one.

Q2: Could you comment further on your statement that unemployment is rare among recent Ph.D.'s?

A: I should have mentioned that my information on this subject is rather sketchy though I believe essentially accurate. My information comes from reports from several universities which have inquired into the matter. For example, one study has been done at The University of Iowa, where for several years a survey has been made each autumn of all the persons who received Ph.D.'s during the previous year. The percentage having jobs related to their fields of study is usually around 95 percent. Other institutions have corroborated these results. Of course, in some fields, especially those where employment opportunities are limited to academic work, the record is less good than the average for all fields.

Q3: Will you please comment further on your recommendation that advanced study should encourage versatility and mobility among students.

A: When I began my formal remarks, I indicated that one of the themes running through this conference is that any field of knowledge may be used in various ways, only one of which is teaching, and that graduate students should be helped to acquire reasonable versatility and mobility in their careers and in their life experiences. I feel strongly that advanced training should be so fundamental that it can be used in many ways, especially in an era of rapid social and technological change leading to change of careers during the course of a lifetime. I feel that in the conduct of a life, a straight line is not always the shortest distance between two points. It does not always follow that to pursue a career out in the distant future you must be trained specifically for that career. As McMurrin said so well, liberal education is in many ways practically very useful. Similarly, advanced training that concentrates on fundamentals helps to produce versatile persons. We ought not think primarily about training scientists or teachers or journalists; rather we ought to think about educating people in fundamentals of a kind that they can use in a variety of ways.

The Philosophy and Future of Graduate Education: A Summary

Walter H. Clark, Jr.

Among the various ways of determining where graduate education is now and what its intentions are or should be, looking to the past and to the future are prominent. Consideration of the future invites imagination and, ultimately, commitment. Consideration of the past invites us first to contemplate the history of the university, but beyond that, to see if we can put into words a whole set of ideals and beliefs implicit in the social form of the institution. One name for this latter activity is philosophy, and it too, leads ultimately to commitment. The immediate cause of this conference on the philosophy and future of graduate education is quite mundane. A drop in college-age population anticipated over the next two decades provides sufficient justification to spend some time trying to assess just where graduate education is now, where its momentum seems to be taking it, what changes in direction are worthy of current consideration. The mundane questions to match the mundane occasion can be asked quite straightforwardly. What are the implications for graduate education of a drop in demand for its services? Do the demographic data give sufficient reason to anticipate such a drop? Can anything, should anything, be done to prevent such a drop?

The central philosophic question, whose relation to the mundane questions will, it is hoped, gradually make itself clear, is, "What is it to know?" Descending from this central question one comes to a question of major importance to the university as social institution, "What knowledge is of most worth?", and then to another of nearly equal importance, "What is the nature of the propagation and transmission of knowledge?" The answering of these three questions, and most especially the one having to do with the worth of knowledge, is not something we willingly leave to philosophers—it is something in which all academics, all citizens, have a stake. And it is fortunate, therefore, that this conference should be concerned not only with matters philosophical, but also with questions of what future commitments to make, since by such an avenue it is possible to find entry into questions which are ultimately philosophical in nature. In consid-

244

ering what challenges will face the university over the next twenty years we might expect the social sciences to be particularly helpful, and I think the papers given at the conference show this to be the case. Nor should one ignore the experience of administrators who have to back daily their anticipations of future developments with actual commitments of institutional resources.

There are, then, two reasons for this conference. One is to consider what may be done for and about graduate education as it enters a period of diminishment. The other is to consider the nature of graduate education in relation to the pursuit of knowledge to which it is dedicated. The first of these questions is considered overtly by the participants and is the ostensible cause of the meeting. The second, or philosophical question, is hidden. Answers to it are often implicit in the comments and opinions in various papers. Very often remarks which are commonplaces of the discipline in which a writer finds his intellectual home will rest on assumptions which would not be accepted by a writer from another discipline. What appear to be exchanges between writers may actually be exchanges between disciplines. A diversity of such dialogues, if unacknowledged, could conceivably constitute an impediment to the university in the process of establishing its collective purposes.

It would be a mistake to consider only questions about the nature of knowledge. The university is a social institution dedicated to certain intellectual pursuits, and as such it is susceptible to description in terms of its role in society. A proposition to which the conferees would doubtless give united assent, though perhaps of varying degrees, is that the university is far from autonomous, indeed, floats in society at large like an organelle in its cell. The simile permits us to suggest that problems affecting graduate education can be categorized under one of the following three heads: (1) Problems originating outside the university, in society itself or the larger environment, which the university is powerless to ward off, but to which it must accommodate itself. (2) Problems having to do with relations between university and society where there are possibilities of interaction and mutual accommodation. (3) Problems arising within the university, having to do with the nature and activities of the various parts of which it is composed. These might concern graduate education in its dealings with some other part of the university, or they might have to do with matters within graduate education itself, as in the case of conflicts between disciplines over matters of educational policy. In the following pages I shall comment on matters arising under each of the three heads.

When we consider the forecasts as to what forces will impinge upon the university from outside in the coming years we are struck by the fact that they range from the seemingly inevitable to the exceedingly hypothetical. Demographers present us with intransigent facts. Economists, on the other hand, seem to array themselves in all shades of prognostication. Science tells us that the energy problem will be solved in due time and we will once again be wealthy, but just when and how is not yet clear. When an intellectual historian tells us, as Veysey does, that our society is moving increasingly toward the legitimization of pleasure and away from the stable family unit we fear the consequences of the movements, but remain at something of a loss to know just how to see them at work.

Still, the difficulties of ascertaining what forces will affect graduate education are less troublesome than the process of deciding how they are to be met. One can envy Pharaoh, who found in Joseph not only someone to translate his dream of trouble, but also someone to tell him what to do about it. If we consider the fall in the birthrate, a simple matter of demographic record, we realize that in twenty or so years a smaller cohort will be reaching the traditional age of entry into graduate school. The question as to whether anything can be done to increase the size of the cross section of the age cohorts entering undergraduate and graduate schools at that time, however, provokes a variety of responses. Veysey's account of the demographic facts is not disputed, but it is most instructive for the reader to compare the conclusions he bases upon them with those derived by Bowen. One cannot employ demographic data in isolation from socioeconomic analysis, intellectual history, and other considerations. Even conferences such as this one may have a bearing on the matter.

However many factors the discussants consider, they can still be divided very crudely into two camps. The optimists are not dismayed by the demographic facts. They see possibilities for expansion of graduate education, partly through increasing the size of the cross section of the appropriate age cohort, partly through expansion of graduate education to take in those beyond the normal age for graduate study. Passmore would like to see students entering graduate study at an earlier age, which would provide a one-time increase in enrollment, but he would also like to see the number of years of graduate study reduced, which hardly makes him an ally for Bowen and Mandelbaum, who are the chief optimists, with perhaps some support from Pusic. An important part of their analysis depends upon the willingness and ability of graduate education to shift its emphasis away from the preparation of teachers, the capacity and willingness of business to further employ Ph.D.'s, and the willingness of society at large to direct resources toward social improvements of the sort which would call for highly-trained personnel. Shapiro is attracted by these ideas, though skeptical. Veysey, Boulding, Pusic, and Harrison are pessimistic on the whole, and foresee a period of declining demand for graduate education. Boulding states:

> We all know that in the 1980s the number in the age group of usual college age will decline very sharply and will perhaps be only 75 or 80 percent of what it is in the 1970s. This will have a "divider effect" on graduate education, for the number of new teachers required will shrink much more rapidly than the total number of undergraduate students, and unless therefore there is a sharp decline in the enrollment in graduate schools, they will be producing a large number of Ph.D.'s for whom there will be no employment in the traditional fields. We are feeling this pinch right now indeed, and even in the 1970s we have been educating a lot of graduate students essentially under false pretenses, for their expectations are most unlikely to be realized.

Harrison, in her discussion of Pusic's and Veysey's papers is even more emphatic. She regards it as out of the question that universities, depending as they do on graduate teaching assistants, will voluntarily cut back on graduate enrollments. Nor does she think that the pressure to enter graduate school will slacken very much. Nevertheless, in the 1980s, according to her calculations, all the jobs in a field such as English (including all openings at the community college level) might be filled by Ph.D.'s from the fifteen foremost institutions. Five out of six Ph.D.'s from the elite institutions will not find jobs in the 1980s. On the face of it, logic as well as numbers would appear to be on the side of the pessimists.

The solutions proposed to these challenges do not sort quite as simply into optimistic and pessimistic. To be sure, both Bowen and Mandelbaum feel that the job market ought to be able to adjust itself fairly easily, that Ph.D.'s formerly trained for teaching careers can be induced to seek jobs in industry and government, and that industry and government will have places for them. Boulding and Pusic see this as the direction to go, but are not sure it will necessarily be easy Harrison describes it as the only way to go, a direction that will be taken in the lack of any other possibility. My own feeling is that these views discount the degree of external pressure which may be brought for the reduction in size of graduate programs. The various tax movements embody a clear threat. At the same time I think these conferees may overemphasize the marketability of the Ph.D. Veysey thinks that graduate education must necessarily decline in size and importance in what he describes as a postindustrial society increasingly concerned with hedonistic values. In his opinion:

> There is only one real recourse. That is to continue to take an intrinsic satisfaction in what we do. Having stared coolly at our prospects, we should turn around and count our many blessings. We do not face extinction. Even if, slowly or more rapidly, we returned to the numerical scale of 1960, we would be enjoying one of the most favorable settings in world history for the pursuit of science and humane scholarship.

Veysey, along with Mandelbaum and Boulding, speaks of an increase in the quality of education as one possible benefit of a reduction in size. None of the conferees seem to feel that there are any other specific advantages to such a reduction, though Boulding identifies quantitative decline as something calling for management.

It struck this writer that there was little discussion of ways in which diminishment in size might be turned to educational advantage. It might be worth noting that forecasts of a decrease in the size of graduate education rest on projections of social and economic trends over the next twenty years or so. There are predictions of growth in the nineties, and one conferee, looking boldly ahead to the twenty-first century, sees the amelioration of scarcity with the coming of nuclear fusion and solar power (see Pusic and Bartell). My own feeling is that the problems which will face the university in those distant times will be much more complex than those facing it over the next twenty years. Expansion may feel better than contraction, but the aftereffects are more painful.[1]

In considering relations between graduate education and society the chief questions seem to be those concerning how responsive education should be to larger social needs, and also how far those values which are peculiar to the academic institution may be made compatible with those of society at large. As already remarked the conferees were very much aware that education does not take place in a social vacuum. Mandelbaum, Bowen, Pusic, Miller, and McMurrin pay particular attention to this aspect. Glazer gives an account of a particular discipline moving toward greater awareness of, and responsiveness to, specific social problems. It is possible that this indicates a trend. As I see it three main issues were raised concerning relations between society at large and the academy. One has to do with the right to graduate education. Another has to do with graduate preparation for nonacademic jobs. And yet a third is the question as to whether some functions now performed by the university might better be taken over by other social institutions.

Does every properly qualified candidate have a right to a graduate education? In the opinion of Bartell, government policy is moving in the direction of establishing a right to higher education. Pusic pointed out that students in Yugoslavia are currently free to pick their fields of study. This freedom, he feels, is not without social implications. Circumstances might arise which would call for its curtailment. Perhaps the most direct statement came from a conferee who remarked during discussion: "To keep people ignorant as a result of something in the job market seems an immoral thing to do."

The statement is one which seems to raise legitimate conflicts between the values of the academy and the concerns of society at large. If I may be permitted briefly to argue the case for society I shall try to sketch a position on its behalf. Society has a stake in the education of every graduate student since it pays for a considerable portion of his study. Why should it pay for the preparation of professionals who will not practice? To the objection that they can be of use in government and business, society replies that cheaper and faster schooling for such positions is already available. To the further objection that some of these professionals have special training in the humanities, society responds by asking why this preparation should not already have taken place in their undergraduate education. Society goes on to point out that it is not only a question of money. During their five to seven years of training the services of these young adults are lost to it, at a time of high creativity and energy in their lives.

A second argument on behalf of the interests of society in the university might go something like this: Resources "wasted" on unused professional training might better be diverted to other functions of the university. The public might prefer that English professors teach freshmen composition in the time they now spend training eighteenth century scholars who will never teach eighteenth century literature. Many people, rightly or wrongly, feel that the medical profession has deliberately restricted access to its ranks, and that this country suffers from a chronic shortage of doctors. Might it not make sense to spend money on preparing more doctors whose services will be used than on preparing Ph.D.'s in fields where there is no demand? Other examples could be added to these. Society is much more likely to agree to the proposition that keeping people ignorant is immoral where it can see social benefit in educating them. The fact that, from society's point of view, the eradication of ignorance in the university proceeds in a selective manner and in ways not always consonant with society's perceived best interests, makes it somewhat reluctant to accept such an argument at face value.

A third brief argument, no doubt presented in carping tones, might go as follows: The eradication of ignorance is not a monopoly of the academy. Libraries and museums, which existed before the university, are still with us, and open to all without restriction. If undergraduate education has not taught a person how to use such resources on his own it has failed in one of its purposes and needs to be reformed.

My own feeling is that society has some pretty good points here. But the purpose of this exercise has not been to demonstrate that the eradication of ignorance is an untenable value, the transmittal of knowledge being a defining activity of the university. The point, rather, has been to suggest that society has legitimate interests in the question as to what knowledge is of most worth, and to whom knowledge shall be transmitted. Another way to put this would be to say that the autonomy of the university, even with respect to its central activities, is not absolute. One might also note in passing that the argument from the eradication of ignorance is a two-edged sword and needs to be handled with circumspection.

The preceding discussion has touched on the question of preparing Ph.D. students for nonacademic jobs. I have argued that where more efficient routes of preparation exist it makes little sense to view traditional Ph.D. programs as offering viable vocational training. This is not to say, of course, that Ph.D.'s should be discouraged from looking to extra-academic fields for employment. In some fields, such as economics, considerable nonacademic demand already exists. Nor, in the current state of oversupply, should humanities Ph.D.'s be discouraged from considering jobs in business and government. Programs which prepare Ph.D.'s to make such a transition can only be praised, but I think it would be a serious mistake to institutionalize the humanities Ph.D. as a route into the business world.

There is another graduate degree, the master's, which has traditionally had a much more varied function than the Ph.D. As the conference progressed it became clear that conferees could be divided into those who felt that the master's should be subordinated to the Ph.D. and those who felt it had a genius of its own. Mandelbaum is representative of the former position. He warns universities to "guard against the danger of diluting the seriousness and the quality of their doctoral programs through admitting into them students whose objectives are different from those of the majority of doctoral candidates." He, nevertheless, concedes that the university may wish to "render service to its community by offering master's degrees for those whose occupations call for additional technical training, as well as for those who have the time and inclination to pursue programs designed for their own personal, cultural enrichment." Implicit in these remarks is a concern that the time and energies of university faculties not be diverted from research and the training of research scholars.

McMurrin, while not speaking directly to the question of tensions between master's and doctoral studies, makes a useful distinction between vocational and liberal education. "There can be little doubt," he says, "that the campaign for career education, whatever its values, has caused a large segment of our people to doubt the value of liberal education, or, indeed, of a university education of any kind." Duffey points out that the audience for public education is growing at the same time that there has been a decrease of support for public education. He, nevertheless, regards the university today as playing a central cultural role. Also worth noting are a number of off-the-record remarks by administrators in the audience, suggesting that a too exclusive preoccupation with the Ph.D. degree, ignoring community needs for certain types of graduate programs, may prove inimical to the university's best interests. This suggests that perhaps the academy should try to steer a middle course between the Scylla of vocationalism and the Charybdis of hothouse scholarship.

The plain fact that doctoral and master's degrees are not necessarily consonant was implicit in many remarks. Master's programs associated with doctoral programs are usually either way stations or dropping off points for candidates deemed lacking. It is hard to be specific about master's programs not associated with doctoral programs because their uses are so various. What can be said is that the Ph.D. degree, like heavy artillery, has weight and range. It has to be dug in, and is best not rushed about. The master's, in contrast, has a kind of academic mobility. It can probe new directions, can be hazarded and withdrawn. Insofar as the territory ahead involves academic accommodation to new social trends and demands, it would seem that the master's, rather than the doctorate, ought to be the degree to employ.

The question as to whether some of the functions now performed by the university might conceivably be taken over by other institutions was hinted at only rather lightly by some conferees, but I believe it is worthy of more consideration. Distinctions already exist between various levels of undergraduate education, most specifically that between the two- and four-year college, and that between lower- and upper-class standing in four-year institutions. There might also be a qualitative difference between the four-year liberal arts education as taught in college and in the university. Graduate lines of demarcation are not so clear, except for the master's and doctorate. Whatever qualitative differences may exist between departments in the university, the principles of instruction are based on allegiance to a discipline, and are derived from the possibilities that a particular mode of knowing makes possible. This allegiance is one which applies equally to students and teachers, and is one of the reasons why it is generally assumed that the melding of research and teaching is a peculiarly happy one for graduate education.

A criticism of this melding addresses itself primarily to the education of undergraduates, or to the preparation of graduate students who are going to teach undergraduates. There the burden of the argument is that too great a preoccupation with research inhibits teaching. The converse of this view, that too great a preoccupation with teaching inhibits research, is one that I should like to raise for consideration. Quinton makes the following remarks in arguing for the separation of university teaching from research:

> I have argued that it is indeed the university teacher, and not the advancer of knowledge through research, with whom the academic graduate school should concern itself. Research proper could well be carried on, as it increasingly is, in separate institutes, which would train their new entrants as apprentices.

Caryl Haskins, writing in a special issue of *Daedalus* devoted to problems in American higher education, cites evidence suggesting that the best path to creative research in the sciences lies, not by way of graduate training at the university, but rather through the research institute itself.[2] There, typically, what teaching does take place is of the apprenticeship sort, and the research staff is protected from inordinate demands of a teaching or administrative nature. Haskins and Quinton provide at least the makings of an argument to the effect that teaching and research are each the healthier where there is a certain distance between them. Such an argument would certainly be disputed by a number of conferees, of whom we might only mention Bowen, who remarks that

American universities and colleges have discharged their research responsibilities well; indeed, there is some opinion that the considerable achievements of America in basic research are in part due to the decentralization of basic research among the universities and colleges.

Whatever our opinions about the relation between teaching and research, it should not surprise us to find increasing amounts of research being carried on either at research and development laboratories of private industry,[3] or under government sponsorship, on the one hand, and on the other at endowed research institutes. One might speculate as to what the implications for the university would be if the pure research institute as presently constituted were to be expanded and students to be invited in at the pleasure of the researchers. It would be interesting to see whether there would be any increase in research of the highest quality, and even more interesting to compare the quantity and methods of teaching carried on by those whose commitment to research is absolute. The results might throw new light on the claim that research and teaching are necessary to one another. In any case, I do not think that such a situation would end in duplication of the kind of arrangement that currently obtains in graduate education.

In the call to the conference Alfred Sussman points out that no great debate has arisen over the issues of graduate education to match celebrated disagreements about the philosophy of undergraduate education. Those who glance hurriedly into this book may come away feeling that the great debate he calls for is not yet afoot. My own feeling is that what may at first appear like a disinclination to discuss the issues of graduate education arises, rather, from disagreements among conferees as to certain issues either prior to, or preemptive of, a philosophy of graduate education. While the questions themselves may not be directly concerned with the philosophy of education, the positions taken on them have definite implications for the way in which graduate education is, or would be, carried out. One such issue has to do with the question as to whether teaching and research conflict with or reinforce one another. Since the participants were philosophers by profession, much attention was paid the humanities. While it can be argued that research in the humanities is qualitatively different from research in the sciences and, indeed, that historically speaking, the present state of research in the humanities suffers by reason of a too great imitation of the style, methods, and modes of

254   Philosophy and Future of Graduate Education

evaluation common to the sciences, I nevertheless believe that the question is also pertinent to the concerns of the sciences.

It is important to say at the start that the conferees were not at odds over the values of teaching and scholarship. Differences of opinion arose out of practical experience and observations of the effects of graduate education on students. It is for this reason that I would say the focus of discussion was not primarily philosophical, though conducted by philosophers. I would argue, nevertheless, that insofar as experiences and observations are conditioned by philosophical beliefs, these discussions do have a philosophical background. I shall, therefore, have the temerity further on to make some observations as to the style of thought reflected in the discussion.

The break came between those who argued that an excessive emphasis on scholarship—especially publication, as the outward and visible sign of scholarly activity—impedes teaching, and those who argued that the current situation in higher education is close to the optimum and should be tampered with as little as possible. The first group, in which I would number Passmore, Quinton, Vlastos, and possibly Frankena, views graduate education in relation to undergraduate education. It takes the job of graduate education to be that of preparing undergraduate teachers who comprehend and are committed to the ideals of liberal education, who have acquired some mastery of the art of teaching, and who have command of a discipline. To have command of a discipline, if I understand correctly, need not commit one to a life of research at the frontiers of knowledge. It calls for an understanding of the basic problems and methods of one's field, as well as its epistemology. Further, mastery of the art of teaching calls for more than the ability to put the knowledge of one's discipline into words. Among other things, it calls for mastery of what might be termed "the rhetoric of instruction," by which is meant an understanding of audience, an awareness of its cognitive and emotional state. It calls for some understanding of the learning process at a more than merely intuitive level. Comprehension of the ideals of liberal education implies not only some awareness of the philosophy and history of education, but also a fair degree of conversance with fields other than one's own and some idea as to how they fit into the broad scheme of undergraduate education.

The opposing position, which I would identify with Mandelbaum, appears on the surface to be only obliquely opposed to that of Passmore, Quinton, Vlastos, and Frankena. But I think it rests on a social philosophy and epistemology which are quite different and imply vastly different consequences for teaching practice. For Mandelbaum the traditional ideals of liberal education are passé, and were, indeed, always of questionable efficacy. "Many liberally educated B.A.'s," he says, "were in later life indistinguishable, so far as their intellectual attainments and cultural interests were concerned, from what they probably would have been had they never entered college." He sees the university of Newman and Mill as having been transformed by social pressures and by the explosion of knowledge, particularly in the sciences, into the multiversity of Clark Kerr. In consequence of the expansion of individual disciplines and an increasing student predilection for graduate study, he sees the old distinctions between undergraduate and graduate education as breaking down. In effect he advocates commencing graduate specialization at the undergraduate level (though not, he says, "putting blinders on a person). It ought not to escape our attention that the kind of institution sketched out here is peculiarly adapted to the needs of the research scholar.

A rapid summary of Passmore, Quinton, Vlastos, and Frankena would reveal the following emphases. (1) The main purpose of graduate education in the arts and sciences is preparation of teachers for college and university work. (2) While the professor must have something to profess ("must be a scholar, in the sense of being an appropriately informed or learned person, as well as an instructor" [Quinton]), he need not be a researcher, one who adds to the store of knowledge. The following brief passage perhaps best exemplifies the kind of criticisms of present-day establishment practices advanced by this group:

> The worst of what is done to the undergraduates is that they are used as course fodder to swell enrollments and strengthen departmental claims to more FTEs and more TAs, without being given due service in return. And what is that? Certainly not to be fed diluted versions of graduate courses, sugared and warmed up. To do this to them is to rob them of their birthright of cultural treasure.
>
> When this happens, why does it? Chiefly, because good undergraduate teaching cannot be a mere byproduct of successful research, as good graduate teaching often can. [Vlastos]

Insofar as a philosophic dispute underlies these disagreements, I think it is of the following nature. An important part of Mandelbaum's position consists in what might be called belief in an open forum for ideas. It relates epistemology to political philosophy in that it applies the ideal of democracy to thought. Every thought must come to market, to paraphrase Frost. If we allow for the greatest research freedom, those ideas which are truest and most useful will persevere. The role of the university is to provide the greatest possible freedom for the researcher and to make his findings freely available to society at large. It is not the role of the university to discriminate between ideas or to make determinations of value on behalf of society.

It is somewhat more difficult to educe or invent a philosophical position for the opposing side, partly because its unity is relative, and partly because the thrust of its argument is to point to what it sees as abuses of the system. Nevertheless, I suspect that the educational system sketched in Plato's *Republic* would be more likely to appeal to Passmore, Quinton, Vlastos, and Frankena than it would to Mandelbaum. I suspect they would hold that knowledge conforms to some kind of general structure, and that the function of liberal education is to bring the student, as far as possible, to an understanding of abstract principles. Believing that it makes sense to talk about the general structure of knowledge, I suspect that they think one can talk about the nature of the university, inasmuch as it exists for the pursuit of knowledge. From the perspective of this position the views of Mandelbaum must appear indiscriminate as regards the treatment of knowledge. From the perspective of Mandelbaum's position, a system such as that of Plato must appear intellectually presumptuous. The development of the university over the last half-century would seem to accord some weight to Mandelbaum's views. Yet the critique of present day graduate and undergraduate education offered by Passmore, Quinton, Vlastos, and Frankena reminds us again of the value to the university of a set of commonly shared beliefs about the nature of knowledge, and about principles of choice which will enable the faculty to agree on a common set of educational aims; some agreement, in short, as to what knowledge is of most worth, and why.

Rather than concluding with an attempt to summarize a series of discussions so diverse in scope as to defy summary, I shall offer a series of responses to ideas raised in the conference. Some will identify what I feel to have been key issues, others will point to directions toward which it seems to me inquiry might continue to flow, still others will consist of mere practical suggestion.

Impressive as the difficulties are, and uncertain the choices facing the university, it may be steadying to remind ourselves of bad times lived through in the past. One has only to recall the poverty of the medieval university, and the ignorance that surrounded it, the long sleep at Oxford and Cambridge mentioned by Quinton, or eighteenth-century student disruptions at Harvard. Compared with such situations, the history of the university for the past hundred years has been one of peace and prosperity, and the uncertainties ahead by no means overwhelming. The perverse notes of courage and hope sounded by Veysey at the conclusion of his paper put me in mind of remarks penned by Santayana upon the signing of the Armistice.

> This war has been a short one, and its ravages slight in comparison with what remains standing: a severe war is one in which the entire manhood of a nation is destroyed, its cities razed, and its women and children driven into slavery. In this instance the slaughter has been greater, perhaps only because modern populations are so enormous; the disturbance has been acute only because the modern industrial system is so dangerously complex and unstable; and the expense seems prodigious because we were so extravagantly rich. Our society was a sleepy glutton who thought himself immortal and squealed inexpressibly, like a stuck pig, at the first prick of the sword. An ancient city would have thought this war, or one relatively as costly, only a normal incident. . . .

> Existence, being a perpetual generation, involves aspiration, and its aspiration envelops it in an atmosphere of light, the joy and the beauty of being, which is the living heaven; but for the same reason existence, in its texture, involves a perpetual and a living hell—the conflict and mutual hatred of its parts, each endeavoring to devour its neighbor's substance in the vain effort to live forever. Now, the greater part of most men's souls dwells in this hell, and ends there. One of their chief torments is the desire to live without dying—continual death being a part of the only possible and happy life. We wish to exist materially, and yet resent the plastic stress, the very force of material being, which is daily creating and destroying us.[4]

I find the distinctive mixture of hope and pessimism in Santayana's attitude appealing and appropriate. Though the lean kine are about to devour the fat kine, the end of the university is not yet at hand. And we may recall that years of famine were the means of reconciliation between Joseph and his brothers.

It occurs to me that universities, though perhaps more willing than other social institutions to examine themselves critically, are no more willing than other institutions to adapt themselves to changing situations until it becomes absolutely necessary. Perhaps this is as it should be, since the role of education has its conservative aspects, education being the nurse of culture. But education is also, to borrow Santayana's words, a creature of aspiration and generation, and as such must assent to the inevitable destructions which accompany growth.

This conference has altered my beliefs on one head. I no longer think that the problems of graduate education can be identified and solved in isolation from the identification and solution of the problems of undergraduate education. It seems to me, therefore, that this conference deserves to be followed by one devoted to consideration of the proper aims of undergraduate education at the present time, and their implications for graduate education. It may be objected that the aims of liberal education have already been canvased to a fare-thee-well. To this I would reply in two ways. The question which underlies concern for the aims of undergraduate education, "What knowledge is of most worth?" is a question we have always with us. To deny the question value is to take a position on it. It may well be that the answers to the question change with the accumulation and/or reordering of knowledge. Even if one holds that the question can be answered in general terms (as, for example, that education must prepare the citizen to make moral and political choices) it may still be argued that the means by which the universal aims are to be achieved must change with the times, i.e., that the curriculum must renew itself, though the purposes the curriculum is intended to serve may remain the same.

The papers of the first day give clear evidence of competition within the university between the demands of teaching and those of research. The question as to whether the tensions are inevitable, or whether things can be done to relieve them, and in the process to strengthen both research and teaching is not one that will be quickly answered. To the various suggestions made by the writers I would like to add one more. I think a comparison of the humanities, social sciences, and sciences, or indeed, of the various disciplines, with respect to the way they define what knowledge is and the ways one goes about doing research, would prove useful. If the differences in modes of apprehending the world which distinguish the various disciplines could be made explicit, that might clear the way for a more ready understanding of shared purposes within the university and also clear up some difficulties which arise from the assumption that all research activities are fundamentally the same.

I shall conclude with a series of rapid comments of a slightly more practical nature. It seems inevitable that the decrease in available jobs will result in the decrease in size of graduate programs and departments. That it may lead to the demise of some graduate programs and departments is, in my opinion, something to hope for, as is the possibility that some programs or departments may join forces.[5] More thought needs to be given to the serendipities of diminishment, and very real care to conserving the vital spirit of the Ph.D. through a difficult period, so that it will be ready to cope with the inevitable return of expansionary times. The continuing quest for working consensus on principles of the educational enterprise is not, in my opinion, a luxury, but a most necessary activity, to abandon which is to invite the politics of power within the university precincts.

NOTES

1. See, for example, Willard Quine, "Paradoxes of Plenty," *Daedalus* 103, no. 4 (Fall 1974): 38–40.

2. Caryl P. Haskins, "Thoughts on an Uncharted Future," *Daedalus* 104, no. 1 (Winter 1975): 240–42.

3. See, for example, Lewis M. Branscomb and Paul C. Gilmore, "Education in Private Industry," *Daedalus* 104, no. 1 (Winter 1975): 222–33.

4. George Santayana, *Soliloquies in England and Later Soliloquies* (Ann Arbor: University of Michigan Press, 1967), pp. 104–5.

5. See Frank E. Manuel, "Clio Vanishes from New York City," *Daedalus* 103, no. 4 (Fall 1974): 126–27. The author argues that there should be a single scholarly center in New York City for the study of history, and that it should draw on all colleges and universities in the area. See also, Martin Meyerson, "Quality and Mass Education," *Daedalus* 104, no. 1(Winter 1975): 316. Meyerson cites a 1971 proposal by Allan M. Cartter that the federal government identify and support between seventy-five and one hundred "national universities."